The Marine Corps Marathon –

George Banker

The Marine Corps Marathon
A Running Tradition

Meyer & Meyer Sport

British Library Cataloguing in Publication Data
A catalogue record for this book is available from the British Library

The Marine Corps Marathon – A Running Tradition
Oxford: Meyer & Meyer Sport (UK) Ltd., 2008
ISBN 978-1-84126-222-2

© 2008 by Meyer & Meyer Sport (UK) Ltd.
Aachen, Adelaide, Auckland, Budapest, Graz, Indianapolis, Johannesburg,
New York, Olten (CH), Oxford, Singapore, Toronto
Member of the World
 Sport Publishers' Association (WSPA)
www.w-s-p-a.org
Printed and bound by: B.O.S.S Druck und Medien GmbH, Germany
ISBN 978-1-84126-222-2
E-Mail: verlag@m-m-sports.com
www.m-m-sports.com

Contents

Acknowledgments

I have completed 65 marathons since 1983 and ran the JFK 50 Miler in November 2006. The 1983 Marine Corps Marathon was the second marathon I had ever run and, as they say, "the rest is history." With the exception of 1986, when I chose to run a marathon in New York City, I ran the MCM for 22 years. The concept for this book started to take shape in early 2005 as a tribute to the MCM as it prepared to turn 30. My objective was to capture the soul of the event and, in so doing, help to explain its enduring popularity among runners. This book was written from my heart and that of others with a personal connection to the race – runners, the race organizers, and their families and friends

The decision to write this book stemmed from a love of the military having grown up around the Marines and for the passion developed for the sport of running. Like many novice runners, there is a desire to go for the "big one," the marathon. The affair started and over the years my involvement with the event increased. The popularity of race was increased as a loyal following developed. Each event has a soul. A friend, Joy Koenig, summed up my feelings – the heart of the race is in the heart of the runners. I could list all of the reasons of what defines the soul of the race but that would spoil the reading of the book. You will be challenged to define the Marine Corps Marathon by your standards and become infected. You may run it only once, but it will be memorable. What keeps me returning is the feeling of duty, honor, and tradition that fills the air around the marathon by the Marines, staff, runners and volunteers. All of the elements had to be documented.

There were numerous people behind the scenes who offered moral support and permitted me to use them as a sounding board while I was writing this book. They all provided much needed encouragement. Unfortunately, space limitations prevent me from naming all to which I owe my gratitude, but I would like to take this opportunity to express my thanks to: Cathlene Banker, Erika Brumbelow, Lauren (ML) Frank, Jackie Concaugh Gruendel, Peter Howes, Rosman Jeffries, Peggy Kaplan, Joy Koenig, Hal Lippman, Joe Lugiano, Mark Mooney, Steve Nearman, David Owens, Mary Salamone, Mara Van Vorst, and Tony C. Willis; my Canadian friends, Angela and Roger Plamondon, along with Karl Kunz of Thailand; two special photographers, Bob Mallet and Victah Sailer; and Pacers Running Store of Old Town Alexandria, Virginia.

I appreciate the positive support of Leatherneck, the magazine of the Marines, a magazine that has been telling the Marine Corps story since 1917. The best are saved for last and goes to those who helped to keep me in the race and on track, the love of my life for 36 years, Bernadette, and our children, Ronald, Yvette, and Andre; the person who instilled lasting values and offered many prayers, my mother Almeta (Perry) Kidd; my stepfather, 1st Sgt George Kidd USMC (Ret.), father, MSgt Alvin Banker USMC (Ret.), and my two stepmothers, Chieko Kidd and Sally Banker.

George Banker

Foreword by Olympian Jeff Galloway

Training for and completing a marathon changes peoples lives for the better. At the beginning of the training journey, the challenge seems over-whelming. On almost every long run, there are significant problems. But as the Marine Corps Marathon trainees follow the well-tested program provided, they will push through self-doubt to find unexpected and powerful spiritual resources inside. Access to these strengths allows marathoners to overcome other problems in life. The crossing of the finish line is an amazing moment of satisfaction and achievement that energizes most for the rest of their lives.

The Marine Corps Marathon is known of as the "people's marathon." While this is a well-deserved nickname, the MCM is much more than this. I've attended hundreds of marathons and have not found any to have the combination of support items, consistently energetic volunteers and staff, all sustained by the "can do" philosophy of the event. A high percentage of the entrants each year are first timers who have little chance of entering many of the local marathons that close their finish line in 5 hours or less, or have a much more restrictive entry process.

After having helped over 500,000 runners reach their goals through my e-coaching, training programs, running schools, books, retreats and individual consultations, I can say that almost anyone can finish the MCM if they use the right run-walk-run™ ratio and do the training necessary. I salute everyone who takes on the challenge and congratulate every finisher. The world is a better and healthier place because of the Marine Corps Marathon.

Jeff Galloway
www.JeffGalloway.com
Runner's World Magazine

Introduction

Marine Corps Marathon

I cried on climbing the hill and knew not why.
The course was long and the winds strong.
I wondered who would prevail.

I had trained the best a neophyte could.
But this race I had never run.

This day had always been a secret wish.
An ambition locked till now in the mind for many years.
As the minutes passed, the pain increased so to mimic life's struggles.

Among the monuments and Capitol we ran.
All symbols of promises far greater than any other land.
The hope of mankind lies here, I thought.
We are a symbol in life's race.

From the cemetery we had come.
Past the Pentagon with power and might.
Across the star spangled Key Bridge we galloped
To Georgetown, it was fun.

The crowd cheered us onto the river and we passed the most recent tragic test
... (Kennedy Center)
How fresh the memory of those young ideals!
On to the greatest of monuments on the Mall.
How well I now understand the weeping of Lincoln for all.

Down the street called Constitution, a test of mine today would prove.
Flanked by a monument to the first President.
And south view of the home of the most powerful man everyday, not just
today, the President of the United States.

Between the buildings of civil servants and museums of mankind's history
we strove.
To the step of the Capitol and in front of the Supreme Court.
Today would be a different test of the system of checks and balances.
Pass the tribute to current technology and challenge of the unknown
(Air and Space Museum).
Once again to make a turn at the Monument of Unity (Lincoln Monument).
In the distance, the monument to Jefferson,

as if strategically placed to test the wind and will.
Far into the park the pain enhances. No crowds to cheer,
only the camaraderie of those with whom we share the agony.
The wind is fierce, the temperature drops, some runners fall, the cramps
become so severe that they force a walk … but victory is now not far off.
So once again to the end we approach … not unlike life itself.

Pass the rows of glistening crosses, total symbols of past struggles, the Flag
Flying High! The band playing a tribute to not just us but a nation.

Today I did not finish first nor last, but I gave as much as I would endure.
And somehow among all these symbols of dreams and promises, I finished
the course and shed a tear of happiness. For the pain I felt seemed nothing
now, for I have shared in a small way today, the struggle of all these dreams
and sacrifices.

- Dr. Gilbert R. Irwin, M.D.

The above poem was written by Dr. Irwin in 1983 and submitted by his daughter, Mary Davison.

Davison explained the origin of the poem, "My dad chose to run in the 1983 MCM as one of his lifetime dreams was to complete a marathon. He chose to run in the Marine Corps Marathon in honor of his second cousin, William Irwin who was killed at Iwo Jima in World War II."

She added, "This poem is special to me as my dad never shared it with anyone until the day I finished my first marathon, which was also the Marine Corps Marathon, in 1996. Growing up, I was a competitive gymnast. My dad had seen me run and always thought that I would be a good runner. As a child and teen, I had absolutely no interest in running as it would have taken away too much time from my gymnastics training. Although my dad wanted me to run, he never forced me into a sport I didn't want to do. After graduating from college in 1994, I again watched my dad train for the MCM and couldn't believe how anyone could possibly run 26 miles! In 1994, after retiring from gymnastics, I began to run casually. Eventually I became hooked and my dad encouraged me to run in the MCM. He said he would train for the 1996 race if I was going to do it. In October 1996, I ran my first marathon and first MCM (3:29:06, 109th place). After the marathon, my dad gave me the poem that he had written about the race. I will always have very fond memories of my first marathon at MCM in 1996. I later went on to finish the 1997 MCM in 3:04:48 (12th female overall)."

Dr. Irwin completed the MCM in 1983 (4:16:19), 1994 (4:55:14), and 1996 (4:50:13). Davison ran the race again in 2000 and finished in 3:08:28 (14th place among the females).

The Marine Corps Marathon was conceived over thirty years ago for the purpose of providing a fitness event for the civilian runner and presenting a positive image of the Marine Corps at a time when the U.S. military was out of favor with the general public due to the unpopularity of the Vietnam War. Every new endeavor has its challenges and race management was not a subject taught to the Marines, but history supported their leadership abilities. As with military missions, the Marines approached the MCM with careful planning, preparation and execution. The first MCM was held on Sunday, November 7, 1976, three days shy of the 101st birthday of the Marine Corps.

In 1978, Race Coordinator, Major Jerry Drucker used the term "The People's Race" and predicted the race would one day achieve national recognition. Through the years, the race has been called "The Run Through the Monuments" because the race passes the Lincoln Memorial, the Kennedy Center, the Washington Monument, U.S. Capitol building, and the Jefferson Memorial. "The People's Marathon" is the name by which the MCM has come to be recognized, nationally and internationally. Unlike other marathons for which a qualifying time is a hurdle to be overcome just to have the chance to run, the MCM is open to all those who have a desire to run.

All marathons are 26.2 miles yet each one has a different personality. In the case of "The People's Marathon," the focus is on creating an atmosphere that will foster memorable moments for each runner. As then–Commandant of the Marine Corps, General A. M. Gray stated in 1989, "We may not be the largest [marathon] in terms of the number of participants, but we do intend to treat each participant with the dignity and respect worthy of their efforts and preparation." When facing the grueling mental and physical challenge of running a marathon, passing by many of the most precious monuments to the history and values of the United States of America, how can running the Marine Corps Marathon not be a memorable experience? Each year, there are many different stories about the motivations and emotions of those who have run the MCM, as well as those on the "sidelines" who have offered their support and encouragement.

This book is a collection of stories of the individuals who have helped shape the Marine Corps Marathon over the past three decades. While these stories are only a fraction of those to be told, they are nonetheless telling of how the race has evolved and endured throughout the years.

The Marathon – A Test of Physical and Mental Endurance

The marathon as an event is not known for making athletes but for testing their physical and mental endurance. "Nike" (Nike in Greek Mythology means triumph and victory and is personified by the goddess Nike), the word shouted by Pheidippides, the Greek soldier who ran 26 miles to report the victory of the Athenians over the Persians, would resonate the essence of what was to become the world's premiere running event. The marathon has challenged countless runners since it was first run in 490 B.C. Throughout the centuries, the marathon kept recreating itself and in 1908, at the London Olympics, the distance and the race was forever changed. The race was routed from Windsor Castle to White Clay Stadium, adding 385 yards so that the race would end at the Royal Box. The marathon, a 26.2 mile race, has retained its regal appeal and is considered the pinnacle race to run.

Accepting the challenge to complete a marathon requires passion and desire. Training for and running in the Marine Corps Marathon is at times a trying yet exhilarating emotional and physical journey. The training starts with asking yourself why you want to run a marathon. The first step is to secure a physical examination. The training will be twofold, the body and the mind must both develop mental toughness. The running will start with short 30-minute runs up to four hours. Depending upon your schedule, you will be running four to six days per week in the rain, humidity, and heat. You may be running in the early morning hours or late evening. The training will cause family, work, and social schedules to be rearranged. There will be changes in your diet to eat what provides fuel for the body. There will be parts of your body that will develop aches and pains along the way. You will be challenged in your desire to seek your goal, how bad do you want it?

It is race day. Just before immersing yourself in the massive sea of runners, you look for the last portable restroom break. You then take your place among the thousands of runners, the aroma from a potpourri of sports balms permeate the air. The adrenaline begins coursing through your body with seemingly accelerating velocity. The reflex is to want to shake the adrenaline off either by literally shaking one's limbs or taking a short jog. To those on the sidelines, these gyrations may look like dancing the "Hokey Pokey" or that one is having reservations about the challenge he is about to undertake and is considering running off in the opposite direction. You cannot contain your excitement and begin talking up the stranger or your running buddies standing next to you. Within seconds you hear the loud boom of the starter pistol and see the cloud of white smoke billow up and dissipate as you run by the starting line.

The first ten miles seem to fly by and your mind alternates between taking in the sights and sounds that catch your attention and parsing through a mental checklist of the elements of your running strategy for the race.

In 2003 and prior, the runners would run south along Route 110 towards Crystal City while the pack was thick and the runners had to be careful not to get tripped. There was a short tunnel where the runners would all yell to hear the echo to express their excitement and the Marine runners who yell out "Ooh-rah!" an expression of enthusiasm. Near the fifth mile, the runners would be several hundred feet away from the Pentagon along Route 27 and then through the North Pentagon Parking Lot. Along the seventh mile, the runners would be along Route 110 and crossing the start line. The spectators were shoulder to shoulder and three to four deep and yelling as the runners did a pass and review before heading to the Key Bridge to cross into the Georgetown section of Washington. Along this point, the sea of runners would begin to thin out.

Starting in 2004, the runners went north along Route 110 towards Rosslyn and crossed the Key Bridge along mile four to five to enter Georgetown.

Between miles 11-15, the anxiety level starts to rise as this is when the first thoughts of wanting to stop and walk enter the mind. There is the fear of not being able to complete the race and dreading that the months of physical and mental preparation invested were wasted. However, you assure yourself that in the absence of debilitating pain, there is no reason not to continue. During these miles, the cheering crowds are invaluable to recalibrating the mental tug of war you are playing inside your mind.

Course changes over the years included the addition of Rock Creek and Potomac Parkways, passing by the John F. Kennedy Center and then onto the large crowds at the Lincoln Memorial as they crowded into the street. The section included Capitol Hill and portions along the National Mall.

The excitement from the start line is on the decline in miles 16-20 as you fill the void with questions. Am I hydrating? How do my legs feel? When and what will hitting the wall feel like? Fatigue sets in as a result of dehydration and carbohydrate depletion. Included in this feeling is depletion of muscle fuels, low blood glucose, increased lactic acid levels and central fatigue. Once again, you must wrestle with the fear that you will not finish the race and now you must also contain the anger that arises from the feeling that your body is letting you down.

The bittersweet area that has been in and out as part of the course is Hains Point, which extends out into the Potomac River. It is where there are the fewest spectators, the terrain is all flat and runners are greeted by "the wall." It is the right locale to find a partner to talk through the pain and forget the ordeal at hand.

At the 21-24 mile point, the muscle fatigue has set in as your pre-race energy supply has been exhausted. Each time your foot strikes it feels like three times your normal body weight and all of your muscles share the pain. The devastating muscle cramps place your finish in jeopardy. It is decision time once again. The will to finish overrides the body and you may alternate between walking and jogging to push forward. Down the road is the hill leading up to the Iwo Jima Memorial.

During the last 2.2 miles, the remaining runners are now along Route 110 and many are down to a slow jog or walking, trying to overcome the calf cramps that have begun to navigate up the leg into the hamstring. The pain is hard to describe but it is real. The enthusiasm of the crowd reaches a crescendo, strangers are cheering you on, and their words of encouragement that "there is little more to go, you are almost there" ring in your ears. A 90-degree turn is made off Route 110 and the runners are face-face with a 100-meter steep hill. The jogging turns into a slow shuffle while some are fighting back tears as they face the ultimate challenge. Your pride is coming back as the 26-mile marker is passed. The trip around the Memorial is slow, although your excitement begins to mount. Reaching the finish line is the only thing on your mind. You see the finish line, the clocks are visible and you see the seconds tick away as you suck up the pain, the crowds are going wild and you know the photographers will be taking pictures. The pain is being internalized. You have left the paved surface and step onto the grass for the last 100 yards. Your brilliant effort ends as you cross under the MCM "Finish" arch. You have no problem slowing down as you make the way through the chutes as you are greeted by a Marine who congratulates you by placing your well-deserved finisher's medal around your neck and wraps you in a space blanket. There are other Marines who remove your ChampionChips from your shoes as many runners can't sit down to unlace their shoes. Each sentence you hear the Marines say ends with "Sir" or "Ma'am."

Architects of the Vision

The success of the present-day Marine Corps Marathon lies within the history of the Marine Corps, which has evolved over the years. On November 10, 1775, the Second Continental Congress passed legislation to create two battalions of Continental Marines. The official birthday of the Marine Corps was being celebrated on various dates. In an action similar to Colonel James Fowler in starting the marathon, Major Edwin McClellan of Headquarters Marine Corps drafted a letter on October 21, 1921, to Major General Commandant John A. Lejeune suggesting the official birthday be celebrated on November 10 of each year and that it be a Marine Corps holiday. General Lejeune issued Marine Corps Order No. 41 Series on November 21, 1921, which set the date.

The guiding principles of the Marine Corps can be found within its core values: Honor, Courage, and Commitment. Through the years, the Marine Corps has undergone changes and leadership. Honor relates to the behavior (moral and ethical) of the Marines and encourages them to act responsibly and be accountable for their actions. Courage is instilled in each Marine through mental, moral and physical strength. Commitment means having the determination and dedication to complete all assigned missions.

A single event that has withstood time and embodies the symbol of the Marine Corps dates back to the morning of February 23, 1945, during WWII. On the island of Iwo Jima, which lies 660 miles south of Tokyo, an assault to the top was launched by the Marines of Company E, 2nd Battalion.

Joe Rosenthal & Bill Genaust
In the late morning, there was a miniature U.S. flag flying atop Mount Suribachi and later in the afternoon it was replaced by a larger one. During the raising of the second flag by five Marines and one Navy hospital corpsman, Joe Rosenthal, a news photographer, captured a still photograph, and Sergeant Bill Genaust, a Marine photographer, captured the motion picture footage. The picture by Rosenthal later received a Pulitzer Prize. Sergeant Genaust was killed in action nine days after the filming.

The Marine farthest from the flag is Pfc. Ira Hayes; Pfc. Franklin R. Sousley is to the right front of Hayes. Sgt. Michael Strank is on Sousley's left and PhM. 2/c John H. Bradely (U.S. Navy hospital corpsman) is in front of Sousley. Pfc. Rene Gagnon is in front of Strank and Cpl. Harland H. Block is the closest to the bottom of the flag staff. Three of the six died later on Iwo Jima.

Felix W. de Weldon

During World War II, sculptor, Felix W. de Weldon entered the Navy as an artist stationed at Patuxet Naval Air Station in Maryland. The Congress commissioned de Weldon to create the Marine Corps Memorial, which took nine and half years. It was dedicated on the 179th birthday of the Marine Corps on November 10, 1954, and is today the center of the marathon.

Colonel Jim Fowler

"After the Vietnam War, the relationship between the military and the civilians was not popular. I thought there was an opportunity for the Marine Corps to establish a race before someone else did. It had to be set up by the Marine Corps. Starting off is always tough if it's new and there were few people with experience. On October 17, 1975, I had drafted the concept paper and presented it to General Ryan. He was asked who was going to run it. The person who submitted the paper was the reply," stated Colonel Fowler.

Colonel Fowler set out to secure the assistance of civilian organizations and companies like the President's Council on Physical Fitness and Sports and Kodak. They wrote letters of support. GySgt Alex Breckinridge of the Financial Systems Branch at Headquarters Marine Corps was an asset since he ran in the 1960 Olympic Marathon in Rome and finished at 30th place in 2 hours 29 minutes. *Washington Post* syndicated columnist Colman McCarthy provided added publicity. He ran the marathon in 1978 in 3:54:44. The plan was to secure experienced people who ran marathons in other places.

To make sure that people knew it was a Marine Corps race, Fowler selected the starting at the Iwo Jima Memorial so that it could be caught by photographers. He wanted a race that all would run and if another city was chosen, people did not want to run where only squirrels and chipmonks would see them. The people wanted to be seen running Georgetown.

In the first year, a portion of the course sent the runners down the George Washington Memorial Parkway, into Old Town Alexandria, Va. They took Abington Road and merged into Lee Street, Oronoco and Union and onto Royal and back to Abington. The runners ran back along the Memorial Parkway.

In the second year, over 2,000 runners registered and that was good growth according to Colonel Fowler. The route was up in front of the U.S. Capitol. There was some resistance but it was overcome by the reputation of the Marine Corps. Colonel Fowler was concerned about the safety of the runners.

"The Marine Corps is not known for road races, but for years it has hosted track and field events at Quantico. The race has gone on quite well the way the Marine Corps has run it and they have taken care of it," commented Colonel Fowler.

"I could not have predicted that 30,000 would be running the race. I wanted a safe race and that one would get lost. There were enough problems earlier to handle. You don't foresee all of the problems and you deal with them the best you can. I think it's been good for the Marine Corps and the participants. We did not need prize money because that changes the nature of the race," he added.

Colonel Fowler comments about race morning as it stirs his emotions, "It appeals to my sense of mischief. I can recall General Ryan saying, 'we give this race and what happens if no one comes?' I replied, 'A few have shown up.' Once the Marines do something two years in a row it becomes a tradition."

General Ryan

General Ryan had conveyed through the years that he was proud of the Marine Corps Marathon. He saw the idea and approved it and supported Colonel Fowler, his Staff Officer.

Colonel Fowler had observed General Ryan walking the course by himself just to see if anything has been overlooked.

It was mid-September 1976, the race course was measured and certified through the Amateur Athletic Union (AAU). The course permit was approved with the signing by Major General Michael P. Ryan, Director Marine Corps Reserve, and Jack Fish, National Capital Parks Director.

General Wilson

The last approval for the marathon in the chain of command was General Wilson, the 26th Commandant of the Marine Corps (1975-1979). He insisted on force readiness, responsiveness, and mobility by maintaining fast-moving, hard-hitting expeditionary units and integrated firepower. Shortly after becoming Commandant, Wilson said, "I call on all Marines to get in step and do so smartly." He was the first Marine Commandant to serve on Joint Chiefs of Staff.

Wilson told Associated Press a month after being named commandant, "If I see a fat Marine, he's got a problem, and so does his commanding officers."

He received a Medal of Honor during an assault on Guam, July 25-26, 1944, while commanding Company F, 2d Battalion, and 9th Marines. President Harry S. Truman presented him with the Medal of Honor on October 5, 1945. After the medal citation, Captain Wilson led his men up the open and rugged terrain at Fonte Hill where, during the night attack amidst hostile enemy fire, he was wounded 3 times during a 5-hour period. After receiving medical attention, he returned and led a 17-man patrol for another objective while engaging in hand-to-hand encounters, intense mortar and machine gun fire. At one point, he dashed 50 yards into the open to recover a wounded marine. They seized a second objective and 13 of his men went down.

J. William Middendorf II
In a letter dated November 8, 1976, Secretary of the Navy, J. William Middendorf II, said to Colonel Jim Fowler, "The first annual Marine Corps Reserve Marathon held on November 7 was an unqualified, outstanding success. Your efforts in coordinating the entire affair were just magnificent, and I predict you will go down in history as the one to receive credit for starting the marathon, which will soon outstrip the biggest of them all, the Boston Marathon."

General Louis H. Wilson,
26th Commandant M. C.
Approved first Marine Corps
Reserve Marathon

Since the first Marine Corps Reserve Marathon on November 6, 1976, the winner receives the Middendorf Trophy. The perpetual trophy was donated by the former Secretary of the Navy (1974-1977), J. William Middendorf II. In 2003, he donated 24 limited edition Franklin Mint replicas of the Iwo Jima Monument, which will be awarded up through 2104 to the top male and female winners.

Major Rick Nealis
Taking the baton for the Marine Corps Marathon in 1993, Major Rick Nealis became the 15th Marathon Director and responsible for continuing the tradition. The move into the position was a natural fit; he had a finance and logistic background, was a runner, and had directed smaller races in the early 1980s for the United Service Organization (USO) for up to 500 runners. He ran in the 6th MCM (1981) finishing in 3 hours 10 minutes 39 seconds and in 1982 he finished in 3:13:08. His personal best was in 1983 with 3:09:50.

Prior to accepting the position he had 140 Marines reporting to him, which he enjoyed but had to give up. In accepting the position, the fear was he would not be able to view the marathon as a runner. He knew the tradition of the Marine Corps. The race had to remain financially solvent because it did not receive any federal funds, it was real business and you had to pay for mistakes.

Middendorf Trophy for 1st Place

Colonel Fowler saw having Rick Nealis as the full-time Race Director as a plus to build up the race. When he attended the new building dedication it took his breath away and he thought what so many others had over the years before the race.

The marathon is taken on as a military operation with civilian components. At the time Nealis arrived, the race had grown from 1,175 finishers in 1976 to

11,262 in 1992. What was passed down? The MCM mission statement, "To promote physical fitness, generate community goodwill and showcase the organizational skills of the United States Marine Corps." In addition, the Operations Order, Operations Plan along with various Annexes, which cover every functional area of the race, were also continued. The preparation and planning is a year-round process with numerous briefs to the Marine Corps leadership and external organizations. The organizational structure includes the marathon staff, Officers-In- Charge (OIC), Non-Commissioned Officers-in-Charge (NCOIC) along with Marines and civilian volunteers. The reporting structure goes from the Marathon Director to the Chief of Staff, Marine Corps Base Quantico, to the Commanding General, Marine Corps Base Quantico. The next reporting official is the Commandant of the Marine Corps.

As each new marathon director came in, there was instant liability. Nealis came on board 90 days into the planning process and was not fully versed in the rules of USA Track and Field when he was faced with having to make a decision about a runner who had cut the course. There were international runners but no staff to act as an interpreter. There was a shortage of portable restrooms near the starting line. He was brought into the event management business. The rewards were still being able to work with the Marines and their "can do attitude." There is the instant feedback from the runners and being around healthy clients (runners) you receive a positive outlook.

"Oprah Winfrey opened the doors in 1994 when she ran the marathon (4:29:15) for her 40th birthday. The second boom had not taken off. The crystal ball could not reflect what Oprah could do in getting the word out. She demonstrated you

L - Fred Lebow, President of New York RRC   R - Rick Nealis, Race Director

could make a change in your life. We have more females in the race," said Nealis. In 1995 there were 2,880 (23%) female finishers, and the following year there were 3,716 (26%) finishers. The number of female finishers has reached 6,700 (41%).

In 1995, Nealis was faced with retirement from active duty. A company from Denver, Colorado, wanted a person to handle security for the Atlantic Olympic Torch Relay, which sounded intriguing. The other option for him was teaching at a school in Wilmington, N.C. The position for a civilian race director became available and Nealis was at the right place at the right time. This ended the era of the two-year rotation of directors.

The financial makeup of the marathon was changing as services were going from free to fee. In 1996, the marathon began a slow crawl into sponsorship opportunities, which changed the dynamics of how the marathon was going to do business. The marathon is known for its organization, it takes care of its runners and it's the race of choice and a credit to the Marines. The race is a quality event and the Marine Corps has been in business for 230 years.

The morning of September 11, 2001 at 9:00 a.m., there was tremendous excitement as the first meeting was scheduled with the architect to discuss the new marathon building. However, after two attacks on the World Trade Center, the meeting was cancelled. The atmosphere of the nation had changed and the sport of running changed. The position was taken that the race would go on as planned. The focus had moved away from portable restrooms, safety pins, and water stops along the course to terrorist threats and to evaluate risk management. Road races across the nation were being cancelled due to security concerns. We had to be concerned with anthrax and having runners use clear plastic bags and banning back packs. The Marine Corps Marathon was on board with President George W. Bush's message for the nation to get back to business.

There were a lot of runners who cancelled and feared coming to Washington, D.C., and the marathon could not guarantee their safety. The Pentagon area where one plane crashed was being treated as a crime scene, which meant planners had to find four miles to replace the section by the Pentagon. The course passed within 40 yards of the scene of the destruction. Five days prior to race, the FBI released the area and the race was allowed to proceed.

"The runners who did run stated it was the most moving marathon. It wasn't about time. Runners who normally ran seven minutes per mile were doing 15 minutes between miles four to five as they stopped at the Pentagon and reflected and took pictures," states Nealis.

The challenges facing Nealis in the upcoming years were how to control the growth. In 2005 the race closed out in 62 hours 19 minutes. Should a west coast MCM be implemented? Thousands of runners are turned away each year. How could they help the metropolitan community economically? How could they help the sport, physical fitness and fighting obesity? How should they continue to help support the Marine Corps and support the mission statement and recruitment challenge?

Nealis has no regrets with the event or his career choice. The running business is upbeat and the MCM helps to make people's miracles happen. He hears people tell their life-changing stories and the MCM is witness to their celebration.

"The MCM is an adopted family. The event business can consume you and you love the consumption. The quality of life, it's love and passion, and I get paid for working my hobby," comments Nealis.

A few highlights since 1993:

1993 – His first year, Nealis was faced with the cutting of the course by Dominique Baroid of Morez, France. The race winner was delayed one full day and this incident received national attention.

1994 – Handling the security and the media attention of Oprah Winfrey.

2002 – The Washington, DC area snipers, John Allen Muhammad and John Lee Malvo, which ended a couple of weeks before the race.

2003 – The marathon through charity partners raised over $32 million. The race was recognized by USATF with the USATF 2003 Charitable Race of the Year.

In order to support the growth of the marathon, the administrative and technical staff increased to 11 people who work year-round. The space in Building 3035 on the main side at Quantico was too small. In 1999, the base Commander Colonel Leif H. Hendrickson had approved the concept for a new marathon headquarters to be located at Quantico. The concept was approved by Congress. The new $3.1 million 11,000 square-foot building included 6,000 square feet of warehouse storage along with a state-of-the-art conference room with up-to-date audiovisual equipment. The building is being financed over 15 years and the funding will come from the race entry fees, sponsorship dollars and licensing agreements.

The facility will take the race into a new era. The Marine Marathon ribbon-cutting ceremony was held on February 23, 2005, the 60th anniversary of the flag rising on Iwo Jima.

Marine Corps Marathon Ad Hoc Publicity Committee

The genesis of "The People's Marathon" centered on the moving force of four individuals, Jim Fowler (referred to as the Founding Father), Herb Harmon, Buff Mundale, and Bill Mayhugh. Armed with only an approval for the marathon, the task was to start the extensive planning process and mapping out the logistics. The bond led to the formation of the Marine Corps Marathon Ad Hoc Publicity Committee, Inc., a 501(c)(03), a non-profit organization.

According to the Chairman, **Colonel Herb Harmon**, USMCR (Ret), "The mission set forth in 1978 was to handle publicity for the marathon and promote the U.S. Marine Corps and physical fitness." Also, the Ad Hoc Committee has helped to maintain continuity through the years. There were 15 race directors between 1976 and 1992 with some serving just one year. They helped to preserve the rich history of the race and shared new concepts to keep pace with the changing aspects of the sport as a form of physical fitness. "The People's Marathon" has found its place within the running community. There is no prize money, only plaques, trophies, and medals. They all serve as constant reminders of their accomplishments.

The committee in 1978 included the following: Col. Herb Harmon, Col. Jim Fowler, Michael Carberry, Jom Coates, Michael Harrigan, Bill Mayhugh, Buff Mundale, and Joe Trainor.

1978

1980

Marine Marathon Ad Hoc Publicity Committee Members
L to R Col. Tom Redden, Joe Trainor, Herb Harmon, Col. Jim
Fowler, Buff Mundale

R - Jerry Traylor L - Herb Harmon –
Chairman, Ad Hoc Publicity Committee,
Hall of Fame Inductee 2001

The Ad Hoc Committee facilitated communication up and down the Marine Corps chain of command. They often addressed non-military matters. During the first 10 years, the race was moving towards a big business operation. The Committee is comprised of members from varied background, both civilians in the private sector and government and military. The common thread is the understanding of the military culture and organization. The people and their leadership are the key to success.

The major accomplishment of the Committee was to help solidify the marathon as one of the premier long distance running events that receive national attention. The provision of the continuity was twofold in that they provided the assistance to the incoming race director to follow recommendations from the After Action Reports, and to maintain a big picture perspective in improving the race. Lastly, the Committee keeps the military and civilians on an even keel to understand the marathon. The growth of the marathon has been a cumulative result over the years. As the race improved, it was through word of mouth that the numbers began to increase. The role of the Committee is not to be in charge of the race but to support the race director. Everything centers on the Marine Corps and the runners.

The success of the marathon came about because members of the Committee propelled their ideas forward to constantly improve the marathon. All of the members are poised to accept challenges and deliver results you can count on for years to come. Committee members share their perspective along with a few of the countless publicity accomplishments. The publicity has attracted exceptional athletes over the years; In 1976, 46-year-old **Pete Strudwick** from La Palma, Calif., a junior high school teacher completed the race in 4 hours 48 minutes and 6 seconds. His mother had contracted German measles and he was born with legs that ended in stumps just past the ankles, a left arm that had only one thumb and a finger, and his right arm ended at the wrist. In 1977, he finished the race in 5:09:09. A detailed report on the second Marine Corps Reserve Marathon (November 6, 1977) was read and entered into the **Congressional Record**, Proceedings and Debates of the 95th Congress, Second Session, Volume 124, Number 39, March 17, 1978.

A quote from the Record, "What is exciting and remarkable about this venture is that it has taken the Marine Corps just two short years to create a sports event which can now take its place among the premier marathons in this country. Indeed, the competition last November was the third largest ever held in the United States."

At the third Marine Corps Marathon in 1978, **Peggy Kokernot** of Houston, Texas, finished in third place (3:05:35). She was on the cover of *Time Magazine* (December 5, 1977). She was one of three who carried the torch the last mile to the first National Women's Conference in Houston. The convention was presided over by Congresswoman Bella Abzug of New York.

The "Voice of the Marathon," **Bill Mayhugh** was the cornerstone from 1976 until 1994 and was heard every year around the race site. He was a radio broadcaster with a mellow-voice at station WMAL from 1964 until 1994, airing from midnight to 6:00 a.m., and Sunday 8:00 a.m. unto 12 noon. He recalled having Ambassador Middendorf II at a pay phone calling back to the radio station to conduct a race day interview. He was selected Washingtonian of the Year in 1984.

In 1985, General P. X. Kelly, Commandant of the Marine Corps assigned **Colonel H. C. "Barney" Barnum, Jr.**, to the Ad Hoc Committee. Colonel Barnum was the Deputy Director of Public Affairs and is a Medal of Honor recipient. The citation reads in part, "For conspicuous gallantry and intrepidity at the risk of his life above and beyond the call of duty as Forward Observer for Artillery, while attached to Company H, Second Battalion, Ninth Marines, Third Marine Division (Reinforced), in action against communist forces at Ky Phu in Quang Tin Province, Republic of Vietnam, on 18 December 1965. When the company was suddenly pinned down by a hail of extremely accurate enemy fire and was quickly separated from the remainder of the battalion by over five hundred meters of open and fire-swept ground, and casualties mounted rapidly, Lieutenant Barnum quickly made a hazardous reconnaissance of the area seeking targets for his artillery.

1998

Photo: George Banker

L - Bill Mayhugh –
The Voice of the Marine
Corps Marathon
Ad Hoc Committee
Publicity Committee,
Hall of Fame Inductee
2003

R - Col. Jim Fowler –
Marathon Founder
Hall of Fame Inductee
2000

2003

Courtesy Marine Corps Marathon

L - Bill Mayhugh – Hall of Fame Inductee 2003
R - Michael Ware

Finding the rifle company commander mortally wounded and the radio operator killed, he, with complete disregard for his own safety, gave aid to the dying commander, then removed the radio from the dead operator and strapped it to himself. He immediately assumed command of the rifle company, and moving at once into the midst of the heavy fire, rallying and giving encouragement to all units, reorganized them to replace the loss of key personnel and led their attack on enemy positions from which deadly fire continued to come." He was the fourth Marine to receive the nation's highest honor.

Colonel Barnum retired in 1989 after 27 and half years of active service and on July 23, 2001, he was sworn in as the Deputy Assistant Secretary of the Navy for Reserve Affairs.

Colonel Barnum states, "The Committee had people who could get involved with issues the active duty Marines could not tackle. The enthusiasm, team work and "can do" attitude of subsequent Ad Hoc committee members was great and strengthen the ability of the committee to get things accomplished."

Photo: Official U.S. Marine Corps Photo

Col. Barney Barnum
Ad Hoc Publicity Committee
Hall of Fame Inductee 2006

He continues, "The committee experienced fundraising restrictions/rules at the beginning and we watched them evolve into the new corporate sponsorship approach. The visibility of supporters like Ambassador and former Secretary of the Navy William Middendorf, II was most helpful and noticeable by businessmen and Arlington County elected officials, police officials and National Parks and DC police. All elements are involved in the planning, coordination and execution of the race."

According to Colonel Barnum, "The bottom line is that we all gave of our time (some more than others) and took pleasure in realizing, mission accomplishment – a successful race. We've proved, 'If it is worth doing, it's worth doing it right.'"

Eric Stradford, Gunnery Sergeant, USMC (Ret), comments, "Colonels Jim Fowler and Herb Harmon, General Samuel Jaskilka, Secretary Middendorf II, and each finisher of 'The People's Marathon' have endowed future generations with a legacy that YOU CAN WIN TOO! This critical value is essential to the nation's security in that it extends 'esprit de corps' beyond the ranks of the Marine Corps and into the community at large."

The steady marathon growth is linked to America's patriotic need. Each year, thousands discover the spirit of "I CAN" in the last four letters of the words "American." The People's Marathon embodies "I CAN" for observers as well as the fast and the faithful distance runner.

The Portofino Restaurant in Crystal City was opened in 1970 by Chef **Sergio Micheli**, his wife Pilar and his father Adelmo. They had a second restaurant on Glebe Road, the Firenze. A post-race reception for 50-60 people was hosted at the Firenze until 1989. In 1990, the reception for the Challenge Cup teams was started.

"I got involved with the Marine Corps Marathon through Bill Mayhugh. I received my U.S. citizenship in 1975 and it was a way to repay this country for what it has done for me. We had a wonderful time meeting the teams. I got to meet General P.X. Kelley, Commandant of the Marine Corps (1990-1994)," stated Micheli.

In order to experience the thrill of the marathon, he did want to run it all at once but did it over three years. The first year he ran 7 miles, the next year was 10 miles and in 1979 he finished the last segment to earn a well-deserved finisher's medal. His TV room at home has all of his Marine Marathon memorabilia.

The name of the race came about as the committee tried to figure out a name and someone said, "People's Marathon." It's a wonderful name and you see people of all ages, nationalities, and from different countries running.

There is a great sense of pride that he feels as being a part of the United States It is through the race that he feels a part of the military. The supporting backbone to the Challenge Cup team and the marathon is way to repay this country.

He came from Italy to the United States in 1962 when he was a member of the Italian Navy. He worked at the Italian Embassy for three years. At the conclusion of his service, he decided to stay. He met a lovely young lady and they were married and the years of happiness continue.

"The feeling you get up on the start platform and you see 30,000 people is indescribable. What is it that causes people to get up so early in the morning to come out and run? For me, to be up there with all of the big shots from the Marine Corps, a poor Italian immigrant, what am I doing up there? I feel so proud," stated Micheli.

In the beginning he didn't know what a marathon was. In those days, he weighed 240 pounds. It was after he met Bill Mayhugh that he was encouraged to start to exercise and it took about four years for him to lose the added weight.

"The beauty of the marathon is, people come from all over the world to run. It's not for money but they love the sport and they want the experience," said Micheli.

The Challenge Cup has been taking place for 29 years and each year the Royal Navy/Royal Marines and the U.S. Marine Corps get together at the Portofino a few days before the race. The two teams assemble for an evening of fine dining as the challenge is "thrown down" by each team captain. It's an evening of friendship before they step onto the field of play.

The tradition will continue for future years. In 1993, three generations of Micheli chefs joined forces as his son Richard, a recent graduate of the famed Culinary Institute of America, began his work at the Portofino.

Photo: Official Marine Corps Photograph – Sgt. Glover

Marine Corps Marathon Ad Hoc Publicity Committee

Marine Corps Marathon Organization

The Marine Corps Reserve Marathon started in 1976 and the name was changed to Marine Corps Marathon (MCM) in 1978. There was an evolutionary process from the day Colonel Fowler developed his concept paper to conduct a marathon. The marathon was not to be in competition with New York or Boston for top athletes but focused on organization. The Marine Barracks at 8th and I Streets in Washington, DC held the responsibility for conducting the marathon.

The growth of the marathon had exceeded expectations and at the end of the 1981 marathon, the responsibility was transferred to the Commanding General, Marine Corps Development and Education Command (MCDEC), Quantico, Virginia. The goal was to establish a self-supporting marathon program. The race director would be assigned for a 12-month period. All military manpower was to be voluntary on the part of each person.

The race was originally started in November to be scheduled near the birthday of the Marine Corps. Over time the race conflicted with the running of the New York City marathon. Starting in 1992, the race date was changed to October.

The framework for the MCM starts with the concept of operations, a broad outline of the commander's assumptions or intentions that cover a series of connected task of the marathon operation. The Operation Plan (OPLAN) includes all phases of the tasked operations. The plan is prepared with all annexes (fluid replacement stations, security, communications, medical support, etc.), diagrams, and policies and procedures. The OPLAN consists of 31 annexes. The Operation Order (OPORD) is a directive issued by the commander to the subordinate commanders to effect the coordinated execution of the marathon.

The present overall responsibility for the planning, organization, and execution for the MCM is the Marine Corps Combat Development Command (MCCDC) at Quantico, Virginia. There are 18 major functional control personnel who provide the operational directives for execution of specific tasks within their assigned areas. The preparation and planning for the marathon is year-round.

The overall responsibility for planning and execution of the marathon is under the Commander of Marine Corps Base, Quantico. The Chief of Staff is the liaison with the internal and external organizations that affect the marathon. He maintains communications with higher Marine Corps leadership. The Marathon Director is responsible for the overall planning and the day-to-day operation of the marathon. He serves as the liaison with all supporting military units and civilian organizations. He sets directions and adheres to policy and regulations, as well as establishing business processes that are effective and efficient. He identifies the functions that are critical to the success of the marathon. He is responsible for the overall financial operations and customer satisfaction (runners, suppliers, and vendors).

Force Protection: As a result of 9/11, there was a shift from crowd control to force protection, a process to protect the runners, equipment, and facilities. Force protection is comprised of planned and integrated application of combating terrorism, physical security, operational security, personal protection service, and is supported by counterintelligence and other security programs.

Since September 11, 2001, many things in America have changed. Race planning is no exception. Before this time, race directors enlisted the support of police to assist in road closures, traffic control and basic crowd control measures. Security requirements in the post-9/11 world require much more planning. Races involve a large number of people crowded into small spaces, a lucrative target for anyone seeking large casualties. Security may increase if controversial agencies or corporations sponsor the race or if the race is located in a city or area that would provide the right message.

When considering security for such large numbers, the means of threat delivery are numerous and often appear innocuous. From the suicide bomber's backpack to the cell phone that can activate an IED, race security has raised to new heights. Often race directors have to determine which risks they are willing to accept.

CWO-4 Kim T. Adamson, a U.S. Marine Corps Reserve and a judge by profession, was mobilized in 2001 and serves as the Anti-Terrorism Force Protection Officer for the MCM. After 9/11, the marathon would have made an ideal target due to number of runners, media attention, and multiple opportunities covering 26 miles. These all presented concern.

CWO Adamson recounts, "In previous years, higher profile security planning was not required. With 9/11, this all changed. Never before had so much coordination between law enforcement, fire and emergency services, and like organizations ever been done. Force protection was a key part of planning the event."

At the 2001 MCM, the crowds were studies for things out of the ordinary. Force Protection planning was being implemented to plan for the worst-case scenarios. Force Protection is defined as the protection of people and assets. All police jurisdictions had responsibility for some segments over the marathon route.

"The MCM plans for criminal activity, mass casualty-producing catastrophic events and the general force protection on and along the race course. Force protection will always be a key component in planning and execution. In 2001, the Marine Corps Marathon had a very visible and public force protection posture and a heightened awareness, second to none," stated CWO Adamson.

CWO Adamson adds, "The personal safety of all runners is always paramount. The Marine Corps Marathon, in coordination with local, state, and federal law enforcement, as well as the excellent liaison with other agencies, has made the Marine Corps Marathon one of the safest sports events out there."

Medical – Provide a comprehensive medical plan to include the placement of medical personnel and equipment along the race course. Identify chain-of-command and provide a liaison for local police and medical jurisdictions. Provide a main medical facility at the race site. Supervise the medical operations during the marathon. Develop a contingency plan for medical evacuations.

Legal – To provide advice and counsel on matters pertaining to sponsorship, vendor contracts and other issues as required.

Business Management – This area provides the overall financial accounting and budget functions for the marathon. This area coordinates with marketing and sponsorship and participates in vendor relations to ensure adherence to guidelines.

Information Technology – This area has the responsibility for the integration of requirements for the need for accurate and speedy communications between the race organizers and the users of the data, news services, and results reporting organizations. Identify new tools that will enable marathon organizers to manage and control the race more efficiently. Identify innovative ways to process data faster to increase efficiency to meet the expectations of the runners. Coordinate the connectivity throughout the race to include hotel, race expo, medical tent, race operations center, and public affairs. Implement a communication plan to provide communication throughout the race course.

Marketing – This area has evolved through the years and has the responsibility for sponsorship, marketing, advertising, and the race expo. The planning and execution of effective strategies that meet the runner's needs, meets the goals of the marathon and conforms to policy. Coordinate activities with external marathon vendors and supplies. Implement controls to manage adherence to marathon policies and coordination through the legal staff.

Operations – To provide the race course layout and design in coordination with course certifier. Provide course management to include course marshals at key locations, appropriate fluid replenishment stations. Provide the race site layout and the traffic flow for the runners and spectators, and coordinate with security.

Logistics – The responsibility in this area applies to the transportation of all equipment, race supplies and personnel to support the race. Provide a transportation plan to coordinate the movement of runners from parking areas to start lines. This area includes warehousing of assets.

Media Relations – This area has the responsibility for the media plan and its coordination, implementation and execution. The plan includes information about the marathon, branding of the marathon, and support for the sponsors. Activities associated with the press conference must be coordinated. This area serves as the liaison to the journalist and other media outlets, print and Internet.

Personnel – The responsibility of personnel is handled by each function area. Civilian volunteers are utilized to augment the military personnel throughout race weekend. On average, 3,000 personnel are required to support the marathon.

"I've been involved in the race all three decades and from different perspectives. First of all, I've never run a marathon. I affectionately say that all those thousands of runners are nuts! Then I look around at all the people running who are older or disabled and think, "I have no excuse not to be doing this!" It has always amazed me, the throngs of humanity all driving toward one goal, and I'm thrilled to cheer them on as they cross the finish line," stated Jenny Holbert, Colonel, USMC.

Photo: Courtesy Marine Corps Marathon

Col. Jenny Holbert

Colonel Holbert served as the Public Affairs Officer for the marathon in 1993, 1994 and 1995. The personality of the race was within her control and there were situations that did not make the front page of the newspaper. She recounts a few moments that remain visible and added to the personality of the marathon.

"My job was to get the story told on the runners, the winners and the race. I'll never forget hearing after one race that a man had a heart attack at the 26-mile mark (I believe in 1995). He finished the race! But MORE incredible was that the very end of the race is an uphill run. This man was going to finish, no matter what. I heard he lived through the experience and have always wondered if he ran another Marine Corps," she adds.

In 1993 she says, "We had a situation where a gentleman from Central America spent all his money getting to the race. He made one big error, thinking that it wouldn't cost much money to get from New York (where he flew in to) to Washington D.C. He made it to D.C., but he got to the race registration just before closing on Saturday. He didn't speak English, had no money and we were 'sold out.' This man was so distraught, almost in tears. This was to be the penultimate experience of his life and he blew it! Once everything was explained to him, he realized he had made so many mistakes getting to the race. But God bless the Marines. The staff quickly found a Spanish-speaking Marine, gave him a complimentary racing bib; got him to the spaghetti dinner for free, then drove him to a shelter to rest for the night. In the morning, a Marine picked him up and got him to the race. That was truly above and beyond, and the gentleman was overwhelmed with gratitude. This was one of those events that made me truly proud to be a Marine."

What better way to relate to the race than being out in front of the action and getting close to the runner while they are in battle along the course as she experienced. "Speaking of proud, the first time I 'volunteered' to work for the Marathon was in the mid-'80s when I was a captain stationed at Quantico. I was one who handed out water at the aid station in Georgetown by the river. It was an awesome day, mostly because the runners, who were at Mile 8, were cheering us Marines on! People were applauding us for serving our country and thanking me for being a Marine. I thought it was supposed to be the other way around."

A memory from 1994, "Then there was Oprah, on her 40th birthday. Her finish time—4:29:15. I'll never forget that time because I always tell first-time runners that they need to beat Oprah Time. Marathons are definitely a great equalizer. Oprah looked just as rough as every runner when she crossed the finish line with no makeup that day. She finished strong. You could see the resolve, tired as she was, in her eyes and that she was very content with her accomplishment. Her running our race created a lot of buzz in 1994 and it was an honor to have her conduct a press conference in my media tent. Thanks to her, CNN chose to cover our race, which was great for increased awareness of the "People's Marathon."

THE BIRTH OF COMMUNITY INVOLVEMENT

The concept of collecting pledges to raise funds for completing some activity is not new. Those who participate in the Marine Corps Marathon (MCM) are often referred to as "charity runners." The correct description is a person who wants to change his lifestyle to get into shape and to raise money for a particular cause for which he feels a personal connection. In the process, the proper training is received.

The birth of the MCM Charity Partner Program was in 1998. There were four primary organizations: The Leukemia Team in Training, National Aids Marathon Training Program, Children's Hospital, and Big Brothers and Big Sisters. In 1998, the MCM was the fourth largest marathon in the U.S. behind Los Angeles, Honolulu, and New York City.

In 2003, the MCM Charity Program raised in excess of $8 million dollars. On May 26, 2004, the marathon received the USA Track & Field 2003 Charitable Race of the Year award. Since the inception of the program, in excess of $32 million dollars has been raised.

The participant is required to raise funds of a specified amount. The amount will vary by organization. In return, they receive an entry into the marathon, certified coach, five-six month training program, and planned group runs.

The organizations have obstacles that they must overcome before using the MCM as a means of raising funds. The program design should be integrated into the organization's mission. The program should have a clear set of objectives to meet the needs of the participants. It should develop a process to the track performance of each participant. The organizations normally receive funds from corporate donations, foundations and individual donors. The program must have resources in place, staff and volunteers and prospective runners. A well-defined runner's training schedule should include education about the sport of running, medical risk of injury, and define the benefits to the participant. They have to be accountable, control all costs and develop a budget.

The organization should be concerned about fundraising (participants and non-participants), participant safety and progress, and raising the awareness for the organization.

Each organization is competing for a prospective runner. There are differences in the services that each may provide and different price structures. The cause of each varies. The organizations must plan for advertising, public and media relations to attract the runners. The public relations will help the public to understand the organization's mission. They must identify any laws and regulations they must follow. Each runner should be educated about the organization to assist them in soliciting for funds.

A major benefit from the various programs is the sedentary person is now on his feet and participating in physical fitness. A popular way of training is called the run-walk-run popularized by U.S. Olympian Jeff Galloway; it incorporates scheduled walked breaks for every mile run. The concept is a way to reduce the risk of injury. Participants come in all shapes, sizes, abilities and ages.

The run-walk-run™ method has been used by Galloway in his training classes dating back to 1973 and was introduced into marathon training classes in 1977. The method is detailed in the following books, which Galloway has authored, *Getting Started, Marathon, Walking, and Galloway's Book on Running 2nd Edition*.

"From the beginning, I knew that there would be a continuing growth of interest in my method because it helps in every way. I have been amazed, however, at the amazing growth in marathoning (because of my method) into people who were totally out of shape at the beginning," stated Galloway.

He adds, "I am very proud to have worked with the charity groups that use my licensed run-walk-run method, because it has allowed totally out-of-shape folks to improve their lives in many ways by finishing a marathon in six months. When they use my method correctly, there is a low drop-out rate and a low injury rate. This means that more

Jeff Galloway
Courtesy Marine Corps Marathon

individuals raise more funds for charity as they accomplish this positive life-changing experience."

There has been criticism from some experienced runners that charity runners take up numbers they can't get into some of the popular marathons, which close early. They run in groups and block the progress of faster runners and are not viewed as real runners of the sport. For example, imagine yourself on the interstate in holiday traffic and you come up on 10 cars driving at 40 miles an hour. The experienced driver gets frustrated and tries to find a way to get around without causing an accident.

"Unfortunately, there are a few charity groups that do not supervise training and do not use my method correctly (or at all). These programs give charity running a bad name and do not help their clients have a positive experience. Due to lack of supervision, a small minority of the charity groups allow their runners to enter the race when they are not trained to do the marathon," adds Galloway.

The members of the Galloway groups are trained to move over to the side of the road when they take walk breaks. At the end of the marathon, not all the finishers are Galloway run-walk-runners.

Some of the benefits of the run-walk-run method include allowing runners at any level to cover the distance, conserving energy to do other daily activities, walk breaks that reduce injury risk, improving finish times, and overall giving the runner control over future fatigue.

"There have been a few vocal critics of charity runners—but they are a tiny minority of runners (probably one-tenth of 1% of the running population). They receive much more publicity than they should receive. Races like the Marine Corps Marathon are open to everyone and therefore are crowded by nature. Faster runners are allowed to qualify for up-front seeding at MCM and can get out ahead of the charity runners if they will simply follow the rules," stated Galloway.

"That they raise hundreds of millions of dollars for charity is a powerful statement and produces a lot of good feelings by those who take part in the charity programs and the race organizations that can claim responsibility for the money raised," stated Phil Stewart, Editor and Publisher, Road Race Management and Director, Credit Union Cherry Blossom Ten Mile Run.

He further adds, "The slower runners present logistical problems in terms of how long courses must remain open, volunteers must remain on duty. There are some who do not display proper running etiquette, such as starting near the front of the pack, running in large packs which block other runners."

The length a course remains opens is up to the discretion of the local jurisdictions where races take place. In large metropolitan areas, tying up streets for seven hours is not an option. In addition to the streets, it creates a drain on police resources and the service is no longer free and can be costly when dealing with such a marathon.

Stewart raises an interesting issue: should the race benefit in a portion of the money raised by the charities? The race organizers perform all of the work to arrange the races and to accommodate their runners. The charity organizers view they are increasing the numbers of participants in the events and conduct their own training programs.

Ryan Lamppa, Running USA, Media Director, offers the following as the attraction to running a marathon:

There are several attractions:

One, the sense of achievement in finishing a marathon (which no other distance has); this is true for the serious, as well as the novice, runner.

Two, training programs have enabled the new, less experienced runner – the main source of marathon growth – to experience the thrill of finishing a marathon.

Three, said training programs have also removed the mystique that the marathon is only for the serious, dedicated, high mileage runner. In other words, the marathon has become more doable/less intimidating and thus, mainstream.

Four, the charity component tied to some training programs is also attracting people to the event, particularly women.

Five, it may seem obvious, but people like doing them and visiting the host city.

He further adds a prediction on the future of marathon running. Lamppa is a former staff member of the USA Track and Field Road Running Information Center, which compiles running statistics for long distance running (LDR) events within the United States.

Our preliminary numbers show a 2-3% increase for 2005 compared to 2004. Unless larger U.S. marathon fields increase (not likely as limits are being reached) or new marathons with greater than 1,000 entrants are added (running out of options/cities here), the U.S. marathon numbers should have slower growth or plateau within 3-5 years.

The Organizations:

Armed Forces Foundation

The Armed Forces Foundation was established to promote the morale, welfare, and quality of life of the United States armed forces community, including active duty military, reservists, and retired personnel and their families. The Foundation organizes a variety of activities and programs to address this need, providing quality support, recreation, and educational services to contribute to the retention, readiness, and mental, physical, and emotional well-being and enjoyment of the military community.

http://www.armedforcesfoundation.org

Injured Marine Semper Fi Fund

On May 18, 2004, a small group of concerned Marine Corps spouses founded the Injured Marine Semper Fi Fund to provide financial grants and other assistance to Marines, sailors, and families of those injured serving our nation. In the summer of 2004, General Alfred M. Gray, the 29th Commandant of the Marine Corps, two retired general officers, and a retired sergeant major joined them.

http://www.SemperFiFund.org

National Multiple Sclerosis Society, National Capital Chapter

The National MS Society was proud to be the first charity partner of the Marine Corps Marathon. The organization joined forces with the event organizers in order to provide individuals the opportunity to train for the event as a cohesive unit, while simultaneously raising funds and awareness about multiple sclerosis.

Participants in the National MS Society's programs have a unique opportunity to commit to a training regimen, and change their lives and physical well being for the better. They are motivated to remain in the training program because of the friendships they develop with their team members and also because they feel they are helping a cause they care about by participating. Often this causes the final event, be it walk or run, to be an even more fulfilling and emotional experience for the participant. The National MS Society, National Capital Chapter walks hand in hand with many of the approximately 18,000 people affected by MS in the Washington metropolitan area and offers a range of services to help these people and their friends and families cope with the everyday demands of living with the disease.

"I always wanted to run (a marathon) but I didn't want to do it alone, so it was a way to meet lots of people in the same situation. The team atmosphere is really awesome. It keeps you going out there week after week," says Laurel Wittman, Marathon Strides Against MS Training Team participant.

"Running the Marine Corps Marathon with the MS Strides team allowed me to absorb my diagnosis and run with folks whose lives had been impacted by the disease as well. It enabled me and the other runners who have MS to show our friends and family that MS was not ruling our lives."

Kate Morse, Marathon Strides Against MS Training Team Participant

http://www.MSandYOU.org

Organization for Autism Research – Run for Autism

The Organization for Autism Research (OAR) was created in December 2001 – the product of a shared vision but unique life experiences of OAR's seven founders. Each has at least one son, daughter, or grandchild with autism, many of whom are adults. One board member has both a son and daughter, now in their teens with autism. All have been active in both local and national autism organizations for many years.

OAR's mission is to apply research to the challenges of autism. In pursuit of this mission, OAR will: Fund applied pilot studies that explore new issues in autism or offer to enhance current knowledge in a significant manner; commission directed studies in areas of high interest within the autism community; and communicate the current "State of the Science" in autism research to OAR's constituents and the autism community at large.

http://www.researchautism.org

Running Strong for American Indian Youth

Running Strong for American Indian Youth® began in 1986. The mission is to help American Indians meet their immediate survival needs – food, water and shelter – while implementing and supporting programs designed to create opportunities for self-sufficiency and self-esteem, particularly for tribal youth. Through long-term development programs, such as organic gardening, housing, water resource development, nutrition and health care, we strive to foster self-sufficiency on Indian reservations across the United States.

Billy Mills, a former Marine, Olympic Gold Medalist and an Oglala Lakota (Sioux) from the Pine Ridge Sioux Indian Reservation, serves as Running Strong's National Spokesperson. He became the first and only American to win a gold medal in the 10,000 meter race in the 1964 Tokyo Olympic Games. Setting an Olympic record of 28 minutes 24.4 seconds, his accomplishment remains a great source of pride to American Indian people. Running Strong's marathon team,

"Team Running Strong," is composed of both Native and non-Natives from across the country who care about the issues facing American Indian families and Running Strong's efforts to empower them.

http://www.indianyouth.org

St. Jude Heroes

The St. Jude Children's Research Hospital was founded in 1962 by the late entertainer Danny Thomas. It was established for the sole purpose of conducting basic and clinical research into catastrophic childhood diseases, mainly cancer. It is the largest childhood cancer research center in the United States in terms of number of patients enrolled and successfully treated.

http://www.stjudeheroes.org

Team Lombardi

Team Lombardi was created in 2001. Team Lombardi is proud to be among the leaders in marathon-in-training charity organizations in the Washington, DC area. Team Lombardi offers an opportunity to move beyond preconceived limits and make a bold statement in the fight against cancer. The end result: a sense of personal achievement, increased public awareness, and crucial funds for treatment, education, and research.

In 1970, the **Georgetown University Medical Center** authorized the establishment of a cancer center named in honor of Vincent T. Lombardi, former coach of the Green Bay Packers and the Washington Redskins, who was treated for cancer at Georgetown University Hospital. The primary objective of the Lombardi Comprehensive Cancer Center is – and always has been – to provide the most advanced treatments available to Lombardi patients and, ultimately, to find a cure for this devastating disease.

http://lombardi.georgetown.edu/events/jointeamlombardi.htm

Team in Training – The Leukemia & Lymphoma Society

The Society's roots stretch back to 1949 when the de Villiers family experienced the devastation of leukemia with the death of their 16-year-old son, Robert Roesler de Villiers. The family members and friends created The Robert Roesler de Villiers Foundation to fund research to find a cure. The foundation later became The Leukemia & Lymphoma Society. The mission: Cure leukemia, lymphoma, Hodgkin's disease and myeloma, and improve the quality of life of patients and their families. Team In Training (TNT) began in 1988, when Bruce Cleland of Rye, NY, formed a team that raised funds and trained to run the New York City Marathon in honor of Cleland's daughter Georgia, a leukemia survivor.

http://www.teamintraining.org

The Carefree Foundation and Foundation for International Medical Relief of Children (FIMRC)

The mission of The Carefree Foundation is to ensure that no treatable condition shall ever be an obstacle to health. Through a combination of foundation programs and social activism, we will work to guarantee that quality healthcare is available to underserved populations in the United States and around the world. Furthermore, it is our goal to promote health and healing not only by providing quality medical and preventative care, but also by creating treatment environments that foster hope.

http://www.carefreefoundation.org.

The mission of the Foundation for International Medical Relief of Children (FIMRC) is to provide access to medical care for the millions of underprivileged and medically underserved children around the world. It strives to accomplish our mission through the following efforts: (1) fundraising for the construction of pediatric clinics in areas currently lacking a reliable source for healthcare, (2) directly influencing the health of children by encouraging and supporting individuals and groups who desire to travel to medically underserved areas of the world, (3) encouraging future health leaders to become involved in our purpose by recognizing their achievements, and (4) lobbying decision makers on behalf of medically underserved children and those who would aid them.

http://www.firmc.org

Big Brothers Big Sisters of the National Capital Area

As the largest and most experienced youth mentoring organization in the country, Big Brothers Big Sisters celebrates 100 years of delivering life-changing mentoring services to children in need.

Big Brothers Big Sisters makes a positive difference in the lives of children through professionally supported long-term, One-To-One® mentoring relationships with carefully screened, caring and committed adults in Washington, DC, Northern Virginia and Suburban Maryland. Big Brothers Big Sisters has a stellar record in helping children on a daily basis make healthy choices to stay in school, out of trouble and on track toward healthy and productive futures. A Big Brother or Sister is someone who has found ways to succeed in life and cares enough to pass on these lessons.

http://www.bbsnca.org

Tragedy Assistance Program for Survivors, Inc. (TAPS)

The Tragedy Assistance Program for Survivors, Inc. (TAPS) was founded in the wake of a military tragedy — the deaths of eight soldiers aboard an Army National Guard aircraft in November 1992. TAPS is a national non-profit organization serving families, friends and military service members who have been affected by a death in the armed services. We offer peer support, crisis response and intervention, grief care and counseling resources, casework assistance, long-term survivor wellness, and community and military education and outreach.

http://www.taps.org

Diabetes Action Research and Education Foundation

The Diabetes Action Research and Education Foundation (Diabetes Action) is a national non-profit organization that was founded in 1990 to enhance the quality of life for all people who are affected by diabetes and its complications. The research funded by Diabetes Action includes projects that examine how nutritional and alternative therapies may prevent and treat diabetes. Diabetes Action emphasizes prevention programs, such as school-based health education programs on American Indian Reservations, free books and free educational programs.

http://www.diabetesaction.org

AIMS India Foundation

The Foundation seeks to bring about a socio-political transformation in India through the collective efforts of hundreds of thousands of like-minded people and organizations spread across the globe. AIMS India was started in 1998 and its mission is:

- To educate the masses of our nation to elect their leaders with conviction.
- To influence the leaders to give the people what they long for.
- To inculcate the seeds of patriotism and sense of allegiance to our nation.
- To make an economically self-sufficient, corruption free, poverty-free NEW INDIA.

http://www.aimsindia.net

National Association for Children of Alcoholics (NACoA)

Team NACoA is comprised of many dedicated individuals from across the country. Walkers, runners, and experienced marathoners support each other and cheer on the team for a cause: bringing hope and help into the lives of millions of children living in homes with a parent who is addicted to alcohol or other drugs.

http://www.nacoa.org

TRADITIONS THAT KEEP THE PACE

U.S. Marine Corps Special Olympics Mini-Marathon

At the Special Olympics, we are more concerned with the quality of a whole life than in the "Speed or distance of an individual performance. More than single victories or trophies, our greatest respect and admiration go to all who try, who make a gallant effort, who stay in the race, no matter where they finish. In Special Olympics, it is not the strongest body or most dazzling mind that counts. It is the invincible spirit which overcomes all handicaps," Eunice Kennedy Shriver.

The Special Olympics was started in December 1968 by the Joseph P. Kennedy, Jr. Foundation. The mission of the Special Olympics is to provide year-round sports training and athletic competition in a variety of Olympic-type sports for all children and adults with mental retardation, giving them continuing opportunities to develop physical fitness, demonstrate courage, experience and participate in a sharing of gifts, skills and friendship with their families, other Special Olympians and the community.

The Special Olympic Oath: "Let me win. But if I cannot win, let me be brave in the attempt."

As Colonel Fowler gave life to the marathon, Major Jim Burke, 1978 Marathon Coordinator was inspired by his brother, Bill, a Special Olympian from New Jersey to start the U.S. Marine Corps Special Olympics Mini-Marathon. The distance was 3,000 meters and he had the vision of increasing the distance in future years. November 5, 1978 marked the beginning of the U.S. Marine Corps Special Olympics Mini-Marathon, a part of the third Marine Corps Marathon. It was hosted by the Kennedy Foundation, the Marine Corps, and the D.C. Special Olympics. There were 100 to 200 entrants from the District of Columbia, Maryland and Virginia, and they ran 3,000 meters around the Iwo Jima Memorial. In 1978, athletes participated from four states and seven in 1979

In the same year, the race was endorsed by the President's Council on Physical Fitness and Sports (PCPFS), which was formed in 1953 by President Dwight D. Eisenhower. The council promotes fitness and health for all ages and abilities through the participation in physical activity and sports.

Between 1989 – 1998 the Chairs for the PCPFS, Arnold Schwarzenegger, Florence Griffith-Joyner, and Tom McMillen provided autographed pictures and letters of encouragement to all of the athletes. Representatives, York Onen and John Butterfield, Captain, US Navy (Ret) both served on the Marine Corps Marathon Ad Hoc Publicity Committee.

"This event really gives the general public an idea of what Special Olympics athletes are capable of doing and how dedicated they can be in pursuing a training program that allows them to qualify for this race. This event is not a 'fun run.' It is a competition for which the athletes have trained. There are rules to be followed, as in any road racing, and our athletes have learned what is expected of them," stated Dolores Enriquez Boehmer.

In 1980, the third Annual Special Olympics Mini-Marathon featured 150 runners from around the country. This was the first nationwide mini-marathon held in Washington, D.C. The runners were selected by their regions to compete in a 3,000 meter or 5,000 meter run. The race course was along Arlington Ridge Road (Route 110).

Photo: Bernadette Bunker

1998

Special Olympics

Photo: Courtesy Marine Corps Marathon

2003

17th MCM
1st Place Special Olympics 5K
LtGen W. E. Boomer

In 1981, the fourth Annual Special Olympics Mini-Marathon was hosted by the Mid-Atlantic Region of the Special Olympics. One participant was Lorretta Claiborne of York, Pa., who had ran in the Boston Marathon and finished in 3 hours and 9 minutes. The following awards to the first place finishers were presented by 28th Commandant of the Marine Corps, General P.X. Kelley. The 3,000 meter male winner was Bob Osika of New York in a time of 11:29 and the female winner was Lois Leos in a time of 14:07. The 5,000 meter winner was Gerrard Legrande of New York in a time of 18:38. The female winner was Loretta Claiborne in a time of 18:56. Currently, she is a spokesperson for Special Olympics and a member of the Women in Sports Hall of Fame, having completed more than 25 marathons. In 1996, she received the ESPY Arthur Ashe Award for Courage.

In the early years, corporate sponsorship funded the cost of staging the race and purchasing awards, arranging accommodation with local families for the athletes and their coaches, and hosting pre-race dinners. The first sponsor was Boeing followed by the Bechtel Corporation of Germantown, Maryland.

In 1983, Dolores Enriquez Boehmer of Sallie Mae was instrumental in securing their sponsorship up through 1995. She remains a member of the Marine Corps Marathon Ad Hoc Publicity Committee.

"I see the participation with the Ad Hoc Committee as a way to continue to raise awareness of the abilities of Special Olympic athletes. This event has always showcased these athletes so that people can see firsthand the results of the Special Olympics philosophy: that through successful experiences in sports, Special Olympics athletes gain confidence and build self-esteem which carry over into the classroom, the home, the job, and the community," stated Boehmer.

A few high points through the years:

- Anytime the Commandant of the Marine Corps participated in the handing out of awards. During 1987-1990, the 29th Commandant, General Al M. Gray, Jr. During 1999-2002, the 32nd Commandant, General James L. Jones.
- For several years the Commanding General from Quantico would visit with the athletes and give them souvenir military coins.
- The race had advances from a 3K to 5K and 10K, and now back to an 8K. The athletes are now mainstreamed with all of the runners in the 8K.
- Runners who started in the Mini-Marathon have progressed to participate in the full marathon.
- Having autographed pictures for the athletes from well-known athletes or dignitaries (one was from Flo-Jo and President Bill Clinton).
- The use of the new timing devices (ChampionChip) worn on the shoes of the athletes. In the early years, the times were scored by hand. The Potomac Valley Track Club, formerly the Potomac Valley Seniors, provided the volunteers for scoring.

- The special t-shirts for the athletes with the marathon and Special Olympics logos imprinted. The Marines provided souvenir patches and finishers medals.
- Radio broadcaster, Bill Mayhugh of WMAL would interview Boehmer from his radio station to help provide publicity.

The challenges for the future:
- Replacing the Marines with qualified volunteers and maintaining continuity.
- Managing the logistics of new race routes and maintaining the continuity of management of the Mini-Marathon.
- Obtaining the sponsorship to cover the expenses, awards, and housing associated with the race.
- There is a need to continue to increase a publicity program for the Mini-Marathon.

The Ground Pounders

Legends are made, not born, and for the MCM it was one foot strike at a time. No one could have predicted on November 1, 1976 how many of the 1,018 finishers of the first Marine Corps Reserve Marathon would continue to return each year. A "Ground Pounder" is a person who has gone the extra mile and shown a dedication to the sport of running and physical fitness.

They are not running for fame or monetary gain but for the thrill of competition. A Ground Pounder is out for the personal challenge, the body against the clock and barriers to completing the marathon. The Ground Pounders have evolved over time, one step at a time. They have learned to balance family, work, and training. They don't just run the race, they compete and complete. Each year the training requires as much effort as that of the top competitors.

The Core Value of the Marine Corps, Honor, Courage and Commitment, can be translated to the runners above. They have witnessed the growth and changes with technology. In 1976 there wasn't a ChampionChip for scoring, heart rate monitors, GPS devices, or any of the sports supplements.

The Ground Pounders represent the living history of the Marine Corps Marathon. They accomplish their mission each year often under adverse weather conditions, and they are accountable. They exhibit the mental and physical toughness in order to endure. They have the determination and dedication to keep the streak going and to tell the Marine Corps Marathon story.

There are 1,018 runners who can make the claim they ran the first Marine Corps Reserve Marathon and only five can make the claim they are still running. Each one knows what they have given up over the years. There were some years when quitting was an option and they were not all Marines, but they had adopted their thinking, adapted and overcome the obstacle. Each year they demand more for their bodies, which may not be willing to answer the call. The speed work is not as frequent nor as intense, and weekly mileage does not peak at 70 to 80 miles. The training program was weeks before, now months as each step counts. Along the race course, they were not out to win every battle but their eyes were on winning the war and receiving the finisher's medal at the end.

It was not until 1994 that an elite group of runners were beginning to come to the surface and in a special ceremony at the *Washington Post* celebrating the 25th Anniversary of the Marine Corps Marathon in 2000 that the five runners received their name, the "Ground Pounders."

Will Brown, Colonel, USMCR (Ret)	Raleigh, NC
Roger Burkhart	Gaithersburg, MD
Alfred Richmond, Colonel, USMCR (Ret)	Arlington, VA
Charles Stalzer, Commander, USN (Ret)	Alexandria, VA
Mel Williams	Virginia Beach, VA

In 2001, Matthew Jaffe of Rockville, Md., was confirmed as having completed each year. In the same year, Charles Stalzer was unable to run the race. Due to a hamstring injury, he was unable to answer the call on October 28, 2001. He continues to run each year trailing by one. Stalzer is the elder of the group running the first year at age 48. The youngest is Will Brown who ran at the age of 30. Five runners from various backgrounds have bonded and continue to keep the elite core of the "Ground Pounders" running into the future.

LEGENDS IN OUR OWN MINDS
Colonel Will Brown, USMCR (Ret) was the youngest of the Ground Ponders in 1976 at the age of 30 where he was able to muster a 3:41:21 finish time. His running began in 1967 and like many others, it was to lose weight to get prepared to join the Marine Corps. He had three months before he was to report to Parris Island, South Carolina for his transformation. He weighed 200 pounds and he dropped 50 pounds (current weight is 125). He retired after 30 years of service in 1998.

To Brown, running is something that he does and something that he is. It has been a part of his life for 40 years. His weekly mileage ranges between 60 to 80 miles per week. The goal for any race is to do his best given the level of training and the weather for that day. When he goes to a race, he looks for scenery, difficulty of the course and interesting people.

A satisfying performance to date has been his 100-mile personal record in 1998, the Umstead 100-Mile Endurance Run (Raleigh, NC), in a time of 24 hours 10 minutes.

The level of training has remained fairly constant through the years. He doesn't do any track speed work. Once a week he does a long tempo run along with a hard and hilly workout. Each year, he races one marathon and three ultra marathons.

In 2000, the 25th Anniversary of the Marine Corps Marathon was a special race for Brown. "I was honored and privileged to be one of the five remaining 'Ground Pounders', as the marathon staff has named us, all of us who have finished all the MCMs. Most of us had not met in person. What a group of guys. Sorry ladies, it's an all-male club, and it's too late to join." Each had singlets with "Ground Ponder" on the back and they all wore race number 25.

He adds, "I was really visible throughout the race because of my number and singlet and, as retired Marine, I took advantage of that to rally anyone with a Marine haircut who was walking in the last mile. My battle cry for them was, 'One does NOT walk a marathon in. Follow me, Marine.' Some did, and I must have looked like the Pied Piper of Parris Island."

There is a sense of camaraderie within the group, he comments. "One of us may be left standing someday, but I didn't feel any sense of competition within the group. I did feel a deep, shared pride in what we've been lucky enough to accomplish. Legends in our own minds, I guess. I'll be genuinely sorry when someone doesn't finish. However, I'll be sorrier if it's me."

Semper Fi.

SPRINTER TO QUARTER-MILER TO MARATHONER

Roger Burkhart, of Gaithersburg, Maryland, ran his first Marine Corps Marathon at the age of 38. He was a sprinter in high school in Iowa in the 1950s. At that time, few people ran year-round so track was limited to the spring. He played football in the fall and fast pitch softball during the summer. In college, he ran cross country, indoor and outdoor track, with summer being a non-running season. While in college, he ran a 52.2 quarter mile. A high mileage week in college then, even during cross country season, was 25 miles and most college cross country courses were less than three miles. One time, when the race was four miles, he remembers wondering afterwards how anyone could possibly run such distances regularly.

For a few years after college, his sport activity was limited to volleyball and only an occasional run. There were few opportunities for competition and in those pre-running boom days, people wondered about old guys in their 20s who were seen running. In 1966, however, he decided he didn't care what people thought and began running again, first just spring through fall but then year-round. After watching the finish of the 1971 Kansas Relays Marathon, he concluded that he could do that and in 1972 ran the Kansas Relays Marathon as his first marathon. In 1973, he moved to the Washington, D.C. area where he soon learned of the D.C. Roadrunners Club and their weekly races and his racing really took off. In 1975, he ran the Boston Marathon after qualifying at the Shamrock Marathon in Virginia Beach. His first, and best, time at the Marine Corps was 3:22:40 in 1972. He has had 15 sub-four hour Marines and 36 sub-four marathons overall. In 1978, he finished the JFK 50-Miler for the first of five times in 1979; he logged 2,000 miles for the year. In 1985, he finished a 100K race, the Great Run Across New Jersey.

Burkhart believes that running is too much work to do unless you enjoy doing it. However, he cautions that when you begin running, you have to be prepared to work through a period of time during which running will be all work until you get into condition. Once beyond that barrier, the fun begins.

Burkhart's primary goal for a race has changed over the years from seeking personal bests to aiming to run at least as fast as the previous year to trying to limit time lost from the previous year. If, at the same time, he happens to place in his age group or finish ahead of other runners who he knows to be about the same in ability, it is a bonus. The Marine Corps Marathon has been a very important race to him and one that he has sometimes forced himself to finish under conditions where he might have dropped out of another race. He realizes that his marathon running days may be coming to an end but hopes to keep running on some level both alone and in races for the rest of his life, and most of all to continue enjoy the running.

During peak marathon training, his weekly mileage will get up to 60-65 and off season it stays around 25 miles per week. He prefers to have his runs in nature and away from the traffic in places like Rock Creek Park, Seneca Park and the C&O Tow Path.

Burkhart noted that his recovery after a race varies with the length of the race, his conditioning at the time, the race conditions, and how hard he ran. However, as he has grown older, it has taken longer to recover even after a shorter race. After a marathon, any obvious stiffness or aches are usually gone in a couple of days, but it may take a couple of weeks for his strength to fully return.

A GOOD SPORT IF YOUR KNEES HOLD UP

At the age of 35, attorney **Matthew Jaffe** of Rockville, Maryland, stepped up to the start with no expectations of becoming a part of the history of the Marine Corps Reserve Marathon. He is the second youngest of the elite club. While attending Bucknell University, graduate 1963, he was on the wrestling team and started running occasionally. In 1966, he graduated from the Georgetown Law Center. In 1976, he finished the marathon with a time of 3:41:38, only 17 seconds behind the youngest Ground Pounder, Will Brown. His best performance to date is 3:01:50, which he ran in 1982 at the age of 41 and it's the second fastest time next to Mel Williams.

In the early years, he was logging up to 90 miles per week but over the years that has been reduced to 40 miles. The runs are less intense and slower and the only time speed work is attempted is when his running partner, his dog Casey, sees a rabbit and gives chase. The racing goals are to finish within the same day since the competitive nature has been relaxed. The Marine Corps Marathon is his favorite as he stated, "Best runner supported and it really is The People's Marathon."

To date, he has logged 17-sub four hour Marine Corps Marathons. A satisfying performance was at the Capital Challenge, a three-mile race around Hains Point where he ran an impressive 17:36. After running a marathon, it normally takes four to six weeks to recover. A good race is made up of a good crowd, good runner's support and fun.

According to Jaffe, the sport of running, "is a good sport if one's knees hold up. Don't overtrain and have a good orthopedist who understands sports medicine."

JUST ENJOY AND LISTEN TO YOUR BODY

"Ground Pounder," **Al Richmond**, Colonel, USMCR (Ret), of Arlington, Virginia, shared some of his thoughts in 1998 as he looked back after completing 22 Marine Corps Marathons. In the summer of 1976, he was coming back on active duty to Headquarters Marine Corps in the Reserve Division. This was the time when Colonel Jim Fowler was in the planning stages of the first Marine Corps Reserve Marathon. All of the service's Reserve units were having difficulty recruiting and the marathon was to showcase the Marine Corps.

"Being on the Reserve Division staff, I didn't have the foggiest intention of running the thing. I was more of a short distance/sprinter type, and only ran long runs when I had to get ready for the Physical Fitness Test (PFT). I was shamed into running it by an older officer and it's been quite a 'trip' so far," stated Richmond.

In high school and freshman year of college, Richmond ran the 440 yards and relays. Once he had to run an 880 yards and felt like he was going to die. He turned his attention to playing football for 10 years.

He ran his first marathon, the Marine Corps Reserve Marathon, at the age of 37 in 4:04:14. Over the next 11 years, he was under four hours with a best time of 3:16:21, which he ran in 1979 and 1982. He started running other marathons and was averaging 3:16 to 3:25 and three were below 3:10. He qualified for Boston with a personal record (PR) of 3:00:52 and competed there three times.

In 1990, from late spring until early fall he did not run for five months as a result of an accident that required several operations. He was able to get in two training runs, three 3-milers and one 6-miler before the marathon. He ran his slowest time of 33 marathons with a 4:41:26, but he managed to run 18 miles before finishing by walking and running.

Running isn't as large a focus in his life as it once was. There isn't enough time to train adequately, and he was logging 12-20 miles per week during non-marathon season and up to 50-60 in the last several weeks leading up to the marathon. In preparation one year, he reached a high of 80 miles in a week.

He jokingly stated that his objective in regard to the marathon is "to finish and LIVE." A reasonable time goal is set based upon conditioning and training and that time going into the race. The recovery time after each race can vary depending upon his training preparedness, race conditions (weather and course), his personal "environment" the preceding week (amount of sleep, food, and other factors), and emotional factors.

"The fascinating thing about the marathon is that, for me, each one (of all 33) has been very different from the others, and I've learned or experienced something new or different from each one," said Richmond.

He stated a satisfying performance of his career was his "marathon PR of 3:00:52, although I would have liked to break 3 hours at some point."

GOING STRONG AFTER ALL THESE YEARS

Mel Williams of Virginia Beach, Va., age 63, a retired university professor, was running to lose weight for wrestling while in high school. Williams did not run competitively while in high school or college. The daily running routine was part of his training while on active duty in the U.S. Army. Williams served from June 1955 to June 1958 with the 11th Airborne Division, as a paratrooper medic.

Williams graduated from East Stroudsburg University, East Stroudsburg, Pa., (B.S. 1962), Ohio University, Athens, Ohio (M. Ed-1963) and the University of Maryland, College Park, Md. (PhD-1968).

While at Old Dominion University, Williams taught mainly Physiology of Exercise, Kinesiology, and Nutrition for Fitness and Sport.

The active running started in 1972 with the formation of a local running club, The Tidewater Striders, out of the Norfolk/Virginia Beach, Va., area.

Williams leads the group of five who have completed all 25 of the Marine Corps Marathons. When it comes to performance, he managed over the years to dominate each of his age groups since becoming a master (age 40 and over). There have been 21 sub-3 hour marathons. A back injury affected his time in 1995, which resulted in a time of 3:10:50, and a hamstring injury in 1996 resulted in a time of 3:31:26, his slowest time ever. His best performance was in 1982 with a 2:34:49, which was good for third master.

In the 40-44 age group, Williams has collected 2 third place finishes. In the 45-49 age group, there have been 3 first place and 2 second place finishes. In the 50-54 age group, there have been 5 first places. In the 55-59 age group, there have been 2 first place and 1 second place finishes. In the 60-64, there have been 3 first place finishes. In the 65-69 age group, he has come in first twice.

The first Marine Corps Marathon (wearing bib number 206) in 1976 (his third marathon overall) was two weeks after running the New York City Marathon (2:55). There were no expectations since he was at a party until 2 a.m., race morning. The lack of sleep did not work against the performance as Williams ran 2:51:41 (86th place overall).

The course in the first year took the runners along the George Washington Memorial Parkway past National Airport and into Alexandria, Va., to the turn around and back up the Parkway.

The memorable year was 1996, when Williams set his slowest finishing time (3:31:26) because of a prior hamstring injury.

"I ran with a hamstring injury that I had been nursing since early September; I did not know if I would be able to complete it or not, and actually had to stop several times to stretch it out as it became somewhat painful. However, the pain began to fade, and I finished at a comfortable eight-minute pace," stated Williams.

To keep the performance up, Williams averages about 50 to 60 miles per week and in his 40s, the weekly mileage was up 100 miles. There is speed work that consists of 200-meters up to one mile repeats about one day per week. His intensity and duration of the training has diminished with the aging process. His recovery time after a marathon can take up to a month, other races up to 25 kilometers, but they do not pose any problems for residual muscle soreness.

"My near future goal is to maintain a high level of training intensity to compete nationally in the 60-year age group. My distant goal is simply to continue to run as well as I can for both competition and health," stated Williams.

Williams accepts that sometimes you need to take days off if injuries arise in order to come back. The best time of day to run is mid-morning, but very early during the months of July and August to escape the heat. A competitive runner with a goal to run the best race possible, he averages about 20-30 races per year.

"My perspective on racing is simply to finish the race, particularly marathons. If I set an objective, such as a particular time, but do not make it, normally it does not bother me unless I made some mistake that contributed to my not making the objective."

Williams enjoys reading historical novels and traveling to foreign countries, especially if there is a marathon available.

"My most satisfying performance is having run all 25 Marine Corps Marathons, and having won my age division about ten times. Also, a first place finish in the 50-59 and 60-69 age groups in the Boston Marathon," said Williams.

Mel Williams joins another elite group, the 2001 Marine Corps Marathon Hall of Fame. There are seven others who share that status.

IN RETROSPECT

"As one gets older, it's tougher to stay in marathon shape primarily because injuries can become more frequent and so one has a harder time managing some chronic problems. I never knew till age 64 what a 'shin splint' or a 'pulled hamstring' was," said **Charles Stalzer** of Alexandria, Virginia, an attorney and former Commander and aviator (US Navy).

"Distance running is something that I got started in the 1960s when I was in the Navy and was the Officer-In-Charge of a small airfield (Webster Field), south of NAS Paxtuent River (Maryland)," said Stalzer.

There was no running boom nor were technological advances being made. The running was for fitness and consisted of a four mile course around the airfield. A test of the level of fitness occurred at the St. Mary's County annual fair where a 20-mile race was held. The course started near Webster Field and went to the fairgrounds in Leonardtown, Maryland. There were five runners in the race.

"The race about 'killed' me since I had no training. I wore Keds and my wife had to follow along in the car to try and get me a glass of water here and there—it was all country roads," recalls Stalzer.

All five starters completed the race. The finish line was devoid of the usual crowds, chutes and tapes. The other four runners told me that the 20-mile distance was not a true marathon, only a twenty mile. "I was aghast," Stalzer stated.

After being persuaded to train for the Boston Marathon, one of the few marathons in the U.S. at the time, "I entered in 1965; the cost was free but I had to pay fifty cents for an AAU card to prove that I was an amateur," said Stalzer.

Late in 1971, at the Boston Marathon at the age of 48, Stalzer recorded what was to become his personal best of 3:15:10 at the age of 44.

The U.S. Marine Corps Reserve Marathon started in 1976 and since Stalzer lived in the Washington area, he entered the race. "What was nice about that (beyond the great treatment given to all runners by the Marines) was that back-in-the-runners like me got to see the elite leading runners moving like 'blue streaks' north on the path as we were heading south to Old Town," stated Stalzer.

The first year in the USMC Marathon, Stalzer (age 48) was sporting race number 138, finished with a time of 3:28:58 and placed 451st overall out of 1,018 finishers.

The strategy and objectives have been revised over the years, but the desire has remained constant. The objectives are simple: finish with a decent time and always finish strong. He offers the following advice. "Don't go out fast; save it for the last six miles. First-timers should do at least one 26 miler in training."

"As I indicated to the USMC Commandant, General Louis Wilson, in my letter to him after the first USMC Marathon, not even Boston executed/administered the marathon as well as the Marines did," said Stalzer.

The elder Ground Pounder was unable to answer the call on the morning of October 28, 2001 due to a nagging hamstring injury. Stalzer, not happy about the situation, was in no position to do anything about it. He will be back to join the fellow "Pounders," just one behind.

2000

Ground Pounders
L to R - Roger Burkhart
Charles Stalzer
Al Richmond
Will Brown
Mel Williams
(Hall of Fame Inductee 2001)
Completed all 25 years

Photo: George Banker

2002   27th MCM

Photo: George Banker

2002   27th MCM

Photo: George Banker

2002   27th MCM

Photo: George Banker

Al Richmond
Roger Burkhart
Mel Williams

2004   29th MCM

Photo: George Banker

Charles Stalzer, age 76 6:31:03
Has ran 28 of the 29 MCM
Former Ground Pounder – Missed 2001

MARATHON LEGENDS

Col. Will S. Brown USMCR
Raleigh, NC

NO	DATE	PL	AGE	TIME	
1	11-07-76	558	30	3:41:21	**RUN# 219**
2	11-06-77	648	31	3:14:37	
3	11-05-78	1776	32	3:29:28	
4	11-04-79	2227	33	3:31:32	
5	11-02-80	2800	34	3:27:16	
6	11-01-81	2804	35	3:34:55	
7	11-07-82	3447	36	3:32:59	
8	11-06-83	3004	37	3:31:07	
9	11-09-84	3546	38	3:43:40	
10	11-03-85	3256	39	3:43:22	
11	11-02-86	1636	40	3:27:18	
12	11-08-87	2256	41	3:28:52	
13	11-06-88	3076	42	3:43:47	
14	11-05-89	4640	43	3:56:48	
15	11-04-90	2574	44	3:38:31	
16	11-03-91	3030	45	3:37:29	
17	10-25-92	3938	46	3:51:59	
18	10-24-93	3294	47	3:41:22	
19	10-23-94	2879	48	3:42:50	
20	10-22-95	2702	49	3:38:53	
21	10-27-96	4035	50	3:57:40	
22	10-26-97	5076	51	4:12:36	
23	10-25-98	2533	52	4:02:26	
24	10-24-99	2044	53	3:52:20	
25	10-22-00	3170	54	4:12:55	
26	10-28-01	2999	55	4:05:33	
27	10-27-02	3328	56	4:14:47	
28	10-26-03	2823	57	4:12:24	
29	10-31-04	3719	58	4:31:26	
30	10-30-05	4380	59	4:21:51	
31	10-29-06	7287	60	4:40:55	

Roger L. Burkhart
Gaithersburg, MD

NO	DATE	PL	AGE	TIME	
1	11-07-76	377	38	3:22:40	**RUN# 59**
2	11-06-77	1531	39	3:48:00	
3	11-05-78	2059	40	3:35:56	
4	11-04-79		41	3:29:20	
5	11-02-80		42	3:23:00	
6	11-01-81	278	43	3:34:37	
7	11-07-82	3766	44	3:36:17	
8	11-06-83	2401	45	3:24:28	
9	11-09-84	3049	46	3:38:40	
10	11-03-85	1733	47	3:23:06	
11	11-02-86	3080	48	3:49:07	
12	11-08-87	4156	49	3:52:00	
13	11-06-88	3362	50	3:47:50	
14	11-05-89	4572	51	3:56:09	
15	11-04-90	5758	52	4:16:34	
16	11-03-91	4141	53	3:49:07	
17	10-25-92	4367	54	3:55:53	
18	10-24-93	6256	55	4:16:50	
19	10-23-94	10174	56	4:50:30	
20	10-22-95	9071	57	4:27:00	
21	10-27-96	13407	58	5:20:37	
22	10-26-97	6097	59	4:23:17	
23	10-25-98	5714	60	4:49:27	
24	10-24-99	6071	61	4:50:10	
25	10-22-00	6737	62	4:57:03	
26	10-28-01	5223	63	4:38:38	
27	10-27-02	6984	64	5:14:03	
28	10-26-03	7981	65	5:23:37	
29	10-31-04	8365	66	5:42:56	
30	10-30-05	8759	67	5:16:52	
31	10-29-06	11719	68	5:49:04	

Matthew E. Jaffe
Rockville, MD

NO	DATE	PL	AGE	TIME	
1	11-07-76	559	35	3:41:38	**RUN# 113**
2	11-06-77	1356	36	3:40:14	
3	11-05-78	1091	37	3:22:36	
4	11-04-79	4296	38	4:09:00	
5	11-02-80		39		
6	11-01-81	1165	40	3:10:23	
7	11-07-82	1090	41	3:01:50	
8	11-06-83	2160	42	3:21:04	
9	11-09-84	423	43	3:37:07	
10	11-03-85	3378	44	3:44:49	
11	11-02-86	598	45	5:12:43	
12	11-08-87	1878	46	3:23:50	
13	11-06-88	5756	47	4:10:52	
14	11-05-89	7316	48	4:41:03	
15	11-04-90	7483	49	4:47:25	
16	11-03-91	8662	50	4:59:07	
17	10-25-92	8244	51	4:56:33	
18	10-24-93	642	52	5:26:34	
19	10-23-94	566	53	5:12:35	
20	10-22-95	13333	54	5:13:40	
21	10-27-96	10384	55	4:47:16	
22	10-26-97	8826	56	5:12:05	
23	10-25-98	167	57	4:45:12	
24	10-24-99	211	58	4:53:31	
25	10-22-00	11409	59	5:03:11	
26	10-28-01	11697	60	5:24:20	
27	10-27-02	85	61	4:56:-9	
28	10-26-03	8956	62	5:48:50	
29	10-31-04	8879	63	5:58:29	
30	10-30-05	11003	64	6:29:14	
31	10-29-06	11672	65	5:47:35	

Col. Alfred C. Richmond, USMCR (Ret)
Arlington, A

NO	DATE	PL	AGE	TIME	
1	11-07-76	754	37	4:04:14	**RUN# 712**
2	11-06-77	938	38	3:24:16	
3	11-05-78	2072	39	3:36:36	
4	11-04-79	1391	40	3:16:21	
5	11-02-80		41		
6	11-01-81	2361	42	3:28:25	
7	11-07-82	2070	43	3:16:21	
8	11-06-83	2178	44	3:21:37	
9	11-09-84	1550	45	3:18:37	
10	11-03-85	3436	46	3:45:38	
11	11-08-86	1751	47	3:29:09	
12	11-08-87	2798	48	3:35:40	
13	11-06-88	5512	49	4:18:28	
14	11-05-89	3072	50	3:37:14	
15	11-04-90	7240	51	4:41:26	
16	11-03-91	6654	52	4:18:09	
17	10-25-92	4580	53	3:57:49	
18	10-24-93	4303	54	3:55:01	
19	10-23-94	5347	55	4:04:25	
20	10-22-95	7627	56	4:16:12	
21	10-27-96	7596	57	4:24:59	
22	10-26-97	5650	58	4:18:37	
23	10-25-98	3544	59	4:17:18	
24	10-24-99	3929	60	4:19:07	
25	10-22-00	4360	61	4:27:07	
26	10-28-01	4197	62	4:22:38	
27	10-27-02	5038	63	4:37:25	
28	10-26-03	5589	64	4:45:24	
29	10-31-04	6011	65	4:59:39	
30	10-30-05	6670	66	4:47:40	
31	10-29-06	10944	67	5:30:15	

Melvin H. Williams
Virginia Beach, VA

NO	DATE	PL	AGE	TIME	
1	11-07-76	86	38	2:51:41	**RUN# 206**
2	11-06-77	167	39	2:51:01	
3	11-05-78	132	40	2:47:50	
4	11-04-79	181	41	2:43:58	
5	11-02-80	130	42	2:38:33	
6	11-01-81	142	43	2:36:48	3rd 40-44
7	11-07-82	79	44	2:34:49	3rd 40-44
8	11-06-83	81	45	2:35:30	1st 45-49
9	11-09-84	63	46	2:36:48	1st 45-49
10	11-03-85	109	47	2:41:10	2nd 45-49
11	11-02-86	72	48	2:38:34	1st 45-49
12	11-08-87	49	49	2:36:56	2nd 45-49
13	11-06-88	60	50	2:40:38	1st 50-54
14	11-05-89	223	51	2:51:40	1st 50-54
15	11-04-90	106	52	2:45:50	1st 50-54
16	11-03-91	101	53	2:43:16	1st 50-54
17	10-25-92	91	54	2:45:24	1st 50-54
18	10-24-93	162	55	2:49:08	2nd 55-59
19	10-23-94	212	56	2:56:11	1st 55-59
20	10-22-95	758	57	3:10:50	9th 55-59
21	10-27-96	153	58	3:31:26	
22	10-26-97	120	59	2:55:03	1st 55-59
23	10-25-98	112	60	2:59:00	1st 60-64
24	10-24-99	157	61	3:03:24	1st 60-64
25	10-22-00	125	62	3:01:40	1st 60-64
26	10-28-01	258	63	3:11:22	1st 60-64
27	10-27-02	227	64	3:11:33	1st 60-64
28	10-26-03	359	65	3:22:26	1st 65-79
29	10/31-04	479	66	3:31:05	1st 65-69 Bib 29
30	10-30-05	624	67	3:26:03	1st 65-69 Bib 30
31	10-29-06	10944	67	5:30:15	59th 65-69 Bib 35

Commander Charles E. Stalzer USN (Ret)
Alexandria, VA

NO	DATE	PL	AGE	TIME	
1	11-07-76	451	48	3:28:58	**RUN# 138**
2	11-06-77	1227	49	3:33:52	
3	11-05-78	1544	50	3:25:47	
4	11-04-79	2490	51	3:36:44	
5	11-02-80		52		
6	11-01-81	3322	53	3:41:57	
7	11-07-82	4943	54	3:48:18	
8	11-06-83	4252	55	3:44:33	
9	11-09-84	2834	56	3:36:09	
10	11-03-85	3256	57	3:43:23	
11	11-02-86	2507	58	3:40:29	
12	11-08-87	3076	59	3:39:10	
13	11-06-88	2641	60	3:38:05	
14	11-05-89	4461	61	3:50:40	
15	11-04-90	3118	62	3:42:01	
16	11-03-91	5567	63	4:02:46	
17	10-25-92	4289	64	3:55:12	
18	10-24-93	6175	65	4:05:40	
19	10-23-94	9294	66	4:39:42	
20	10-22-95	9660	67	4:31:18	
21	10-27-96	11439	68	4:56:45	
22	10-26-97	7090	69	4:35:53	
23	10-25-98	3985	70	4:24:08	
24	10-24-99	5432	71	4:41:33	
25	10-22-00	8189	72	5:21:29	
26	10-28-01	Injured			
27	10-27-01	8283	74	6:01:01	
28	10-26-03	9334	75	6:07:05	
29	10-31-04	9414	76	6:30:55	
30	10-30-05	10236	77	5:50:37	
31	10-29-06	12574	78	6:29:02	

The Challenge Cup

Legend has it that on November 6, 1977 Royal Navy Commander John McDonough participated in second Marine Corps Reserve Marathon. The Commander wearing number 2022 finished in 3 hours 56 minutes 48 seconds, which placed him 1,706th among men age 30-39. An annual challenge was proposed between the Royal Navy/Marines and the U.S. Marine Corps. Hence, the first Challenge Cup started in 1978. The British donated an 1897 Victorian silver cup, which is awarded to the winning team. When the British won, the Cup was to be displayed at the British Embassy in Washington, D.C., and when the Marines won, it was to be displayed at Marine Corps Headquarters. Starting in 2005, the Challenge Cup will be permanently displayed at the marathon office in Quantico, Virginia.

"Back in 1976, a certain Commander, John McDonough of the British Naval Staff, entered the race and also, as a wager, challenged some of his USMC colleagues. Afterwards he thought it would be a good idea if a proper RN/RM team could challenge the Marine Corps. We needed a trophy to race for. Enter HMS Temeraire (RN school of physical training). A search was conducted in the old trophy store and a suitable one was selected. It is generally thought the trophy was once aboard HMS Victory," stated Ed French, member of the first team, finishing in 2:44:12.

It has been a natural fit since 1978 for the Royal Navy / Royal Marines and the United States Marine Corps to continue the Challenge Cup competition; it goes beyond the time on the clock. Athletics is a universal language among nations, and each service places their best athletes in head-to-head competition.

Members of the 1st Challenge Cup Team
L to R - Jim Loveday 2:47:42, Ed French 2:44:12
Al Rich 2:37:23, Colin Carthy 2:38:08

Photo: Fleet Photographic Unit HMS

Ed French at Finish 2:44:
Challenge Cup Team Member
Royal Navy / Royal Marines

The success of the Challenge Cup is rooted in several factors. The main factor is the lasting friendship developed among all of the athletes. There is also the pride in representing their branch of service and country. The personal pride runs deep within each runner. The competition goes to a new level each year as it is filled with lasting memories.

The Challenge Cup has been transformed into an institution within the marathon. According to Commander Andy Rhodes, British Defense Staff, "It is a competition between friends. There is no one you want to beat more than your friends or peers. A challenge against friends in any sport is self-motivating; it's a fact of life."

Commander Rhodes is the liaison between the Royal Navy / Royal Marines and the Marine Corps Marathon. Like the other liasons before Commander Rhodes, they all served a three year tour in the United States.

"The spirit of the competition is extraordinary, and the Attaché and I are embraced into the marathon organization and by the Marine Corps. The whole event is fantastic and the challenge is part of the fabric of the long-term maritime relationship between our countries. We have always worked closely together, co-operated and been friends," added Commander Rhodes.

The members of the Royal Navy/Marines Team must qualify to run and team selection is based upon the performances at the London Marathon. The athletes look upon the Challenge Cup, and running in the United States, as a special honor.

Photo: Fleet Photographic Unit HMS

Photo: Courtesy of Ed French

L - Ed French,
R - John McDonough *(Founder Challenge Cup)*

At the conclusion of each race, a sports signal is transmitted back to the United Kingdom from the Embassy with the outcome of the race.

"Winning was my thought. I was willing to go 2:17 – 2:18 pace. I wasn't going to make a move until after Hains Point. You need consistence and not have any ups and downs. Then you look for the extra edge to improve," stated Mark Croasdale of the British team after his third attempt to become the overall winner in 1999 with a time of 2:23:27. His prior times were 2:25:24 (3rd 1996), 2:31:33 (2nd 1998).

"It's difficult to get a marathon right every time. I had a groin injury which did not affect me but you lose your edge without speed work. I wanted to stay with the group, and I found out if you don't do the work, you don't get the win. The crowd was big going back to mile six; it was deafening. I did walk at mile 23 and 24 and up the hill where I was passed, I just wanted to finish the race. If it were not for the Challenge Cup competition against the Marines, I would have dropped out," Croasdale said in 2000 after finishing in 2:29:38 (4th place).

The cornerstone of the British Team was Commander Al Rich who helped to mold the team in the early years. In the first Challenge Cup, he ran 2:27:23 at the age of 27. He was a two-time masters champion in 1991 (2:34:02) and in 1992 (2:24:55) he posted his best Marine Corps Marathon finish time at the age of 42. He ran a total of 12 times. In October 2002, Commander Rich was inducted into the Marine Corps Marathon Hall of Fame.

A standing tradition on the Wednesday or Thursday prior to the race is the Challenge Cup Dinner, which is hosted by Sergio Micheli (member of the Ad Hoc

Winners Royal Navy /
Royal Marines Challenge Cup Team

Committee) at the Portofino Restaurant, Arlington, Virginia. Upon Commander's Rhodes arrival in 2003, he had the honor of laying the challenge down for the Royal Navy/Marines.

Through 2004, the score was British Royal Navy/Marines (RN/RM) 19 and U.S. Marine Corps (USMC) 8 wins. The finish time of the top three male runners from each team are added and the lowest total combined time is declared the winner. A female Challenge Cup was held 1998-2003 and the score was three wins for the RN/RM and three wins for USMC.

Starting with the 2005 race, the scoring methodology was change to form mixed teams (males and females) for scoring. The finish time of the top three fastest males and the first female are combined and the lowest combined time is declared the winner. The record through 2006, RN/RM 21 wins and USMC 9 wins.

"As a Marine, the Marine Corps Marathon and the Challenge Cup mean a lot to me, and I will always check the results. Aside from the competition itself, I looked forward to meeting the Brits every year. Those guys are a riot, and they amazed me with the relaxed way they approached the race each year. I remember in 1989 we went out to dinner a few nights before the race and they were having a few beers, and there I was encouraging them to have another and thought that there's no way these guys would make it half way. Well, I was wrong. Although they didn't win that year, they ran a very strong race and I never took them lightly," stated Farley Simon, retired Gunnery Sergeant, USMC, the only active duty Marine overall winner in 1983 (2:17:46), and the only retired Marine to win the master's title in 1995 (2:25:25, 4th place overall).

Women's Challenge Cup – Winner
L to R - Capt. Rhesa Ashbacher (3:26:01),
1stLt. Patricia Restrepo (3:29:52),
Lt. Patty Bouvatte (2:59:29),
Capt. Bridget Brunnick (3:11:44).

Team Marine
L to R - Capt. Rhesa Ashbacher (3:26:01), 1stLt Patricia
Restrepo (3:29:52), Capt. Steve Schmid (2:37:10), SSgt Albert
Martinez (3:04:33), **Front** *- SSgt Matthew Zammit(2:55:16),*
Lt Patty Bouvatte (2:59:29), Capt Bridget Brunnick (3:11:44).

"I believe I have been on two Marine teams that defeated the Brits (1995 and 1997), but the drought in the Challenge Cup has been substantial. This year we changed the scoring system and combined what were previously separate men's and women's competitions into one competition where the top three men and top woman score. We lobbied for this move as a way to level the playing field because of the success of our women runners over the last few years. Ironically, we would have won the men's competition under the old scoring system, but lost because the Brit females ran so well this year. Perhaps it was some sort of cosmic justice for meddling with tradition, but I still think it is the right move for this day and age as the military services become more gender integrated (although the RMC is still an all-male institution which requires them to include RN women)," stated Major Alexander Hetherington, team captain.

Hetherington adds, "what makes the Challenge Cup so special is the historic relationship of the USMC and RMC/RN. After all, the original USMC was entirely modeled on the Royal Marine Corps. What makes the Brits so successful is the UK's proud running, cross country, and amateur sports tradition, and the opportunities that they have to train and compete, which generally exceed those available to USMC athletes.

However, the USMC has a larger pool of athletes to choose from, and in recent years I think the tide has been gradually turning in our favor as the Brits appear to be unable to find new young athletes while we are starting to have greater success at identifying young talent (remarkably, their top two finishers were the top two masters finishers in the race, and one of them, Steve Payne, retires from the RMC this November after 31 years of service). Although I say it every year, I

1st Female Marine Capt.
Bridget Brunnick (2:58:23)

Mark Croasdale 2:23:27
Royal Navy/Royal Marines Challenge Cup Team
Courtesy Marine Corps Marathon

feel more sincerely than ever that next year will be the beginning of a period of Challenge Cup domination by the USMC."

He adds, "what also makes the race so special for me is the sense of camaraderie I have experienced between the Marine Team members, the Royal Navy/Marine Team members, other Armed Forces Teams, and the Marathon Staff. From year to year, many of the faces remain the same and they have become some of my closest friends."

Major Hetherington is an AH-1W Cobra pilot by occupational specialty and participated in Operation Anaconda in Afghanistan in March 2002 as part of the 13th Marine Expeditionary Unit, and flew in support of Operation Iraqi Freedom as a member of Marine Aircraft Group 39 from March to May 2003. He currently is the Alpha Company Commander at The Basic School, Quantico VA, preparing to take 270 newly commissioned Second Lieutenants through a six-month course where they will be trained as provision rifle platoon commanders and assigned their follow-up Military Occupational Specialties, a job that he considers the highlight of his career as a Marine.

"Every time I go out running, the Marine Corps Marathon is vaguely in the back of my mind ... It combines the two things that my family and friends know me as, and that I think of myself as, a Marine and a runner, and it has been the source of some of my proudest moments in both categories. The course is inspiring and scenic, and generally requires some experience to run well on. I have participated in the last 12 MCMs in a row and 13 total. My best finish was 5th in 1996. I have broken 2:30 twice and cracked the top ten three times (1995, 1996, 1998).

Over the last 12 races, I have been in the top 25 every year, and I have been the first Marine finisher three times, the second Marine finisher six times, and the third Marine finisher on three occasions (which is the statistic that has become my benchmark for success as my times have generally slipped to the mid 2:30s over the last four years). I was asked to be a member of the All-Marine Marathon Team after the 1994 Marathon where I finished as the third Marine overall and have made it a priority to be prepared to compete on the team every October," said Hetherington.

"I felt so fortunate to be a part of the competition. It is such an awesome tradition and the Brits really make us work for it. It is a really special camaraderie we have and one that will stand the test of time," said former Marine Captain Mary Kate Bailey.

"My feelings about the race have always been serious, and I was so proud to be representing the Marine Corps. Lindsay Gannon is someone who I look up to and can remember saying to me, as she ran by me in 2001, "I will see you at the finish." She made it look so easy and inspired me to take marathoning more seriously," added Bailey.

During the period from 1978 to 2004, the Challenge Cup team scoring was computed by averaging the total of the top three finishers. In 1998, a female Challenge Cup was started with the top two times averaged to determine the winner. Starting 2005 there is only one Challenge Cup with a team composed of five males and three females. To determine the winner, the averaged chip time would be comprised of the top three males and top female. The low total would win. The first Challenge Cup started with the third Marine Corps Marathon (MCM).

Challenge Cup Teams
L - U. S. Marines Corps, R - Royal Navy / Royal Marines

Top Male Finishers In The Challenge Cup

Year	USMC	Time	RN/RM	Time
1978	Royal Bricker	2:32:57	Keith Cawley	2:30:32
1979	Chris Mollahan	2:22:12	Barry Heath	2:21:42
1980	Barry Heath	2:20:54		
1981	Michael Healer	2:24:55	Barry Heath	2:23:49
1982	Keith Cawley	2:27:38		
1983	Randy Hoyles	2:33:22	Barry Heath	2:20:46
1984	Thomas McKeown	2:27:57	John Stephen	2:24:57
1985	Chris Cortez	2:33:12	Michael Derrane	2:29:23
1986	Ronald Kronlage	2:40:27	John Stevens	2:24:06
1987	David Robisheaux	2:38:07	David Bennett	2:28:30
1988	Robert Bernal	2:37:46	John Stevens	2:22:27
1989	Farley Simon	2:22:37	David Bennett	2:27:13
1990	Douglas Marocco	2:37:12	William Nixon	2:29:31
1991	Manuel Estrada	2:34:34	Steven Ginge Gough	2:32:08
1992	Michael Romer	2:39:10	Chris Robison	2:26:27
1993	Douglas Marocco	2:34:24	Steven Ginge Gough	2:29:29
1994	Bern Altman	2:33:11	Steven Ginge Gough	2:27:56
1995	Farley Simon	2:25:25	Steven Ginge Gough	2:28:12
1996	Alexander Hetherington	2:39:39	Mark Croasdale	2:25:24
1997	Steven Schmid	2:32:39	Steven Ginge Gough	2:35:07
1998	Alexander Hetherington	2:44:33	Mark Croasdale	2:31:33
1999	David McCombs	2:34:58	Mark Croasdale	**2:23:27***
2000	Rob Adams	2:33:11	Mark Croasdale	2:29:38
2001	Alexander Hetherington	2:38:05	Steve Payne	2:31:27
2002	Aaron Nichols	2:35:53	Mark Croasdale	2:30:46
2003	Alexander Hetherington	2:37:07	Mark Croasdale	2:30:20
2004	William Edwards	2:35:16	Mark Croasdale	2:32:54
2005	Alexander Hetherington	2:35:23	Dauvio Roberts	2:30:39
2006	Timothy Tapply	2:34:40	Dauvio Roberts	2:34:55

Top Female Finishers In The Challenge Cup

Year	USMC	Time	RN/RM	Time
1998	Patty Bouvatte	2:59:29	Lindsay Gannon	3:08:42
1999	Bridget Brunnick	2:58:23	Lindsay Gannon	2:59:14
2000	Mary Kate Sullivan	3:11:23	Lindsay Gannon	3:05:27
2001	Mary Kate Sullivan	3:04:31	Lindsay Gannon	2:54:46
2002	Mary Kate Sullivan	3:02:24	Wendy Scott	3:17:16
2003	Ginger Beals	3:11:21	Lindsay Gannon	2:58:46
2004	Mary Kate Bailey	**2:48:31***	None	
2005	Tara Smith	3:12:00	Wendy Scott	2:59:09
2006	Tara Smith	3:19:36	Zoe Rooke	3:21:41

* Overall Male/Female Winner

Male Challenge Cup

Year	USMC	Win	British RN/RM	Win
1978	USMC	Win	British RN/RM	
1979	USMC	Win	British RN/RM	
1980	USMC		British RN/RM	Win
1981	USMC	Win	British RN/RM	
1982	USMC	Win	British RN/RM	
1983	USMC	Win	British RN/RM	
1984	USMC		British RN/RM	Win
1985	USMC		British RN/RM	Win
1986	USMC		British RN/RM	Win
1987	USMC		British RN/RM	Win
1988	USMC		British RN/RM	Win
1989	USMC	Win	British RN/RM	
1990	USMC		British RN/RM	Win
1991	USMC		British RN/RM	Win
1992	USMC		British RN/RM	Win
1993	USMC		British RN/RM	Win
1994	USMC		British RN/RM	Win
1995	USMC	Win	British RN/RM	
1996	USMC		British RN/RM	Win
1997	USMC	Win	British RN/RM	
1998	USMC		British RN/RM	Win
1999	USMC		British RN/RM	Win
2000	USMC		British RN/RM	Win
2001	USMC		British RN/RM	Win
2002	USMC		British RN/RM	Win
2003	USMC		British RN/RM	Win
2004	USMC		British RN/RM	Win
2005	USMC		British RN/RM	Win
2006	USMC		British RN/RM	Win
Total		8		21

Female Challenge Cup

Year	USMC	Win	British RN/RM	Win
1998	USMC	Win	British RN/RM	
1999	USMC		British RN/RM	Win
2000	USMC		British RN/RM	Win
2002	USMC	Win	British RN/RM	
2003	USMC	Win	British RN/RM	
2004	USMC	Win	British RN/RM	
Total		4		3

Significant Memories of Marathon Runners 1976-1985

A collection of events and runners that stand out as significant in the history of the MCM.

November 7, 1976 was the first Marine Corps Reserve Marathon, a test for the U.S. Marine Corps to host what was to be the third-largest marathon in the United States. The course selected was used for the first year only. To the surprise of many, the race attracted 1,175 registrations and they paid the $2 entry fee. The temperature was 40 degrees. There were 1,018 finishers (994 males and 24 females) and 155 males and 8 females who qualified for the Boston Marathon.

The start was at the Iwo Jima Memorial and down to Route 110 South to the North Pentagon Parking Lot and back out to Route 110 to access and run across Arlington Memorial Bridge using the sidewalk. The course continued up to the Lincoln Memorial and around the right side of Memorial Circle onto the path along the north side of the Reflecting Pool (parallel to Constitution Avenue). At 17th Street, it followed the path up the far side of the Reflecting Pool and back towards the Lincoln Memorial. At Daniel French Drive, a left turn to cross over to Independence Avenue to Ohio Drive.

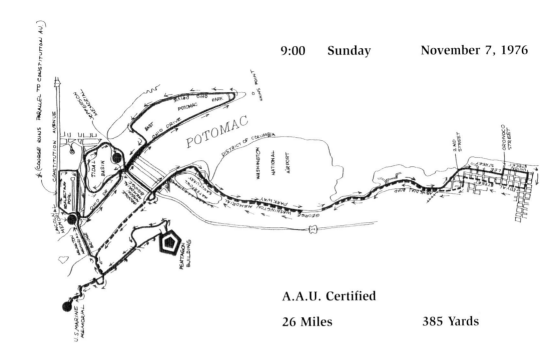

9:00   Sunday   November 7, 1976

A.A.U. Certified

26 Miles   385 Yards

From Ohio Drive it continued to the end to cross over the Inlet Bridge to proceed to the tip of Hains Point (East Potomac Park) along the river side. Follow the Channel side back up to Buckeye Drive and a left turn and a right to go back to across the Inlet Bridge. The path follows around the Tidal Basin to cross in the inner section of the Kutz Bridge and then around to the Jefferson Memorial to cross over the George Mason Memorial Bridge.

The runners proceed past the Water Fowl Sanctuary and past National Airport, then follow the George Washington Memorial Parkway going south into Old Town Alexandria (Washington Street). There is right turn at Abingdon Road and down to Lee Street and a left turn at Oronoco Street and Union Street to King Street over to Royal Street up to 2nd Street to get back to the George Washington Memorial Parkway. Just before the Arlington Memorial Bridge, there is a left turn to loop back onto Route 110 to go north back to the Iwo Jima Memorial.

The race standout was two-time Olympian **Kenny Moore** of Eugene, Oregon. He graduated from North Eugene High School in 1962 and the University of Oregon in 1968. He trained under Bill Bowerman. At the 1968 Olympics in Mexico City, he placed 14th in the marathon. On December 7, 1969, he broke the American marathon record (2:13:28) at the 22nd Fukuoka International Marathon in Japan by placing seventh in 2:13:28. The following year, he placed second in 2:11:36. He was the U.S. Marathon Champion in 1971 with a time of 2:16:49 – the fastest time since 1925 and the first runner to go under 2:20. At the 1982 Olympics in Munich, Germany, he placed fourth in 2:15:40.

Moore had an impressive record coming into the race and a sub 2:20 time was possible. As the race developed, he got lost in the area of National Airport and lost valuable time. He won the inaugural race in a time of 2:21:14.

He later became a senior writer for *Sports Illustrated* 1980-1996. He wrote "Best Efforts" in 1982. Moore was the executive producer and co-writer of the movie "Without Limits," a feature film about Steve Prefontaine. He has appeared in two films, "Personal Best," and "Tequila Sunrise." He was inducted into the Hall of Fames for the Road Runners Club of America in 1988 and in 2001 the National Distance Running in Utica, New York.

"I found Kenny to be focused as most world-class marathoners are, and of course, an intellectual sort of athlete, and I always admired his writing tremendously; it's very poetic and unique. What gives him power in writing about marathoning is he knows that part of the sport that only a few can know," said **Bill Rodgers**, 1976 Olympian, a 4-time winner of the Boston Marathon, 4-time winner of the New York City Marathon, 4-time winner of the Washington, DC Cherry Blossom Ten Mile Run, Contributing Editor for *Running Times Magazine*. He was ranked #1 in the world in the Marathon by *Track & Field News* in 1975, 1977, and 1979, and #2 in the world in 1978.

Years later, Rodgers provided commentary on the Marine Corps Marathon (1995). "I have done a few clinics at the marathon (one with George Sheehan), but also remember doing TV at the finish. No one who was a certified member of the first running boom predicted the extra large boom that followed the first one, and that races like Marine Corps would grow so huge."

"As I was standing on the knoll Sunday in the cool morning air, I sensed a true solidarity among the runners. It is something I have felt at races before. Because of the large number of fellow servicemen, it was even more intense than usual. The Marine Band played the National Anthem, and I saw the crowd rise. With the band playing, the flag waving in the breeze and the moment in the foreground, I was truly inspired. It is a scene I shall never forget," stated **Samuel R. Maizel**, Cadet Captain of the Marine Corps Marathon Team from West Point, second place in 2:25:02 in 1976.

Cadet Maizel was riding high in the saddle at the beginning of the race as he recounts, "I had a decent chance to win the Marine Corps Marathon, which would have been a big deal for an Army cadet. I went to the front at the beginning of the race and really started to believe that maybe I could do it. After about five miles, a tall fellow in a green uniform pulled up alongside me (I am 6 feet, and he was taller). After a few minutes, I realized it was Kenny Moore, the Olympian in the Marathon. We ran stride for stride for about 16 miles. When we hit the 20 mile mark, he realized I was not going away voluntarily and he shifted into another gear I did not have. He steadily pulled away from me for the next few miles, and I started thinking about hanging onto second."

He suggested that the race should promote a military marathon championship to increase the team size up to five instead of three. In addition, it should establish awards for the top military runners. He further added, "This is not to imply cutting civilians out of the race, but there is a golden opportunity for the large military running community to gain some recognition."

The day was not without drama, which he recounts, "I showed up at the finish line with no racing socks, so I decided just to race in my flats, with no socks. By the end of the race, I had taken the skin off the tops of all my toes, and after I finished a Marine Corps Corpsman saw my feet, which were bloody, and tried to clean them off with hydrogen peroxide. I fought him off and insisted he do it with just water, which stung plenty enough. I ended up having to attend classes for days at West Point wearing my black bedroom slippers because I couldn't get my leather shoes on my feet, and they would not let me wear my sneakers with my uniform, because my sneakers were white."

Maizel attained the rank of Lieutenant Colonel and served during Operations Desert Storm and Desert Shield and received the Bronze Service Medal (meaning he distinguished himself by heroic or meritorious achievement or service, in connection with military operations against an armed enemy).

There were a few more notable finishers:

Episcopal High School teacher, **Max White** of Alexandria, Va., was a local favorite and finished in 2:26:33 (6th place). Jennifer White placed second in 2:58:03.

Susan Mallery of Columbus, Ohio, was the winning female in 2:56:33. She was a graduate of Washington-Lee High School in Arlington, Va.

The grandnephew of General Ryan, **Kevin Fisher**, age 17, a student of El Segundo High School, California, ran a record of 2:39:58 (28th place).

Hugh Jascourt, age 41, finished in 3:58:21. In 1961, he founded the District of Columbia Road Runners Club. Since 1977, the club holds the Hugh Jascourt 4-Miler. He was a former Road Runner Clubs of American President (1962-1966).

The Deputy Assistant Secretary of Defense, Energy, Environment and Safety, **George Marienthal**, finished in 2:53:35 (101st place).

Winston Brown, age 11, of Portsmouth, Virginia, finished in 3:07:08.

Overcoming all odds was **Peter Strudwick**, age 46 of La Palma, Calif., finished in 4:48:06. He was born with a birth defect that left him with only the front portion of his feet and two fingers on each hand. He wore specially constructed shoes. A high school math teacher, a former psychologist in the space program, and author of the book, "Come Run With Me," he ran his first marathon at age 39 in 1969.

Henley Gabeau (then Roughton) comments: "I had only started running the year before, in 1975. Eleven girlfriends and I had organized the first women-only running club, the Washington RunHers Limited Club, in the fall of 1976. We did this because, back then, the other running clubs in the area did not encourage women to run – most of the members of the other clubs were 'wives of' the real running members: male. Sometime between 1975 and 1976, we started seeing ads for the first Marine Corps Marathon. Since the racecourse was located in Washington, DC, Arlington and Alexandria, it was attractive to us since we knew the streets and the course very well. We ran those streets all the time. I had never run a marathon before and it sounded very formidable, but a wonderful challenge too, being in our own backyard."

She was inducted into the Road Runners Club of America (RRCA) Hall of Fame in 1985, and is a former Executive Director of the RRCA. She shares her thoughts from the experience of the first Marine Corps Reserve Marathon (MCRM):

"The RunHers, in our gaudy purple and green outfits, had been winning most of the races we entered as a team, and to run the MCRM was attractive to us. Six RunHers entered. I, personally, was both very excited and scared of the distance, and thrilled that I might be able to accomplish it. It was a personal challenge, for I had never run that far, but having five other RunHers also training for it was tremendously encouraging, and made it a lot more fun."

"Being one of only 24 women in the race did make us feel unique, but probably more as freaks than outstanding athletes. Women runners were still looked upon at that time as kind of weird. I don't recall any particular notice from the race organizers, pro or con. Women didn't get much recognition in those days. Keep in mind that there was NO women's marathon in the Olympics yet either. The scuttlebutt — even in *Playboy* — was that our uteruses would fall out if we ran long distances. Those of us who did run long distances intimately knew the joys of it, and knew that it was not hurting us physically."

"That was the first year that Boston had instituted its time limits for entry into that marathon. All of us had that goal of qualifying, and we had to run at least 3:30 to get into Boston. I ran about 3:22:42 (6th place). Jennifer White (Haas) was the first RunHer, and second overall (2:58:03), I think Barbara Jones was second. Caroline Hahn (Morris) ran 3:24:24 (7th place) and squeaked under the time limit, and Valerie Nye ran 3:32:53 (10th place) while Ellen Wessel ran 4:43:40 (21st place). They were just over the 3:30 and petitioned the Boston officials to let them in, which they did. Yes, I felt very competitive and was determined to qualify for Boston."

"I remember, on Hains Point, being thrilled to be running near Kenny Moore's then-wife. That was significant because an article she had written in *Sports Illustrated* about a year prior to that, about her beginning running, had inspired me to start my own running."

"*The Washington Post's* coverage of the entire race, male or female, was paltry and minimal. I think it was about one column in the back half of the sports pages the next day. I wrote to George Solomon, venting my frustration at the lack of *all* coverage – not just because the women's race was not covered."

"And yes, I did feel that women's participation would grow. As president of the Washington RunHers, I was fielding call after call from women who wanted to join and/or wanted more information about running. A year later, Jeff Darman appointed me the RRCA liaison to the State Department's Women's Torch Relay, which went from Seneca Falls, NY to Houston, the site that year of the International Women's Year conference. There I met Jacqueline Hansen and Leal Ann Rinehart, the American record-holders in the marathon and advocates for a women's Olympic Marathon. Their enthusiasm ignited in me the drive to push for a women's Olympic marathon. I worked through the RRCA and was asked to work on other national committees to accomplish that goal. Of course, we got it, and in 1984, American Joanie Benoit won it."

Gabeau ran a total of three other Marine Corps Marathons (1981-3:15:35, 1978 --DNF, 1995 -4:39:24) and over the years did a lot of volunteer work at the behest of the marathon to organize women runners' clinics for them over the years.

"The Marine Corps Marathon was special, and I feel honored to have run in the very first one. It was a thrill to run by all the monuments, be cheered by the tiny groups of people along the route here and there to clap for us, and to be one of 24 women to have accomplished it in 1976. As my very first marathon ever, it will *always* have a special place in my heart, personal running history, and memories."

U. S. Army Major **Robert Nakamura** comments, "By 1976, I had already run three marathons. In 1972, I was living in Heidelberg, Germany, assigned to the NATO Central Army Group. My first marathon was in Mannheim that year and I ran 4:02. In 1972, the summer Olympics were held in Germany and Frank Shorter won the marathon and Kenny Moore finished fourth. I was there in Munich before the terrorist hit the Israeli Olympic Team. I think that Frank Shorter's victory at the Olympics was the inspiration that started the running craze that is still going today."

He states further, "In 1976, the Marine Corps Reserve Marathon made its debut. By this time, I was working at the Defense Logistic Agency at Cameron Station in Alexandria, Va. The first year was great weather (cool) and I saw Kenny Moore running alone back toward the Pentagon while we were still running south toward Alexandria. I don't remember many women in the race." His time was 3:15:11.

The second Marine Corps Reserve Marathon, Sunday, **November 6, 1977,** was marked by improvements. The turns were marked with traffic cones, a police escort was provided for the leaders and course marshals throughout the course. The course was changed to be more scenic and the George Washington Parkway and Old Alexandria was eliminated and the course was extended to include Capitol Hill.

The temperature was in the 50s with winds 10 to 15 miles per hour. The registration and finishers numbers doubled over the first year. There were 2,279 male finishers and 87 women. There were 591 returnees from 1976.

It was **Kevin McDonald**, a health system planner from Greenvile, S.C., who was the victor in a time of 2:19:36 the first time in 15 marathons since 1973 that he went under 2 hours 20 minutes. He was a native of New Jersey and a Villanova University graduate. In the 1975 Boston Marathon he placed 25th in 2:20 and at the 1976 Olympic Marathon Trials in Eugene, Oregon, he finished in 2:21. McDonald won 9 of 12 long distances races in 1977. Susan Mallery, Columbus, Ohio, made a successful defense of her title and lead wire-to-wire to win the women's division in 2:54:04. She lowered the record from 2:56:33.

Kathryn Ann (Kitty) Consolo, a junior at Wake Forest and runner up in 3:08:09 commented, "I had traveled with some fellow students from Wake Forest University in Winston-Salem, NC. I had high hopes of breaking 3 hours because I had run a 3:14 in my first marathon in June 1977, the Toledo Glass marathon and even took first place in the women's. I had done long runs this time and more miles, around 75 miles a

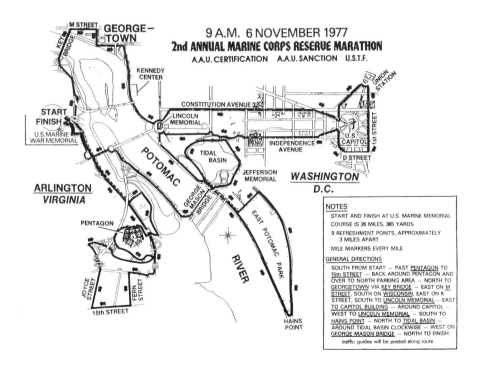

Place 1977 Kitty Consolo
4th 3:08:09

week and felt the 3-hour mark would be mine. However, I went out too fast, at a 2:54 pace for the halfway point. I remember starting to slow even before 20 miles and realized it would be another struggle in. While I managed to finish 4th place in the women's, I was so disappointed to be so far from 3-hours."

Boston University student **Cindy Patton** made her debut and finished in 4:51:28 to claim the first wheelchair title. Patton is paralyzed from the waist down as a result of a skiing accident.

Washington Post editorial writer **Colman McCarthy** finished in 3:26:43.

It was a family affair for the **Levri** clan of Rockville, Md., the father, age 44, Elvio.A. finished in 3:19:00, Ann L., age 16, finished in 4:20:04, D.M., age 7, finished in 4:20:05, Edward M., age 12, finished in 4:22:30, and Phillip C., age 14, finished in 5:53:50.

The Marines were given a training guide that addressed the "collapse point." The collapse point was a theory based on a physiological study that **Ken Young** read about the endurance capabilities of trained mice (running inside a wheel). Their maximum capability was roughly three times what their average daily training was. Couple that with the observation that it takes about eight weeks to show a training effect (muscle capilarization), and you have the collapse point as three times your average daily mileage over an eight-week period. The collapse point actually refers to the point at which muscle glycogen stores are exhausted and the body has to rely on the breakdown of fats to produce the energy needed to run. To properly train for a marathon, divide the distance by three and that should be your average daily mileage (minimum). 26/3 = 8.67 miles / day or 60.7 miles per week. Add a small cushion to 63 miles a week.

"I tested the theory on myself and found a reasonably good correlation. It wasn't until I was running more than 70 miles a week that I could run strongly all the way through a marathon. When I ran a 100 mile race, my collapse point was roughly 48 miles and I remember my pace was fairly good through 50-52 miles," said Young.

"I think this is a valid concept and advise people training for a marathon to maintain a minimum of 63 miles a week while training for a marathon. Of course, you can complete a marathon on willpower and 35 miles a week but I don't think it would be a very pleasant experience," adds Young.

Ken Young has a Ph.D. in the physical sciences; he won the 1978 Pikes Peak Marathon in 3:50:44. A founding member of the Association of Road Racing Statisticians, he set up the road-record keeping system in the United States in the early '80s, the Data Running Center.

The organization for the marathon was transferred from the reservist to the active duty Marine Corps, and the Third Annual Marine Corps Marathon was held on Sunday, **November 5, 1978**. The temperature at the start of the race was 58 degrees at 9:00 AM and during the course of the race it rose up to 70 degrees. It was a day for heat exhaustion, blisters and cramps. Two aid stations ran out of cups and there were not enough portable restrooms along the course.

The race continued a steady growth as 4,462 males and 238 females finished the race. The race entries were being accepted up to one hour before the start of the race. The race did not command the top athletes because the Department of Defense Code of Standards precluded commercial sponsorship or payment of money for runners' expenses. The race continued to attract runners from across the United States and foreign countries.

The Marine Corps Marathon was endorsed for the first time by the President's Council on Physical Fitness under President Jimmy Carter. Governor Jerry Apodaca served as the Chair.

The Kennedy Foundation in cooperation with the Marine Corps Marathon sponsored the 3,000 meter Special Olympics race. It was the Middle Atlantic Regional Cross Country Championship. It was officially called "The U.S. Marine Corps Special Olympics Mini-Marathon."

Lydia Monice, age 20, a resident of Baltimore, Maryland, was Miss Black America 1978 and she sang the National Anthem. She was a 1976 graduate of John F. Kennedy High School in Willingboro, NJ. She attended the Peabody Conservatory of Music where she was a member of the Peabody Chorus and Concert Singers.

Entering a balanced field was **R. Scott Eden**, a medical student from Duke University and a Richmond, Virginia native. He started running in 1966 and participated in seven NCAA Championships, five AAU Championships, won six individual Atlantic Coast Conference Titles, and the NCAA Cross-Country All-American (1973-1974). He had a marathon best of 2:20:28 when he won the marathon in 1977 in Greenboro, N.C.

It took Eden 14 miles (corner of First Street NE and Maryland Avenue by the U.S. Capitol) before he was able to shake the lead pack of Charlie Maguire of State College, Pa., Dan Rincon of College Park, Md., and Jeff Peterson and Will Albers of Fairfax, Va. Eden set a new event record with 2:18:07, and it was his first time going under 2:20.

Eden explains after the move, "There was no need to continue to push myself any harder when there was no one there. At mile 20, a friend yelled, How do you feel? My legs were dead and I had no experience with that feeling. I was coming up from the 10,000 meters and 10-milers. At Hains Point, it was a mental challenge and the hardest part."

"I selected the Marine Corps Marathon because it looked like a fast course. I thought the field was a good level of competition. It was comparable and not as big as Boston. I know the medical school got some mileage out of the win by saying that medical school is not too bad since I had time to win the race. I was dating my future wife and her parents did not want to come and watch the race because they thought it would not be worth it. I had never had a Marine guard before, and after the race he walked around with me," said Scott Eden, the winner and new record holder, 2:18:07.

Trying to drink water from cups is a challenge, so to eliminate the cups, he and his future wife (Jane Bird) hide his Gatorade (in the plastic ketchup squeeze bottles) around the course.

Eden has a family practice in Annapolis, Md., and is a volunteer assistant coach at Annapolis High School. His wife, Dr. Jane Bird is an OB/GYN Specialist. He holds a personal best for six miles of 28:09, and marathon time of 2:16:41 in 1979 at the Houston Tenneco Marathon (Texas). He placed 4th in the 7th Perrier Cherry Blossom Ten Mile Run on April 1, 1979.

Arlington, Va., resident and Episcopal High School teacher, **Max White** was making a third attempt for top honors. In 1976, he placed sixth in 2:26:33, in 1977 he was third with his best finish in 2:21:32, and this year (1978) he finished seventh in 2:25:55.

Returning was **Kitty Consolo** and armed with experience to chase the sub-3 hours that eluded her in 1977.

"I really liked the Marine Corps Marathon course, and I felt confident, I could break 3 hours this year. I went out a little wiser in the first half of the race. However, at 14 miles, the back of my sock slipped down and I could feel the back of my heel starting to rub. I didn't want to stop and lose more time so I kept going," said Consolo.

The long training runs did not prepare her for the sequence of distractions that affected her mental state as she continued, "I also was getting a lot of chafing between my legs with some new shorts I had and in those days, there were no running bras for women so I was getting a lot of chafing there, as well. I remember though how close my halfway split was to breaking three hours."

Consolo recognized that her overall position was in jeopardy and some measure was needed within the closing miles. She had to make changes. "I focused on a man's red shorts in front of me for the second half of the race. I never saw the Washington Monument, Tidal Basin or any other landmarks, as I was focused on the red shorts ahead of me. Finally, with a mile to go, I took a quick look at my shoe and it was covered with blood from heel to toe."

The last mile was passed and it was not a time to panic but a time to plan that last assault to finish what she had started. Realizing that her goal was no longer attainable, she said, "I felt a little queasy and started slowing a bit but wasn't too concerned as I had been running a strong second place overall for women. As we neared the final hill, a woman and a man passed me. He turned to the woman and said, 'You got her now, she's done.' That comment really got me mad, and I found some extra energy and ended up finishing second by just 2 seconds. Once I finished, I could hardly walk due to my heel – the skin was worn off almost down to the bone. A very nice Marine carried me to an aid station. I had to wear sandals for three weeks. I am thankful for the better running shoes and clothing we have today and maybe I will get back to the Marine Corps Marathon."

In the previous 24 months, she had ran 47 races and placed first in 27 and second in another six. In preparation she had been training 85 miles per week. Currently she is an assistant professor at Ohio University Zanesville, Ohio where she teaches a variety of health and physical education classes along with human anatomy and physiology.

The road to the start line was filled with notoriety for **Peggy Kokernot** (now Kaplan), a 25-year-old physical education instructor from Houston, Texas. A series of events served as a catalyst that would have lasting effects on her life as a person and athlete. The race was in the era of the women's equal rights. Title IX was recently enacted giving women equal funding for sports. In 1974 while at Trinity University, San Antonio, Texas, she organized the first women's track team.

The National Women's Conference was scheduled in Houston for November 18, 1977. A torch relay was planned form Seneca Falls, New York (the site of the first women's rights convention) to Houston, Texas – 2,610 miles. A 16-mile stretch had met some resistance and there was no runner to carry the torch. She was contacted by Houston relay committee, Mary Ann McBrayer to run the leg. An invitation was extended to have Kokernot and two other athletes run the last mile to the convention center in Houston

On November 17, she entered the Convention Center and ran to the stage where two former First Ladies (Betty Ford and Lady Bird Johnson) and the current First Lady, Rosalyn Carter, to whom she presented the torch, were present.

During the opening ceremony, a *TIME* magazine photographer took a picture, which later was on the front cover of the Dec. 5, 1977 issue of *TIME*. On January 21, 1978 she won the Houston Marathon in 3:01:54. The publicity she received was shaping her life into becoming more of activist for the equal rights movement.

Robert Nakamura
832ⁿᵈ Place 3:16:00

"I knew I wanted to run the Marine Corps Marathon. It was one of the top races in the country, one that so many runners talked about. Just coming off my experience with the Houston Women's Conference, plus my win in the Houston marathon, I knew this would be the race to run and possibly break 3:00. To my great surprise, a group of Marines in Houston raised funds to send me to the race. There was no way I could afford to do this on my own limited budget. I remember the T-shirt they made up for me. It was red and the back was covered with yellow iron-on letters, all full of Marine lingo about the group that sent me north.

"I traveled with a dear friend who also was going to run the race, Mary Cullen. She was one of my biggest supporters and a good training buddy. She believed in me and I believed in her. Together we took D.C. by storm, seeing the sights and preparing to run the race ... remembering the hospitality offered by all the Marines we met that weekend.

"The race day came and we both made our way to the starting line. What I remember most was all the noise at the start with Marines making some kind of loud yell (Oo-Rah) and some running by me wishing me luck. I think they did that because of what I had on my shirt.

"It was not the kind of race I had planned to run. About midway through the race, the orthotics I had in my shoe began pressing on a nerve in my foot. Instead of taking a minute or two to untie the knots in my laces, I ran on the side of my foot. Of course I slowed my pace down and finished with a time of 3:05:35 in pain.

"For me, racing the marathon was different than just running to complete or finish it. It wasn't about winning or losing the race but doing my best on a specific day; reaching deep within to make a goal, to challenge myself unlike any other physical endeavor I had tried before ... but still I should have stopped and untied the knot. So I was a little stubborn or stupid at that moment. We all make mistakes. In the finish line chute, my spirits were lifted when a nice Marine approached and asked if he could stand in line for me so I could go and get something to drink or eat. Never had I had this happen before in a race.

"It was shortly after the Marine Corps Marathon that I was invited to the White House along with the women who organized the Houston Women's Conference in 1977. They would be presenting the results of the conference to President Jimmy Carter in hopes of having an Equal Rights Amendment for Women. As I stood there in the White House, my legs still sore from the marathon only weeks before, I had a lot to think about. I was fortunate indeed.

"It was by chance that my picture was snapped and I appeared on the cover of TIME. But it was not by chance that I found the marathon and decided to make it my own. It became part of who I was and continue to be today. Simply "passing through life" was never an option for me. Running it and digging deep into my soul is my only option."

Leading up to the Olympic Marathon Trials, she qualified on April 8, 1984 at the D.C. Marathon where she placed first in 2:49:05. At the Trials on May 18, 1984, she ran 2:53:28. The overall exposures led to a local CBS television station doing a weekly program on running tips. Later she became a host on the ABC affiliate in San Antonio for *P.M. Magazine,* a syndicated show.

"Marathoning gave me the strength to take on causes near to my heart … to challenge myself to be an activist in life; to see a finish line and cross it, to be a passionate person who wants to make changes in this world, especially for those who cannot speak for themselves. In my case, it is the animals on this earth that have no voice. You never know when you will run your last best race. For me, it was on May 12, 1984. I had another passion in my life and I needed to devote myself to that the way I had devoted myself to running, so I stopped racing. I began to focus 100% of my attention on animal welfare; to be the voice for the voiceless. Instead of just doing a little to help animals, I was now ready to do more".

Overcoming challenges was nothing new for 40-year-old **Harry Cordellos** who was born with glaucoma. He is an accomplished athlete. He ran his marathon in May 1970 at the Golden Gate (3:50:14) and he is a skier, water skies, bicyclist, hang-glider, swimmer, diver, and kayak-paddler. He holds a Master of Science in physical education and is an author, lecturer, and photographer. At the 1975 Boston Marathon, he ran 2:57:42. He finished the Marine Corps Marathon, in 3:07:34. Navy Commander **John Butterfield** ran alongside Cordellos.

Cordellos wrote after the race, "Visiting the Nation's Capitol is one thing, but running 26 miles past many of the most well-known monuments and buildings in the United States and being cheered and encouraged every step of the way is something very special. I ran my best marathon in 18 months on your course."

Maryland Congressman **Goodloe Bryon** was registered for the race this year but died suddenly while out jogging October 11, 1978. He was commissioned a first lieutenant in the U.S. Army in 1953 and served a legal officer with the Third Armored Division in Germany. In 1957, he joined the Maryland National Guard where he served as the aide-de-camp to Maj. General William Purnell. He served in Congress from January 3, 1971 until his death.

An award in his memory was given to first Maryland finisher and was presented by a family member. The recipient was **Joseph Suggs**, age 19, who finished in 2:37:01.

The Fourth Marine Corps Marathon, **November 4, 1979**, welcomed the first active-duty female Marine winner (2:58:14). 1st Lieutenant **Joanna Martin** was stationed at Camp Pendleton, Calif., and was a graduate of Woodbridge High School in Virginia. This was her second time running as she finished fifth in 1977 (3:10:26).

"When I was in college, there was no women's track, only field days and I was a dancer. The year of the race I was stationed at Camp Pendleton, Calif., and being a Marine made it easy and meant that I was skilled at something that men could do. The shoes I had were Adidas SL72; they had no support. The highlight was when the Commanding General of Camp Pendleton gave me a call after the race and had people congratulate me," said Martin.

A Marathon press release quoted the following from **Dr. George Sheehan**: "For every runner who tours the world running marathons, there are thousands who run to hear the leaves and listen to rain and look to the day when it is suddenly as easy as a bird in flight. For them, sport is not a test but a therapy, not a trial but a reward, not a question but an answer."

Dr. Sheehan, was the head of the Department of Electrocardiography and Stress Testing at Riverview Hospital in Red Bank, New Jersey. He ran his best marathon time at the fourth Marine Corps Marathon in 3:01:04. While in the Navy and during World War II, he served as a doctor on the USS Daly. He was diagnosed with prostate cancer in 1986 and died November 1, 1993. He wrote eight books, lectured and was the Medical Advisor for *Runner's World* magazine.

Top Three Winners
1st Phillip Camp 2:19:35, 2nd Will Albers
2:20:14, 3rd David McDonald 2:20:45.
L - Ambassador J. William Middendorf II
(#1) Hall of Fame Inductee 2000

MCM Start Line

The Fifth Marine Marathon, **November 5, 1980,** was marked with a short course that rippled through all of the running headlines. The official finds by A. J. Vander Wall who was the course certifier for The Athletic Congress (TAC) were that the course was 1,725 feet short, which invalidates all of the posted times.

To determine the correct time, according to Vander Wall, the runners had to convert their finish time into seconds and multiply their time by 1.012625 and then reconvert their time back to hours, minutes, and seconds.

At mile 24, off I-395 near the exit for the North Pentagon parking lot along Boundary Channel, the lead pack included **Michael Hurd** of the British Royal Air Force. Hurd made a quick exit from the course to relieve an upset stomach. He made a swift recovery and caught back up with the leaders and went on to win in 2:18:38.

The Sixth Marine Corps Marathon was held **November 1, 1981**. A directive was issued by the General P.X. Kelley, Assistant Commandant of the Marine Corps to transfer the operation of the marathon after 1981 from the Commanding Officer, Marine Barracks, Washington, D.C., to the Commanding General, Marine Corps Development and Education Command (MCDEC).

President Ronald Reagan wrote the following to all of the runners, "I send greetings to each runner in this outstanding field and salute you for participating in the ultimate challenge of foot-racing – the 26.2 mile marathon. I hope the running revolution which has captured the imagination of this nation will continue to inspire citizens of all ages to become involved in this healthful exercise throughout their lives."

Dean Matthews of Atlanta, Ga., a graduate from Clemson University, had an impressive record coming into the Marine Corps Marathon. In April 1979, he ran 2:14:48 at the Boston Marathon and in December the same year he set a new course record at the Honolulu Marathon with a 2:16:13. Matthews won by 1 minute 20 seconds over **Hank Pfeifle** of Kennebunkport, Maine (2:17:52).

In the master's ranks, it was consistency that dominated. **Bill Hall** proved his staying power over the years. His longest standing record remains on the books. He adds "In 1979 I ran with a friend, Scott Eden, who was an All-American at Duke in cross-country. He ran very well at the Marine Corps the following year. I knew I had the record in 1981, but no, I didn't think it would last as the amateur running boom was just beginning. The competitive level wasn't an issue for me, as I always raced the clock. Running marathons for me was similar to conducting scientific experiments. My hypothesis was that if I train in a certain way, I will improve. Unfortunately, my hypothesis was usually false. My feelings on the last stretch were always the same – depleted and dehydrated.

I tried to focus solely on keeping my sails trimmed and not stopping until the end." His time in 1981, 2:24:36, stands as the master's event record where he placed ninth at the age of 41.

Hall had made several prior appearances at MCM. In 1977, he placed fifth in 2:22:54, and in 1978 he placed eighth in 2:27:00. In 1979, he ran 2:21:01 for fourth place, and he was the oldest person to qualify for the 1980 U.S. Olympic Trials. He returned later in 1983 and placed 22nd in 2:25:49 at the age of 42. Today, Hall is a professor in the Department of Neurobiology at Duke University.

Conrad Hall gives a perspective on the years the family observed his father's quest for excellence, "Going up to D.C. to watch my dad race the Marine Corps Marathon was something of fall tradition for several years for my brother and me when we were children (I was ages 6, 7, 8, 10, and 12 for Dad's five Marine Corps Marathons), and I have many memories from the marathon. It was a great course, for spectators especially. My mom, my brother, and I would move as fast as we could from the start to various points on the course / on the mall and then to the finish, seeing the race in several spots and cheering Dad on. I recall walking the bridges to the mall area and cheering for the race near the reflecting pools and the Lincoln Memorial.

"I do also distinctly remember the Iwo Jima Memorial near the finish. This sculpture always had a big impact on me as a child. I think this image, as well as my parents' explanation, gave me a real sense that the men in the sculpture were engaged in great effort, service, and sacrifice for some higher cause. It is, to this day, a moving image for me, as I'm sure it is for many. My parents would also read us the Gettysburg Address and Lincoln's 2nd Inaugural, which are carved on the walls of the Lincoln Memorial, which is right on the race course. These words had a similar impact on me as did the Iwo Jima Memorial. I would also add that going to D.C. to watch Dad race was always a big treat for us as children – I'm thankful that the event brought me up to D.C. so many times as a child. That I'm a high school American history teacher today (as well as a track & cross country coach) might be coincidence, but I'm sure these early experiences at the Marine Corps Marathon had a meaningful impact on me," he adds.

His son closes with the following account: "There was something unique about this marathon and the scenic course it took through D.C. We watched Dad race in scores of marathons as children, but the Marine Corps (along with Boston) are the ones that stand out most. I know it was a special one for Dad too, as he liked the course and liked racing through the monuments. His memories of the race are filled with fatigue and pain I'm sure, but I know he looked forward to the Marine Corps Marathon and Boston above all others each year. He also ran his best time ever at the 1979 marathon."

Cynthia Lorenzoni (formerly Wadsworth), of Charlottesville, Va., grew up in Farmington, Connecticut. She was a scholarship athlete (recognized for her academic and athletic abilities), attended Michigan State University (MSU) and was team captain in track and field and cross country. She was the top Spartan at the Big Ten Championships in 1976 (17:21 – 2nd place) and in 1979 (18:16 – 5th place).

She returned to competition after training with Olympian Margaret Groos (UVA graduate) who set school records from 1,500 meters to 10,000 meters. The two would do long runs every weekend of 10-15 miles. In 1981, the weekend before the Marine Corps Marathon, she ran 20 miles and then she decided to enter the race to see what see what it was all about. She ran the distance at a 6:30 pace. She won in 2:50:33.

Lieutenant General **Richard E. Cary**, Commanding General, MDEC, Quantico, Va., finished the race in 3:19:29 and placed 1,739.

Retired jockey from Ocean City, Maryland, **Ed Benham**, age 74, finished in 3:37:07 (overall 2,972). He set a U.S. single age record for 20 miles at 2:48:47 in 1981. His first marathon was in March 1981, the D.C. Marathon in Washington finishing in 3:32. At the age of 77 he set a U.S. age group record (75-79) for 20-miles at 2:42:38 (DCRRC Greenbelt 20 Miler, December 1984). He went on to set another age group record (80-84) at the age of 84 for the marathon at 4:17:51 (October 1991).

The top male marine finisher was 2nd Lt. **Michael Healer** of TBS, Quantico, Va., in 2:24:55 (11th overall).

The top female finisher was Sgt. **Judith Sagerian** of Marine Detachment, Indian Head, Md., in 3:26:47.

Photo: Official Marine Corps Photo

Harry Cordellos

The Seventh Marine Corps Marathon was held **November 7, 1982**. The race entries reached all-time high of 11,525 with 8,516 finishers (7,513 males and 1,003 females). The race day temperature was a cool 50 degrees. The race entry fee was increased to $10.00 and the post race refreshments included free beer, soup, soda and cookies. The Sheraton National Hotel, Arlington, Va., race headquarters was charging $38.00 per night. Race registrations were accepted until 10:00 P.M., Saturday, November 6, 1982.

"When I was 19, I ran my first marathon (2nd Maryland Marathon November 30, 1974, 2:29:22) and finished eighth. I graduated from Towson High School and was born in Baltimore so I was a 'local' boy. My training partner in Cumberland, Md., had run the Marine Marathon, Dave Rinehart in 1981, and he finished fourth (2:22:51). He told me what a great race and it was and what a fast course it was. I had just run a personal record (PR) for 10K (30:30) and felt I was ready for a marathon," said **Jeff Smith** of Cumberland, the overall winner in 2:21:29.

"I came through the halfway point in around 1 hour 10 minutes in 13th or 14th place and felt strong. I started to pass people and around Hains Point (miles 20-21), I was in sixth place. I came upon a group of three running together. They looked like they were struggling and I was still feeling fairly fresh. I went by them and moved into second," said Smith.

Smith was beginning to start his final assault as he continued. "With about a mile to go, I saw a press truck up ahead. I didn't realize it was the leader at first. I thought maybe it was a wheelchair racer or something. I passed Bill Stewart of Winchester, Va., at the bottom of the hill with about a half mile to go." Bill Stewart finished in 2:21:54.

"All of a sudden I was leading the race and it was almost over! I crossed the finish line and threw my arms up in the air. I don't think it had really sunk in that I was going to win. It was very exhilarating. My family was there and all very excited. It took awhile to sink in that I had actually won and still today sometimes it is hard to believe! It was one of my proudest moments in running along with a high school cross country championship and ACC 5000 meter title," added Smith.

Cynthia Lorenzoni, Charlottesville, Va., became the second female back-to-back winner joining Susan Mallery (1987-2:56:33, 1977- 2:54:04). She took first place in 2:44:51. Her husband Mark they own the Ragged Mountain Running Shop in Charlottesville.

In 1982, she felt that she could run a sub-2:40. She was running in a pair of Converse that caused problems, "At mile 19, my feet were bleeding and I was in so much pain, I was going to drop out. I saw my husband at mile 20 and he told me the leader, Laura DeWald had dropped out and that I was in the lead and had to finish," she said. She continued for the win in 2:45:51.

At the Boston Marathon in April 1982, she placed 13th with a 2:46:02. In 19th place (2:48:14) was Kitty Consolo the second place finisher in the 1978 Marine Corps Marathon (3:03:33).

Captain **Irene Janet Volodkevich**, USMC, completed the Marine Corps Marathon on November 7, 1982 and finished in 4:03:46 (place 6,148), wearing run number 6608. Her last billet was as Protocol / Assistant Aide de Camp to Major General D.M. Twomey while stationed at the Marine Corps Development and Education Command at Quantico, Virginia. Her parents were natives of Russia, and she grew up in Elyria, Ohio along with her two sisters and brother. While growing up, her family referred to her as being the jock of the family.

She graduated from Ohio State University in 1980, having walked onto the women's swim team with no high school swim team experience. After graduation, she joined the Marines. In her officer training class, she was the only woman to max all the physical fitness tests in boot camp. Prior to the marathon, her longest distance was a 10K. A few fellow marines then introduced her to triathlons, which turned out to be a very natural fit with her abilities.

Irene's sister, **Joy Koenig**, said, "I'd flown out of Maryland in May of that year, to watch her do a 'tin man' (now called a half-Ironman). It rankled that I was 23-years old, and yet these 50- and 60-year-old men and women were in better shape than I. Irene had laughed, and said, 'Just because you're the smart one in the family doesn't mean you can't also be a jock.' She encouraged me to find out how much of a jock I could be. Through her love and support, I signed up for, and completed, my first sprint distance triathlon (0.75K swim, 20K bike, and 5K run)."

Captain Volodkevich's passion for triathlon increased, and in 1984 she resigned her Marine Corps commission and moved to La Jolla, California, to devote herself full time to her training. By this time, she had completed at least three triathlons. Her dream was to compete in the Hawaii Ironman Triathlon, which did not require qualification at that time.

In March 1985, she was diagnosed with malignant melanoma, a deadly form of skin cancer, which was detected in a mole on her back. Her dream of doing the Hawaii Ironman was broken, but not the drive to continue with the sport that she loved. Her last event was the Pepsi San Diego International Triathlon (February 1988), where she did the 1,000 meter swim leg as part of a relay. Just five short months later, on July 8, 1988, she lost her battle with cancer.

Remembering when her sister's cancer was diagnosed as most likely fatal, Joy Koenig said, "I'll never forget her phone call to me, telling me that her cancer had metastasized. I was sitting on the floor of my apartment and can still feel the carpet under my hands as she said, 'Don't be upset. I'm not. This gives me my respectable way out. I do well with physical challenges. Fighting this, as long as I want to, will be a challenge. Now I don't have to figure out a career.' I remember too, how deeply I understood her pain, and the trace of envy that I felt toward her. We were both exhausted, and her finish line was eminent. Who knew how much further until my finish line? At that time, I, too, was exhausted and struggling to stay in the race." She was referring to their shared history of childhood sexual abuse and aftermath of being raised by a bipolar alcoholic mother.

As a final note, Joy added, "Triathlon was the tool my sister gave me, that helped me to see I was more than our past, and more than my academic abilities. This sport will always hold a special place in my heart and in my life. Irene is the inspiration for the freedom with which I now live. Her death catalyzed my life in an entirely different direction than the one I laid out prior to her death. Our lives were very different on the outside, yet we knew our motivations and values were similar. The Marine Corps Marathon is what launched her into what she truly loved (triathlon), and ironically, the Marine Corps Marathon is what launched me into my Ironman triathlon in her memory."

Finishing in 4:06:33 was **Fred Lebow** (June 6, 1932 – October 9, 1994), president of New York City Road Runners Club and race director of the New York City Marathon (1970-1993). He was born in Transylvania, Romania as Fischel Lebowitz. The club started in 1970 with 270 members and in twenty years the members grew to 31,000. This would be the last year an American would win the New York City Marathon, **Alberto Salazar** in 2:09:29. In 1978, the race started paying award money. **John Block** was the Secretary of Agriculture (1981-1985) under President Ronal Reagan. He finished in 3:12:55 (1,836[th] overall). He graduated from West Point in 1957 and served three years with the U.S. Army 101st Airborne Division at Fort Benning, Ga.

The Eighth Marine Corps Marathon was held **November 6, 1983**. It was a proud day for the Marines as one of their own captured the Middendorf Trophy, the first male Marine to win the race overall, Sgt. **Farley Simon** from Alea, Hawaii. In 1981, Simon had to drop out after 12 miles with leg cramps. He won with a 2:17:46 and the second fastest winning time in the history of the race since Dean Matthews set the record in 1981 (2:16:31). In the process of winning, he qualified for U.S. Olympic Marathon Trials.

Simon was born on the island of Grenada, West Indies. Two weeks earlier, a force of Marines and Army paratroopers had landed in Grenada after the leftist government was overthrown in a coup. He came to the United States in 1971 with his family, which settled in New York. He joined the Marine Corps in November 1979.

Simon commented, "In 1983, I was fueled by the unbelievers who didn't give me a chance and a comment I had overheard two years prior in the media tent. A reporter congratulated the Marine Corps for putting on one of the best races in the country and then said too bad they don't have one of their own that could run at

Photo: Official USMC Photo by SSgt Becki Wass

Sgt. Farley Simon holding trophy,
*first active duty male Marine to have
won MCM 2:17:46
Hall of Fame Inductee 2000*

Sgt. Farley Simon crossing first,
*first active duty male Marine (2:17:46).
Hall of Fame Inductee 2000
Holding finish tape is Assistant Commandant of the Marine Corps
General J. K. Davis and Major General D.M. Twomey,
Commanding General MCDEC, Quantico, Va.*

the front. I immediately made a promise to myself to be the first Marine champion
and for two years I trained with that goal in mind (it was sweet victory)."

The top five females qualified for the 1984 women's Olympic Marathon Trials:
Suzanne Carden of Strousberg, PA., in 2:45:55, **Julia Burke** of Beverly, MA, in
2:47:19, **Juleann Quigley** of Vernoa, NJ in 2:50:25, **Christine Gonzalez** of New
Orleans, LA, in 2:51:04, and **Patricia Sher** of Jacksonville, FL in 2:51:06. The
cutoff was 2:51:16.

"I attempted to sign up the day before the race as I did the prior year (3:32:02).
To my shock, I was told I couldn't run because the race now required pre-
registration. Desperately, I sought advice and was told by one of the Marines if I
could find someone with a number who wasn't running, I could use that one, so
long as I reported it to an official," stated **Fred Gedrich** of Annandale, Va.

He tells about the ending of the race, "I came up the hill knowing I had a shot at
a sub-three hour marathon. So at about 250 meters to go, I unleashed a pretty
good kick and the fellow on my left went with me. We raced all the way to the
finish line and I finished a couple of steps ahead of him (2:58:21 to 2:58:23). As
I bent over gasping to catch my breath after finishing, he sort of collapsed on my
back. At the time, I had no idea who it was. It wasn't until I got the photo that I
realized it was the Redskins General Manager, Bobby Beathard, he was a member
of National Capital Track Club (GNAT). Bobby and I subsequently raced quite a
few times against each other, and I always seemed to have a little advantage most
likely because I was several years younger than him."

A victory celebration was held at Champions in Washington, DC for Senator
Larry Pressler (R-SD) who finished in 3:53:36 (790th in the age group 40-44).
The average age for the registered men was 35.5 and 32.2 for the women. The
number if first-time marathoners was 5,984 for the men and 1,108 for the women.

The Ninth Marine Corps Marathon was held **November 9, 1984**. Former Marine artillery officer, **Brad Ingram** of Mansfield, OH, while stationed at Quantico, Va., ran in the 1979 Marine Corps Marathon and finished in 2:35:01 (65th place). He returned in 1982 and finished in 2:22:49 (4th place), and in 1983 when he finished in 2:20:36 (4th place). Along the section he knew well, Hains Point (miles 18 to 20), which is flanked by the Potomac and Anacostia Rivers, the chase pack included attorney, **Jim Hage** of Rockville, Md., and Lt. Cmdr. **Thomas Bernard** of Hayes, Va.

Ingram stayed the course and held off the competition to capture his first win in 2:19:40. Hage had second place but in the closing miles, Bernard began to reel him in and took second 2:20:45 to 2:22:40. Bernard ran his first Marine Corps in 1983 and finished in 2:24:14 (16th place).

Defending women's champion (2:45:55) and 1982 runner-up (2:54:33), **Suzanne Carden** of Stroudsburg, Pa., was going for a repeat. **Beth Dillinger** of Blacksburg, Va., was the 1981 runner-up (2:53:48). The two were denied of their win by **Pamela Briscoe** of Chevy Chase, Md., with a finish time of 2:43:20. Briscoe ran a 2:54:03 at the Boston Marathon in April 1984. She ran the Marine Corps in 1979 and finished in 3:18:44 (27th place), and in 1981 and finished in 3:14:40 (36th place). Carden finished in 2:56:39 (9th place), and Dillinger finished in 3:02:50 (13th place).

Wannie Cook of Richmond, Va., who lost both legs while in combat with the 101st Airborne while in Vietnam took first in the wheelchair division with a 2:23:04.
It was a family affair for retired Marine Colonel **Herbert Waters**, Jr., of Dartmouth, Mass., he finished with a 3:42:00 with his sons' finishing, Chris 3:22:53, 2ndLt Michael Water 3:24:02, Mark 3:42:00, and Captain Herbert Waters, Jr., 3:47:37.

Ruth Rothfarb, age 83 of Cambridge, MA, finished in 6:50:36. She was born in Russia on June 18, 1901, and her family immigrated to the United States in 1913. At the age of 75, she entered her first race, which launched an impressive running career that included 22 single age and age group records.

Winner Pamela Briscoe
(2:43:20)

1st place Brad Ingram
(2:19:40)

2nd place Jim Hage
(2:22:40)

The 10th Marine Corps Marathon was held **November 3, 1985**. The overcast, light drizzle had an effect on the total finisher, which ended a three-year growth to 7,819 (6,640 males, 1,179 females), the lowest male finishers since 1981 (6,312). The race entry fee was a modest $12.00.

Near the 23rd mile, the runners cut seven meters off the course coming off Hains Point going towards the Thomas Jefferson Memorial before going to the 14th Street Bridge. A Short Course Prevention Factor (SCPF) was applied during the measurement process to avoid any short courses. The course was verified as the true marathon distance.

Brad Ingram from Mansfield, OH, was returning for his fifth appearance and as defending champion. The competition was from runner-up Chief Petty Officer **Thomas Bernard** of the Coast Guard from Hayes, Va., and third place **Jim Hage** from Rockville, Md. By Hains Point along Ohio Drive (miles 20-21) the race was down to Ingram and Bernard.

Ingram was denied a second win as Bernard finished with 2:19:16 to 2:19:47. Hage was reduced to another third place finish with 2:23:30.

The participants and spectators had the pleasure of seeing **Grete Waitz** of Oslo, Norway as she ran with her husband in the opening miles of the marathon. Her husband dropped out at mile 23 due to cramps. Waitz was coming off her seventh career win of the New York City Marathon (October 27, 1985) with a 2:28:34. She was the silver medalist at the first women's marathon at the 1984 Olympic Games. She won five world cross-country championships.

Run It and You'll Remember the MCM 1986-1995

The 11th Marine Corps Marathon was held **November 2, 1986**. This was the first year there was a conflict in dates with the 17th New York City Marathon, which had to be rescheduled, and the two ran on the same date. New York made the change due to a religious holiday.

The top winners of the New York City Marathon received $25,000 plus a Mercedes-Benz and had 20,141 runners. The Marine Corps Marathon had 11,255 registered with 7,913 finishers (6,719 males, 1,194 females). The packet pick-up was held open until 11:00 p.m. on Saturday night. The official race starter was the Commandant of the Marine Corps, General P. X. Kelley. The Marathon office was notified that selected runners would have to undergo urinalysis testing. A three-page letter was sent all registered runners. At first it was to be the top 25 males and females, but was later changed to the top three males and females and then a random selection of four others out of the 25 for a total of 10. If a runner refused, he would be disqualified. The Marathon office offered to refund the race fees if a person did not want to compete under the rule. The New York City Marathon was notified they would be subject to drug testing.

This year was the awaited rematch of former Marine **Brad Ingram** of Mansfield, Ohio, and Coast Guard Commander **Brad Thomas Bernard** of Hayes, Va. Ingram was attempting to become the first male to have two wins. The race conditions proved to be less than ideal; the rain had stopped by race start at 9:00

a.m., the temperature was 55 degrees at the start, the humidity was 100% and later in the morning the temperature rose to 65 degrees. Ingram was running his seventh Marine Corps Marathon and Bernard, the defending champion, was running his fourth. Each had an opportunity to collect a second win. It was not easy with the likes of **Rudy Robinson** of Washington, DC and **John Stevens** of the Royal Navy / Royal Marines. Stevens was in competition for the Challenge Cup against the U.S. Marines.

The early pack of runners by the 24th mile began to fall off the pace, which included Bernard (finished in 2:26:37, 14th place), Stevens (finished in 2:24:06, 2nd place). Robinson was third in 2:24:32. He was the winner of the 6th D.C. Marathon in 2:25:02.

Ingram became the first male to collect two wins with his 2:23:13. His best performance was in 1984 (2:19:40). **Ken Archer** of Bowie, Md., captured his fourth wheelchair win in a time of 2:10:01. **Kathy Champagne** from Plattsburg, NY was entering her first marathon. She had set a course record at the Lake Placid Half-Marathon two months prior in 1:15:36. She ran cross county and track at the University of New Hampshire. Second place went to **Lucia Geraci** of Dunwoody, Ga., who finished under the Olympic Trials standards (2:49:59) with 2:48:58.

Marine Staff Sergeant **Martin (Marty) Albert Wurst, Jr.**, age 32, was the first fatality in the history of the race. He was from Warminster, Pa., and a mechanic stationed with the Headquarters & Maintenance Squadron – 49 (H&MS-49) at Naval Air Station Willow Grove, Pa. He went down near the 15 mile mark along the Mall just before to the Washington Monument around 10:40 a.m. and was pronounced dead at 11:42 a.m. He ran in 1985 and finished in 3:04:07 (151st in the age group 30-34). He died from occlusive coronary atherosclerosis, a severe narrowing of the arteries that feed the heart caused by the build-up of cholesterol and other fatty materials.

Photo: Tom Bartlett, Leatherneck Magazine

1st place
Kathleen Champagne
2:42:59

Photo: Tom Bartlett, Leatherneck Magazine

1st place
Brad Ingram 2:23:13
at tape

Official USMC Photo by Sgt. Michael M. Kronak

Wheelchair winner
Ken Archer 2:10:01
Hall of Fame Inductee 2006

The 12th Marine Corps Marathon was held **November 8, 1987**. The temperature at the start was 60 degrees and 73 degrees at the finish with winds at 10 miles per hour. For the first time in the history of the race, television coverage was provided by WTTG-TV, Channel 5. The commentators included Steve Buckhantz, Bill Rodgers, Missy Kane and Angela Robinson. Larry Matthews was broadcasting on WMAL and Mike Ritz was speaking with runners along the course at the Lincoln Memorial.

Race entries reached a history record of 12,091 (10,193 males, 1,898 females) with 8,809 finishers (7,505 males, 1,304 females). The race entry fee was $15.00. Due to the high temperature from last year, water stations increased from 9 to 14. The U.S. Olympic Marathon Trials would be taking place in 1988 and to qualify, males had to run 2:20 or less and females had to run 2:50 or less. The temperature was in the low 50s but the air quality was not good because of forest fires burning in West Virginia.

Brad Ingram was making his seventh appearance and **Tom Bernard** was making his fifth. The score was 2 to 1 in Ingram's favor. On average, 60% of the marathon runners in the Marine Corps are first timers and Ingram and Bernard had **Jeff Scuffins** of Hagerstown, Md., to worry about, a late entrant wearing bib number 11464 and his running mate **Chris Fox** wearing bib number 11463. Another contender making his third Marine Corps was **Darrell General** of Temple Hills, Md. In 1984, at age 18, he ran 2:24:36 and in 1985 he ran 2:26:52.

Scuffins ran 4:27 per mile while at North Hagerstown High School (Maryland) and was the record holder for 5,000 meters (13:52) at Hagerstown Junior College. His best 10,000 meter time was 28:40 and for 10 miles was 47:50. He is a 1985 graduate of Clemson University. Going into the 11th mile, Scuffins found himself in total control. The chase pack began to fade as Bernard dropped back and Ingram dropped out at mile 22 while by mile 24, General was out fading.

Scuffins was on record pace and shattered the event record (2:16:31 by Dean Matthews, 1981) by two and one-half minutes and ran 2:14:01. General placed second with 2:19:08 and the two qualified for the Olympic Marathon Trials. Ingram dropped out at mile 22 and Bernard finished in 72nd place with 2:39:09. The Ingram-Bernard era came to an end.

"We started off very slow and it took us five to six miles to get to the front. Jeff was on his game immediately, and I had to keep asking him to hold back. We were having a fairly leisurely, for us at the time, 5:15 to 5:20 pace tempo effort. I knew I was going to get out between 10 to 15 miles. We kept picking it up and Jeff was talking as if we were on one of our training runs in Williamsport, Md., on the C&O Canal towpath," said Chris Fox. From 1987-1994, he was a member of the Nike-Athletics West Team. Fox has a best mile time in 3:59.10, 5000m in 13:21, 10,000m 27:53, and the marathon in 2:13:40. Presently, he is the head cross country and track and field coach ay Syracuse University.

Leaders in Pentagon parking lot,
L - Chris Fox (#11463),
L Center - Darrell General (#93),
Center - Jeff Scuffins (#11464 eventual winner
and record holder 2:14:01),
R - James Glidwell (11925)

Leader Mary Robertson at Pentagon
parking lot, Bob Dalrymple driving
motorcycle 1987. The winner 2:44:34
Hall of Fame Inductee 2005
Presently Mary Wittenberg (formerly Robertson)
is the Director of the New York City Marathon
and President of the NY City Road Runners Club

Fox dropped out of the race and Scuffins was on his own. "Jeff was glad I was gone so he could go faster. He dropped the pace to 5:10. I saw him a few more times during the race and he looked under complete control. He finished with very bloody feet from blisters, the worst I have seen in my long history in the sport. He did not really complain and he was untouchable that day. Two hours after the race we were at White Flint Mall having lunch and people were recognizing Jeff from the great live TV coverage they had. I remember it as a great day for my great friend and everyday training partner. The record will stand as long as it remains a 'race for the people,'" added Fox.

The women's race started out with a newcomer, **Mary Salamone**, age 24, an IBM engineer from Centreville, Va. She had explosive energy and went through mile four in 23:54 (5:32 pace) through the halfway in 1:19:22 and 15 miles in 1:31:25. Going across the 14th Street Bridge, Salamone was falling off her earlier pace as **Mary Robertson**, age, 25, a lawyer from Richmond, was running her second marathon. Robertson had been closing in slowly and by the 24th mile she was in total control. Robertson took the win in 2:44:34 and Salamone was second in 2:46:18. **Elizabeth Andrews** of Norfolk, Va., was third in 2:47:46, followed by **Sally Strauss** of Washington, DC in fourth in 2:48:49. The top four females qualified for Olympic Trials.

Salamone recounts, "The race was extremely organized and orchestrated due to the commitment of the Marines. This was my first experience seeing the military in action, and I was proud to be an American that day. They treated every runner like they had won the race. I got scared by that hand coming out of the ground on Hains Point. I had never been there before, and as you well know, it's lonely out there and you're into the 20s mileage wise, so the brain starts doing funny things, along with the body. The press helicopter also came down low and blew up a bunch of debris in my face. I was tempted to gesture but that would not have looked good on TV."

She continues, "I was passed at mile 24 and a spectator, who was also a member of NOVA, the track club I belonged to, told me to go catch her. I had hit the proverbial wall and was concentrating only on putting one foot in front of the other (i.e., keep moving forward no matter what the pace). Where was the finish line anyway so I could stop? Yes, the finish line. Up that vast mountain to the Iwo Jima Monument, which appeared to be a brief hill on a training run. I actually thought I had gotten lost and would never find the finish line.

"Crossing the finish line and thinking I could not run even another step consumed me. I was so disappointed in my performance (being passed so late in the race due to those sub-6 minute miles early on). Then I got to meet Bill Rodgers, who so kindly said in response to my voicing my disappointment that he did not even finish his first marathon. The marathon king, humbled himself to make me feel better. Those silver blankets were cool, too," added Salamone.

Chuck Moeser, then living in Thornton, NH, recalls his performance (1st age group 35-39 2:26:32, 7th place). "That was the year there were forest fires in WV so the air quality was considered quite bad, and it was very hot. The start of the race really surprised me as at the mile, my split was 5:30 and I was in 100th place. It wasn't until five miles that I felt I was working my way up to the top 20. My half

1987

Mary Robertson 1987 winner 2:44:36
being interviewed by Angela Robinson of WTTG TV
Hall of Fame Inductee 2005
Presently Mary Wittenberg (formerly Robertson) is the Director
of the New York City Marathon and President of the NY City
Road Runners Club

Photo: Official USMC Photo by Sgt. M.G. Lindee

1987

2nd place Mary Salamone
(2:46:18) lead for 24 miles

split was 1:12. There was a young man pushing his way to the start of the race and elbowed me off of the start line. He was sort of small so I shoved him back and we started a shoving match to see who was going to put their foot on the start line. I remember him well because he was the only black guy on the front line, and being from New Hampshire I didn't recognize him, it was Darrell General."

Moeser was drafted in 1971 into the Army and served with the 101st Airborne in Fort Campbell, Ky. He signed up for the Green Berets at Fort Bragg, NC but that did not work out. He went to Ranger school and excelled. He was sent to West Point to train Cadets on how to patrol through the jungles of Vietnam. He was discharged in 1974. Bob Dalrymple started leading road races in 1977 while a U.S. Park Police Motorcycle Officer. In or around 1981, he was contacted to drive a special modified motorcycle for the New York City Marathon. Later, he did Chicago, Montreal, Cleveland, Boston and a few other races around the country.

"While doing MCM, I always feel a sense of pride and patriotism in the men and women of our armed forces, especially since I served in the U.S. Navy. The pre-race ceremony by our military is so moving. I enjoy leading the race and seeing all the runners as they jockey for position and then as they cross the finish line, the excitement of the fans lining the race course, cheering and waving the American flag," Dalrymple said. He continues, "I always have a feeling of accomplishment when the race is over safely with no incidents and no interference with a runner. This is difficult at times when I am asked to go back into the pack. Since I have been doing these races I have never had an incident with any runner or race official. For this I am very thankful."

The 13th Marine Corps Marathon was held **November 6, 1988** under moderate conditions. The temperature was 55 degrees at the start and 65 degrees at the finish, the winds were 10 to 15 miles per hour with gusts up to 25 mph. It was another record year for entries, with 12,198 (10,114 males, 2,083 females), and 8,998 finishers (7,504 males, 1,494 females). The race was ranked the third largest marathon in the U.S. The race continued to operate without major sponsorship or offering financial incentives to attract top-name runners.

It was Murphy's Law day at the races; the starter's pistol was raised to begin the race but misfired, not once but twice. The runners were frozen, an arm was raised and lowered and the 105mm howitzer did the job as the front line broke free.

Brad Ingram, the only two-time winner was back for his eighth race. On the line to see if the third time would be a charm was lawyer **Jim Hage** of Lanham, Md. Ingram had shut down Hage twice before, and he finished in third place in 1984 (2:22:40) and 1985 (2:23:30). They ran in the U.S. Olympic Marathon Trials in April. Ingram placed 14th (2:18:45) and Hage was 26th.

Ingram was the aggressor as every move that was made to take to lead he was in contact. Bennett had the lead but he fell off around mile 20, and it was down to a two-man race, Hage and Ingram. With less than a quarter mile to the finish, Hage unleashed a kick that gave him the victory with 2:21:59 and Ingram finished in 2:22:18. **John Stephens** finished in third with 2:22:27 and **David Bennett** was next with 2:22:53.

Jim Hage returned after a two-year absence to settle an old score. He was coming off a strong 1987 season with a PR at 10 miles at the Nike Cherry Blossom 10 Mile Run of 48:35 and 1:04:30 at the Philadelphia Distance Run (half-marathon). The focus for 1988 was on winning. The confidence was supporting Hage as he recalls, "I felt pretty good, stayed with Ingram through 20, where I had faded twice previously. This time, I felt good enough to challenge him with a surge, but he stayed right with me. I surged a couple of more times, and Ingram hung tough each time. Because I was dictating the action, I grew more confident that I felt better than he did, but I still couldn't shake him."

The determination was strong. "As we passed the 25-mile mark, I tried to drop him again — I didn't want to have to sprint up the hill at the end. But Ingram matched my every move. As we made the left turn with a half mile left to go up the hill, I knew it was going to hurt, but I didn't want it to hurt in vain, so I went as hard as I could for as long as I could, and Ingram finally released."

But the race was not over. "I was still wary and continued to push hard, but I felt like I had just dropped a very big anchor. After the finish line, we embraced and *The Washington Post* ran that photo on A1 the next day, which was very cool. I felt fortunate to have beaten a proven champion and a heck of good guy." Hage took the win 2:21:59 to Ingram's 2:22:18 – a 19-second margin. It was the closest win in the history of the race.

Photo: Tom Bartlett, Leatherneck Magazine

Leader Jim Hage (#A9806 eventual winner 2:21:59) Buckeye Drive over Brad Ingram (A5, 2nd place 2:22:18)

2nd place Brad Ingram (2:22:18)

The 14th Marine Corps Marathon was held **November 5, 1989**. The temperature at the start was 47 degrees with a projected high of 60 degrees

This year saw the match-up between two formidable champions, Marine Sgt. **Farley Simon** (1983; 2:17:46), and **Jim Hage** (1988; 2:21:59). Depending upon the victor, Simon could become the only Marine to collect two titles and Hage would become the first back-back to winner. Simon was going after the record set by **Jeff Scuffins** (1987; 2:14:01).

At 9:10 a.m., the runners were off and due to cross back over the start area near the seven-mile mark. The two lead runners were Simon and running mate Sgt. **Randy Hoyles**, both of whom were stationed in Okinawa. The two were part of the Marine team competing against the Royal Navy / Royal Marines for the Challenge Cup. Hage was within eyesight of both runners. A spectator jumped onto the course and handed a water bottle to both Simon and Hoyles. They maintained a blistering pace, which kept Hage almost a minute behind but Hoyles began to fade in the later miles.

Near the Jefferson Memorial (mile 23) Simon was following the lead vehicle and he cut off 20-30 yards of the course. The Athletic Congress (TAC) local official ruled that since it was not intentional a disqualification didn't take place. Across the 14th Street Bridge, Hage closed the gap and managed to put Simon away without a fight. Hage broke the victory tape in 2:20:23, which was held by Marine Commandant General A.M. Gray and Lt.Gen. William R. Etnyre, Commanding General, Quantico, Va. Hage became the second runner to have two victories and the first to make a successful back-to-back defense. Simon placed second in 2:27:37 and in third was Paul Okerberg of Marietta, Ga., in 2:25:16.

General Gray Letter

"I was a marked man, even wearing bib number 1. Marine Sgt. Farley Simon and I ran together for about eight miles and then he took off. I didn't think I could match that pace so I let him go, thinking I might well be running for second place. Simon had a big lead on me at 16 miles, so much so that my family wouldn't tell me how far back I was when I asked," Hage said.

As in 1988, Hage relied upon his determination and strength to stay the course. "But at mile 18, I could see Farley way in the distance and I sensed that he was slowing down. I still didn't catch him until the 14th Street Bridge and he wasn't too happy to see me. But I roared past him the best I could and he fell apart. I remember seeing my coach, Dan Rincon, at mile 25, and he was still concerned that I might fall apart myself. But I knew I had it and when Dan raised his hand for a modest high-five, I just about knocked him over. I was pretty pleased to win back to back."

Hage took first in 2:20:23 and Farley was second in 2:22:37. Hage became the first back-to-back winner.

Former area resident, **Laura DeWald** of Grands Rapids, Mich., was the favorite over the defending champion, **Lori Lawson** of Philadelphia, Pa. (1988-2:51:26). DeWald a graduate of the University of Virginia, a veteran of 25 marathons, was ranked eighth on the All-Time U.S. Rankings – Women's Marathon by *Track and Field News* in 2002. She set the event record at the Washington's Birthday Marathon in 1981 (3:01:29), which is the Washington area's most difficult three-loop course.

DeWald ran the MCM in 1979 and finished third (2:59:25). In 1980 she finished second (2:42:55). She was going for the win.

Lawson led the race through 10 miles as DeWald began to gradually close the gap. Near mile 20 along the Potomac River side going towards the tip of Hains Point, DeWald took over the lead and went on to capture first place in 2:45:16. Lawson was second in 2:48:26 followed by Christine Snow-Reaser of Stafford, Va., in 2:50:16. DeWald was two minutes and eighteen seconds off a new record. The official record was set in 1986 (2:42:59) by **Kathy Champagne** of Plattsburgh, NY. Jan Yerks of Buckingham, Pa., was credited with the record (2:41:54-1980). The course was short in 1980.

The first to win overall and the master's title was Navy Commander **Phil Camp** from Sigonella, Italy. In 1979, he was the overall winner in 2:19:35. This year he was the first master in 2:28:25. In 1977, Camp was runner-up in 2:20:09.

Courtesy Marine Corps Marathon

1989

14th MCM Winner Jim Hage (2:20:23)
Two-Time Consecutive Winner (1988-1989)
Hall of Fame Inductee 2003

1989

14th MCM Winners
Jim Hage 2:20:23
Two-Time Consecutive Winner (1988-1989)
Hall of Fame Inductee 2003
Laura DeWald 2:45:16

On Thursday, November 2, 1989, **Bob Wieland** started his journey for the Marine Corps Marathon on behalf of the National Rehabilitation Hospital (NRH). The president of NRH, Edward Eckenhoff was on hand to wish Wieland success. At the age of 23, he was an Army Medic. On June 14, 1969, while stationed in Vietnam, he lost both legs from an 82mm mortar round. He was in Vietnam for three months. He made a decision that his life was not over. He walked across America on his arms in three years, eight months and six days (1982-1986), 2.784 miles. Wieland sat on a pad made out of bullet-proof type material and used his arms to raise his lower body and push forward. He is a former four-time world record holder in the bench press with a best lift of 507 pounds. In 1988, he finished the Ironman Triathlon in Kona, Hawaii (128 hours, 1 minute and 46 seconds).

On the first day, he covered nine miles and the rain started to fall along with the temperature and he was not properly dressed. The next day, he covered 7 miles and the last day 10.2 miles. Wieland stated, "I reached a point where I wanted to stop along mile 22 (Hains Point). The other runners were an inspiration and provided the additional coverage for me to finish. The Marine marathon was the best because I felt more involved by being on the course with the other runners."

He explained that he did the marathon, "To bring attention to persons with disabilities and that what is being sought is not special treatment but equality to include having adequate services and facilities." Also, for the recently injured he added, "Don't be a square, but a triangle. A person should develop three elements – their body, soul and spirit."

He finished the race at 11:00 p.m., Sunday night in 79 hours and 57 minutes. During the last mile, a troop of 100 Marines marched along with him. He was given the Most Inspirational Award.

There was a pre-race build-up between **Kenny Carnes** of Morningside, Md., and **Abigniew Wandachowicz** of Poland. Last year, Carnes lost a 62-mile race in Poland and he returned this year to beat Wandachowicz. In 1989, Carnes had 25 wins and 10 losses and a world's record for 100k 5:13:43, which was set in Poland.

By the seventh mile, Carnes had built a sizable lead and he rolled to take the win in 1:54:23. Kevin Sanders of Corpus Christi, Texas was second in 2:19:40 and third went to Wandachowicz in 2:28:20.

This year, the Marines tried a new registration process using a computer-generated form that required completion with a #2 pencil. About 75% of the applications were processed using the new form. By the end of each day, all applications were processed, according to Major Olmstead.

The 15th Marine Corps Marathon was held **November 4, 1990**. The race entries closed for the first time in the history of the race at 13,000. The temperature was projected to reach a high of 75 degrees under a sunny sky. The Marines were staffed with 14 water stations, main medical facility at the start/finish area, eight aid stations staffed by 300 personnel, 20 ambulances along the course and 80 volunteer ham radio operators.

Runners were asked to sign a statement declaring their support against illegal drug use in American sports and that they were drug free. According to Marathon Coordinator, Capt. Marshall Fields, "the idea of a drug-free marathon is really the logical extension of the original goals of this event, which we are to emphasize the value of physical fitness and a healthy lifestyle."

He added, "In our marathon every runner is treated equally. We do not pay big-name athletes to participate. The race is about endurance, dedication and resolve, characteristics that made our country and the Marine Corps what they are today."

The females did not have any of the finishers from 1989. The favorite was **Olga Markova**, age 22, from Leningrad, a sergeant in the Soviet Army who had completed three marathons and set a personal record of 2:38 in the Hamburg International Marathon, Germany. She was a middle distance runner, with a 1500m time of 4:24 and 3,000m outdoor time of 9:30. She won the 1989 Soviet Cup 20K National Championship in 1:09:19.

Soviet runners Markova, **Albina Galiamova** and coach, Gregory Vinjar (1975 Soviet Marathon Champion 2:14), were hosted by C.W. and Marny Gilluly of Washington, DC. Markova and Galiamova tied for first place in the Army 10-Miler

Courtesy Marine Corps Marathon

Olga Markova, 22
Lennigrad, USSR (2:37:00)
Female Record Holder

L - Marny Gilluly (3:13:19)
1st DC Female Finisher
R - Olga Markova (2:37:00)
New Female Record

a few weeks prior running 58:41. Last fall Gilluly was invited to participate in the first Moscow Marathon in Leningrad (June 23, 1990), where she was the only American.

Off the start line and running in fourth place was **Matthew Waight** from New Britain, Pa., an electrical engineer graduate from Iowa State. He was 22nd at the Twin Cities Marathon in 1988 (2:25). Waight managed to get a 150 yard lead over Simon by mile 10 (near the Lincoln Memorial) and at the halfway point he was 1:08:29.

Farley Simon had failed after mile 20 due to a knee problem that was affecting his performance. By mile 21, Simon dropped out. Waight got the win in 2:21:32, the 12th fastest winning time.

At mile 23 after Hains Point, **Robert Rollins** (a corporal in the Royal Air Force) was in sixth place. He pressed hard over the closing miles and near the finish he took second place away from **Barry Holder** of Hagerstown, Md. Rollins ended 2:26:41 and Holder 2:26:45. Holder stated, "This was my first marathon and I was training 80 miles a week. At the half, I was 1:13 and no one had passed me and gradually I had started to pick off people until I moved up to second place."

He continued, "I was running on empty the last half of the race and in a zone. I had a tough time getting up the hill to the Iwo Jima Memorial. I remember all the people (crowd) cheering/screaming about something ... then approximately 250 to 300 yards to go this guy flies by me. I did not have enough energy at that point to stay with him, so I just continued to cruise to the finish line."

Top 3 Females - 1st Olga Markova 2:37:00,
2nd Suzanne Ray 2:44:48
3rd Lynn Patterson 2:51:03

3rd Place Barry Holder (2:26:45)
L - York Onnen President's Council on Physical Fitness

Markova took advantage of the ideal race course and weather and was destined to set a new course record. She captured the title with a 2:37:00, which broke the old record of 2:41:548 that was credited to Jan Yerks in 1980. Markova was in 40th place overall.

Second place went to **Suzanne Ray** from Anchorage, Alaska in 2:44:48 followed by Lynn Patterson of Fairfax, Va., in 2:51:03. Last year, Patterson was eighth in 2:54:33.

The trip from Anchorage, Alaska to Washington, DC was an easy choice, Ray had won a race in Anchorage that offered a free trip to a race outside of the state as part of the development of local runners.

"I chose the Marine Corps Marathon because a lot of Alaskan runners had done it several times and they told me it was a great race. Several things stood out about it. I had never been to Washington before, therefore, was awed by the course," said Ray.

"It was interesting to be overwhelmed with a case of severe patriotism while running a very painful race. I specifically remember the bagpipes playing as somewhere past half way and realizing for the first time why they were such effective instruments of war, since they gave me a dose of fighting spirit just when I needed it." She continues, "I also remember running through some sort of underpass where there were so many people cheering that I sped up to faster than my planned pace. An Alaskan friend who I was running with at that point in the race warned me not to let the crowds affect me since I was used to the spectator-less courses in Alaska."

The memories are vivid in her mind. "The finish up the hill is also etched in my mind. Knowing that I was on course for a marathon trials qualifier, if I could just make it up that hill without slowing down, made it both wonderful and horrible. I was 39 when I ran that race and it was the first time that I realized that I could actually be competitive outside of Alaska."

Ray began to run races across the U.S. as a Master and had three wonderful years competing on a national level. At age 42 she was chosen as the Master of the Year in 1994 by the Road Runner's Club of America (RRCA). Today, at the age of 53 she works hard to stay at the top of her age group.

The master's division for the men was tight as **Lucius Anderson** of Silver Spring, Md., edged out **Bill Hart** of Virginia Beach, Va., 2:32:28 (17th) to Hart's 2:32:46 (18th place). **Alvin Rich** of Dorchester, England captured third with 2:34:36 (25th place). Rich was a member of Royal Navy / Royal Marines who were competing for the Challenge Cup against the U.S. Marine Corps. The British took the overall win with an average time of 2:32:23 to 2:45:16.

The female master division was captured by defending champion, school teacher, **Rose Malloy** of Annapolis, Md., with 2:58:11 (6th female). Last year, she ran 3:03:45. The second position was captured by **Ann Davies** of New York with 3:03:53 (16th female). **Sandra Jensen** of Madison, WI, was third in 3:04:16 (18th female).

In the wheelchair competition **Kenny Carnes** of Morningside, Md., was on a mission to dominate the event. He rolled to first place and established a new event record in 1:40:22, almost 14 minutes better over last year. On August 11, 1990, Carnes was the winner of the 10th Moscow Marathon in 1:42:16. **Ken Archer** of Bowie, Md., was second in 1:52:39.

Diana McClure of Charleston, WV, was the top female wheelchair winner in 2:33:57. Rolling in second was **Brenda Smith** of Gaithersburg, Md., in 2:34:48. **Marny Gilluly** managed to be the first District of Columbia female finisher and received the Bill Mayhugh Award with a time of 3:13:19 (32nd female). The male winner was **Jack Cleland** in 2:32:22 (15th place). Cleland was last year's winner in 2:3131.

Team Hoyt, father Dick (retired Lt. Colonel Air National Guard) and son, Rick, who is pushed in a racing chair completed the race in 2:51:12. He was born as a non-speaking spastic quadriplegic with cerebral palsy.

Courtesy Marine Corps Marathon

Ken Carnes
Wheelchair Record Holder (1:40:22)

Photo: Bernadette Banker

Kenny Carnes, New Record (1:40:22)
Hall of Fame Inductee 2000

The Marine Corps Marathon is one of the favorite marathons of Team Hoyt, as Dick states, "Our personal best time for a marathon was set at the Marine Corps Marathon. The first year we ran the marathon, Rick went out and bought himself a Marine uniform so he would be dressed as a Marine while competing in the marathon!"

He further stated, "The Marines do an awesome job with the organizing, directing and actual running of the marathon. The efficient organization of this event places it high in the rankings of marathons around the country. The Marine Corps Marathon was the first marathon that we ever ran in without having any problems about being 'officially entered.'"

For the second time in the history of the race, there was another fatality. At 4 hours 15 minutes into the race (1:15 p.m.), Midshipman **Lisa B. Christiansen**, Navy ROTC, age 19, Boston University sophomore (Cheshire, Conn.) she collapsed on the 14th Street Bridge, near the 24 mile mark, the Route 110 turnoff, 2 miles from the finish. She was taken to Arlington Hospital by the Wheaton Rescue Squad and pronounced dead at 2:45 p.m., from a congenital condition. She was running in her first marathon.

A spectator was attempting to cross the race course at 200 feet from the finish line. Marines instructed the spectator not to cross but she proceeded and cut into the path of the runners. The spectator was struck to the ground and taken to the medical tent. It was determined she suffered a broken (fractured) wrist and possibly fractured her face.

Photo: Bernadette Banker

Team Hoyt (Dick & Richard)

Courtesy Marine Corps Marathon

General Al Gray
29th Commandant of the Marine Corps

The 16th Marine Corps Marathon was held **November 3, 1991**. The registrations jumped to 14,515 and there were a record number of finishers 11,288 (9,224 males, 2,064 females). The race used the computer–generated registration form which had to be completed using a #2 pencil. The temperature was a comfortable 50 degrees. Through the years, the course has changed, race coordinators have passed batons, but the mission of excellence has been the motivation of the U.S. Marines to give the runners and spectators a first-class event.

In a letter from the President's Council on Physical Fitness and Sports, "The Sixteenth Annual Marine Corps Marathon is the only race in the world endorsed by the President's Council on Physical Fitness and Sports. It is a symbol of the popularity of running for sport and exercise, with over half the runners going the full marathon distance for the first time, not for prize money, but to test themselves and enjoy the camaraderie of fellow athletes. We see this race as a tribute to physical fitness for all Americans," stated Chairman Arnold Schwarzenegger and the Executive Director John Butterfield.

The New York City Marathon was being run on the same day; the top male would win $25,000 plus a Mercedes Benz sedan and a time bonus for sub-2:10 of $35,000. The female winner would receive $20,000, the car and a time bonus of $25,000 for a sub-2:30.

This year, a further community bond occurred with the cooperation of the public transportation system, Washington Metropolitan Area Transit Authority, by opening the stations early so the runners could get to the race site. The only

1991

General Carl E. Mundy
30th Commandant Marine Corps Marathon

1991

Winners Carlos Rivas (2:17:54),
Amy Kattwinkel (2:44:27)

returning champion was the 1984 (2:19:40) and 1986 (2:23:14) winner, **Brad Ingram** from Mansfield Ohio, a former Marine artillery officer. He has made eight other appearances, including the first in 1979 where he placed 65th in 2:35:01 while being stationed at Quantico, Va.

Near mile five at the Pentagon, a leader surfaced, **Carlos Rivas**, a sailor in the Mexican Navy, and he shook all possible contenders. Mile after mile, Rivas remained alone and unchallenged. At the halfway point on Capitol Hill his time was 1:07:39. He continued with his assault to win with 2:17:54 (the fourth fastest time). Rivas had completed 26 marathons with a personal record of 2:12 at the San Diego Marathon (December 1988). Fellow countryman, **Rene Guerrero**, managed to protect second place with 2:21:12. Third place and first American was **Craig Fram** of Hamstead, NH with a 2:23:33. The fourth position was reported as **Peter Mullins**, which turned out to be incorrect due to a bib number mismatch. The runner was **Brad Ingram** in 2:24:30, his third time taking fourth place.

At the halfway point, **Jodie Foster** of Sandy Hook, Conn., was in the lead. She was running her ninth marathon. Closing in was **Amy Kattwinkel** of Charlotte, NC (a cross county runner while at Wake Forest). At the Boston Marathon, she ran 2:51:32. At mile 23, Kattwinkel worked to take control and had a gap on Foster and **Christine Snow-Reaser** of Old Orchard Beach, Maine. Kattwinkel won with 2:44:27 (12th fastest winning time). She qualified for the Olympic Marathon Trials. Foster continued for second place in 2:46:12 and Snow-Reaser was third in 2:47:50.

The men's masters was led by **Alvin Rich** of Dorchester, England with a 2:34:02 (24th place overall). Rich is a member of the Royal Navy/Royal Marines team. **Mike Zeigle** of Sun Prairie, WI, was second in 2:37:33 (47th place) and **Lucious Anderson** of Silver Spring, Md., was third in 2:38:40.

Rose Malloy of Annapolis, Md., the defending champion (2:58:11), was first in 2:55:13 (12th females). In second was **Joyce Ploeger** of Norfolk, Va., in 3:12:46 (30th place). **Linda Mills** of Salisbury, Md., was third in 3:09:29 (34th place). **Steve Lietz** of Salisbury, Md., was the top wheelchair in 2:02:58 followed by **Patrick O'Brien** of Williamsville, NY in 2:30:48. **Skip Sanders** of Panama City, FL, was third in 2:46:32.

The female chair winner was **Brenda Smith** of Rockville, MD., in 2:41:33. Second place was **Shelia Luellen** of Richmond, Va., in 3:41:04. The New York City Marathon had a 1-2 finish by Mexican athletes, **Salvador Garcia** with 2:09:28 and second was **Andres Espinoza** in 2:10:00. The female winner was **Liz McColgan** of Scotland in 2:27:23 and second was **Olga Markova** in 2:28:18. Markova set the Marine Corps record last year (2:37:00).

WUSA-TV-9 sportscaster, **Glenn Brenner**, age 43, of Bethesda, Md., finished the race in 4:26:53. A statement was released the day after the race that Brenner had been hospitalized and diagnosed with a brain tumor.

The 17th Marine Corps Marathon was held **October 25, 1992**. The runners had to face 25-30 mph winds and the temperature was 51 degrees at the start. The clocks were turned back so the runners had an extra hour to sleep.

The line up included defending champion (2:17:54), **Carlos Rivas** and **Rene Guerrero**, (the runner-up 2:21:12). The two were part of the team from the Mexican Navy, which included **Ricardo Galicia** and **Francisco Lugo** (2:33:51 last year). The master division had defending champion (2:34:02), **Alvin Rich** of the Royal Navy / Royal Marines. In his first Marine Corps Marathon, in 1978, he ran 2:37:23.

The top returning female was fourth place finisher (2:50:12) **Judy Mercon** of Clearwater, Fla. The top master was three-time defending champion (3:03:45-1989, 2:58:11-1990, 2:55:13-1991), **Rose Malloy** of Annapolis, Md.

Record holder in the wheelchair division, **Kenny Carnes** of Morningside, Md, was rolling off against 19-time winner **Ken Archer** of Bowie, Md.

A pack of six led through the eighth mile, the dominant runner was Guerrero in his first marathon and Galicia. The two worked the race until the 18-mile mark along Hains Point as **Michael Whittlesey** of West Wellington, Conn., took the lead briefly. Leaving the tip of Hains Point to the Jefferson Memorial, the runners faced the strong headwind. The race was down to three as Guerrero pulled away from the pack at mile 23 and took the win in 2:24:09. Whittlesey denied a Mexican 1-2 finish by taking second in 2:25:26. Galicia was third in 2:26:23.

Starting Line along Route 110

9th Place Carlos Rivas (2:31:52)
1991 Winner 2:17:54

Mercon took the lead for the woman in Crystal City (mile three) and continued to open a lead. The closest competitor was **Kelly Flanagan** of New Vernon, Fla., who finished 23rd place last year in 3:06:37. Mercon went unchallenged to win in 2:47:58 and Flanagan held in for second in 2:50:25. **Denise Metzgar** of Jacksonville, Fla., was third in 2:53:33.

Carnes out rolled the 20 chairs in the race to capture his third win in 1:48:46. Archer was second in 1:49:41.

Al Rich defended his master's title and won in 2:34:55. Bennett Beach of Bethesda, Md., was second in 2:35:05.

Rose Malloy managed to collect another master's win in 2:56:42. Maddy Harmeling of Merrick, NY was second in 3:01:54.

Team Hoyt (father Dick and son Rick) rolled to finish in 2:40:47. The Hoyt Fund was established in 1992 to enhance the lives and mobility of people with disabilities. The goal of the Hoyt Fund is to integrate the physically challenged into everyday life. One way to accomplish this is to educate the able-bodied, making them more aware of the issues that the disabled face every day. Another is by actively helping the disabled to participate in activities that would otherwise be inaccessible to them.

Harry Cordollos of San Francisco, Calif., a visually impaired runner with a guide, John Butterfield, Executive Director, President's Council on Physical Fitness and Sports finished in 4:01:58.

Winner Rene Guerrero (2:24:09)
Ambassador J. William Middendorf II
LtGen W. E. Boomer

3rd Denise Metzgar (2:50:33)
LtGen. W. E. Boomer

The 18th Marine Corps Marathon was held **October 24, 1993**. The race started with a few good men and women. The new race coordinator, Major Rick Nealis, was faced with a major decision. For the first time in the history of the race, there would not be a declared winner at the awards ceremony. To be declared a winner, the runner must run the 26.2 mile course as measured. The core of the race remains to promote physical fitness and fairness of competition.

Dominique Bariod from Morez, France was making his U.S. debut and was observed on several occasions cutting the corners along the course. The practice was acceptable in European countries. However, it is the runner's responsibility to know the rules and course of each event they participate in. Officials along the course alerted him of his actions but he could not understand English. The second place finisher, **Esteban Vanegas** of Ecuador was observed on a couple of occasions cutting corners.

The first mile was hit in 5:13 with Bariod in a pack of four runners, which included **Dominique DaLuz** of Silver Spring, Md., and Mark Hoon of Bethesda, Md.

Going into the 10th mile after the Kennedy Center a pack of four passed in 53:44 which included Bariod, Vanegas, **Ramon Cenlenoayala** of Puerto Rico, and **Dave McCormack** of Falls Church, Va. The pace passed the halfway point along Louisiana Avenue going up to Union Station in 1:10:15. Bariod made a move to break up the pack and took sole possession of the lead and he never looked back.

Bariod crossed with the slowest winning time in 2:23:56 followed by Vanegas in 2:24:20. **Chuck Lotz** of Charlotte, NC was third in 2:24:50. Finishing in 12th place was the defending champion **Rene Guerrero** from Mexico in 2:28:19.

Lead pack beyond the Kennedy Center
#644 Estaban Vanegas, #10551 Dominique Bariod
#10527 Ramon Centenoayala, Dave McCormack
10.5 Miles at Kennedy Center.

Dominique Bariod, Mile 18
Eventual Winner (2:23:56)

Female Winner Holly Ebert (2:48:41)

1st Master & 1st Female Military (3:01:4⁙
Sandra Jensen

Holly Ebert, a mother, waitress, and hardware store employee from Ogden, Utah took the lead off the line in her fourth marathon. At mile five, Ebert clocked 30:36 and maintained a steady but demanding pace. At mile 10 she was 1:10:30, a pace of 6:09 per mile. Ebert kept on rolling, and at mile 15 she was 1:33:21. Ebert crossed the line in 2:48:41.

Second place was captured by **Mary Gaylord** of Alexandria, Va., in 2:53:33. Gaylord had prior times at the Marine Corps of 3:18:52 – 1987, 3:15:21-1989, 3:02:25 – 1991, and last year 3:23:04.

The wheelchair division was dominated by 44-year-old **Ken Archer** of Bowie, Md., in 1:49:12, his 10th Marine Corps win. A short and steep ramp had been added near the Lincoln Memorial, which required brute force to roll up. The second chair was **James Arendt** of Westwood, NJ in 2:10:56.

The top male master was **Michael Zeigle** of Sun Prairie, WI in 2:34:32. In second was **David Dunne** of Ridgewood, NJ in 2:38:42. **Sandra Jensen** of Milwaukee, WI, was top female in 3:01:45. Jensen ran 3:07:39 in 1988. **Eunice Phillips** of Frederiction, Canada was second in 3:04:09. The 1987 winner (2:44:36), **Mary Robertson** form Richmond, Va., finished in 3:06:15 (221st place). **Donietta Bickley**, age 79, of College Park, MD, finished in 5:47:28. **Karl Hackbarth**, age 77 of Montclair, VA finished in 3:55:23.

Runner, author, philosopher, and doctor **George Sheehan** died November 1, 1993 four days before his 75th birthday. He had run and conducted several clinics at the Marine Corps Marathon.

Julius Becza, age 58, from Point Pleasant, NJ, a professor of education at Monmouth College, became the third fatality in the race history. He was 4 hours

Courtesy Marine Corps Marathon

Photo: George Banker

1993

Donietta Bickley, 77

1993

1st Wheelchair Ken Archer (1:49:12)
Hall of Fame Inductee 2006

13 minutes into the race when he went into cardiac arrest between miles 22-23 (Thomas Jefferson Memorial and the 14th Street Bridge). He had completed the race in 1991 (4:27:04) and last year in 4:36:18. The medical examiner of the District of Columbia indicated that Becza's death wasn't caused by the marathon. The condition was cardiomegaly with occlusive coronary arthersclerosis, meaning an enlarged heart with blocked vessels.

There was to be no disqualification of Bariod or Vanegas and their 1-2 position would stand. Major Rick Nealis, after consulting with various local race officials, concluded there was no unfair advantage and the distance was insignificant.

The 19th Marine Corps Marathon was held **October 23, 1994**. Mother Nature was out to test the wills of the participants by releasing rain that started Saturday night and continued through Sunday afternoon. It was another record year for registrants, 16,211 (12,427 males, 3,764 females) and total finishers, 12,675 (9,795 males, 2,880 females). The registration was closed on October 12, 1994 because the limit had been reached.

The race this year was dedicated to those men and women who fought and died almost 50 years ago in the Battle of Iwo Jima. The battle is largely remembered by the historic flag raising atop Mount Suribachi (February 23, 1945), which was captured in print by Associated Press photographer Joseph Rosenthal and in motion picture footage by Sgt. Bill Genaust. On November 10, 1954, the monument was dedicated.

On Thursday, October 20, 1994, **Oprah Winfrey**, America's number one rated talk show host announced on her show that she would be running the Marine Corps

Photo: Official USMC Photograph LCPL Vincet Aropesa

Courtesy Marine Corps Marathon

Steve Bozeman (w/US Flag)
Hall of Fame Inductee 2000

Oprah Winfrey, #40
1st Marathon (4:29:15)

Marathon. This was to be her first marathon. She was assigned bib number 40 to match her age. Major Rick Nealis stated in a press release, "She was impressed that it was 'The People's Marathon' and that the Marine Corps Marathon had so many first-time runners like herself." Last year, Winfrey completed a half marathon in 2 hours and 16 minutes. Under her training program, her weight had dropped from 225 to 155. She stepped on the start line as a runner with a personal mission and to fulfill a dream. The rain did not seem to affect her quest. While running along the courses, there were words of encouragement. Her first mile was 8:15. The pre-race goal was 4:10:00 and she ran 4:29:15. Winfrey commented, "It's the best feeling I've ever had. It's better than an Emmy, I tell you."

The race began to take shape coming off Hains Point. After mile 20, it was flooded as the runners had to take to grass, which quickly turned muddy and shoes sank and almost were pulled off. **Graciano Gonzalez**, a 34-year-old sergeant in the Mexican army, started to make a move and began to reel in the top runners. Along the 14th Street Bridge, he closed in on **Gordon Saunder**, a soldier from Fort Campbell, KY. The next in line was **Bob Schwelm** of Bryn Mawr, Pa., and **Ginge Gouge** of the Royal Navy/Royal Marines. Gonzalez continued to pull away and he returned the control of the Marine Corps Marathon back to Mexico and took first in 2:22:51. This was his 12th marathon and he has a best of 2:17. Sanders held in for second in 2:25:06 and third went to Schwelm in 2:25:37.

It was a wire-to-wire win for Charlottesville, Va., special education teacher, **Susan Molloy** running in her first marathon. She finished in 2:39:34, which was 2 minutes and 35 seconds off a new women's record. The runner-up (2:49:46) was **Callie Malloy**, a 1stLt in the Air Force station at Randolph AFB, in Texas. The third place was captured by **Kimberly Markland** of Dayton, Ohio in 2:53:22. Molloy and Malloy both qualified for the 1996 US Olympic Marathon Trials.

The wheelchair division was dominated by **Ken Archer** of Bowie, Md., in 1:53:31 for a total of 11 wins. **Cisco Jetter** of Woodbridge, Va., was second in 2:15:21. **Dana Jackson** of Laurel, Md., was third in 2:22:01. He stated, "This was the hardest event, and I was emotionally drained at he end." Near Capitol Hill, the coating on the tires came off which almost sidelined him and he adds, "I was in third and I kept telling myself, don't get caught."

Peggy Gray of the Carlisle Running Club, PA, relates a high point in her running career as she accompanied her daughter, **Kate**, to the completion of her first marathon. She states, "Having experienced her first tooth, first word, first step, first grade, first date, first job, I thought I was prepared. Not a chance! As we made our way to the starting line of the 1994 Marine Corps Marathon, all I could focus on was the steady downpour, the ocean of runners and my own churning stomach. I wondered what was going on in Kate's mind but we seemed to have an unspoken pledge between us not to verbalize our fears as we slogged along. After the cannon boomed and the wave of runners rolled on, I saw my daughter, the runner. Dressed in her Penn State T-shirt and my 86 Boston Marathon cap, the usually quiet Kate constantly offered cheer and encouragement to fellow runners as the miles wore on and the rain continued."

They continued to tour the course and she recounts, "The miles and hours in training paid off as we were able to enjoy the beautiful course. The Washington Monument, the Capitol, the Lincoln Monument all helped pass the miles, as did the ever-present Marines, who offered encouragement and hoo-ras as we ran. At mile 20, we passed the medical tent where Kate was pulled from last year's effort with a stress fracture. I remembered 1993 and our long limp across the bridge to the car, the tears we shared and the bond we formed."

The two ran past Hains Point and by the Awakening statue and on across the Potomac River for the final stretch to the finish line. "By now I was feeling some pain and was anticipating that Kate might have to walk a stretch but she had entered the 'zone' and so on we ran. When the bell tower finish came into view, Kate suffered a surge of emotion and indicated that she might have to walk but we talked it through and headed up the infamous Iwo Jima hill and into the bedlam of the cheering crowd. Crossing the finish line a step behind Kate, I watched as she was awarded her medal and turned to hug me. I saw her as a child, a grown woman, a runner, and I felt truly blessed to have been part of the journey as well as the marathon."

She closes, "I also knew that in her heart she now truly understood why I run, why we all run – alone but always together, sharing our lives, our disappointments and accomplishments. And so I share with all of you my pride and my love for a daughter who is a winner all the way!"

The 20th year had plans in the making according to BGen M. R. Steele, Commanding General, Marine Corps Base, Quantico. "We are anticipating even greater interest for the 20th Marine Corps Marathon; therefore, I have announced in the runner's application that the field will close October 6, 1995, to alert runners to apply early. The registration acceptance again will be on a first-come, first-served basis since this system worked very well in previous marathons. There currently is no intention of beginning a lottery to control the number of runners."

The 20th Marine Corps Marathon was run **October 22, 1995**. The ties of this event are with the novice runner and providing a platform for their introduction into the world of marthoning. The elite runners are welcomed but there is not the usual financial incentive. There were a record number of finishers 14,618 (10,902 males and 3,716 females). The course offers a tour of the historic monuments in Washington, DC but at a price, 43 turns along the course.

There was a break in the tradition. The Race Coordinator position was filled for two years by an active duty Marine who was rotated out and replaced. Major **Rick Nealis**, off active duty, had accepted the position as a civilian to maintain the continuity in leadership.

The marathon is unique and takes a mental and physical commitment. Some of the runners were here for themselves and others were there to represent others. The number 3072 was assigned in 1994 to runner LtCol. **Paul D. Ice**, USMCR (Ret) from Okalahoma (a US Customs Agent). He ran 4:11:48.

On April 19, 1995, the bombing of the Alfred P. Murrah Federal Building took the life of LtCol. Ice. The Marines retired the number and a group of Oklahoma City runners ran in memory of their friend and fellow runner.

The starting line-up included the only male Marine Corps winner, **Farley Simon** (1983- 2:17:46). The favorite was **Darrell General** of Mitchellville, Md., making his fifth appearance (1983- 2:58:55, 1984- 2:24:36, 1985 – 2:26:52, and 1987 – 2:19:08 second place). His personal best marathon is 2:14:42. At the 1990 Boston Marathon, he was the first American and 14th placed with a time of 2:15:28.

The race opened quickly and General was in charge going into the first mile. An unregistered runner jumped into the race and was not removed. **Eron Ferreira** from Brazil ran without shoes and he stayed with General until the Lincoln Memorial where he dropped out. At Capitol Hill, the halfway point General passed in 1:08:05. He had fallen off the pace to break the record (2:14:01) set in 1987 by **Jeff Scuffins**. Holding the tape at the finish line was Gen. Richard D. Hearney, Assistant Commandant of the Marine Corps and BGen. E.C. Kelley, Jr., Commanding General, MCB Quantico. General crossed in 2:16:34, the third fastest winning time.

Francisco Hernandez of Mexico was second in 2:20:19 and in third was **Nelson Shertzer** of Lancaster, Pa., in 2:24:11. Simon placed fourth in 2:25:25 and was the first master. He is the second person to hold an overall title and master win. The first was Navy runner **Phil Camp** open winner in 1979 (2:19:35) and master's in 1989 (2:28:25).

Claudia Kasen of Williamsburg, Va., took the race out from the start and led the entire way. She coaches cross country and track at Walsingham Academy in Williamsburg, Va. Kasen was fourth in 1992 (2:53:35). She went on to win in 2:49:21. **Maria Pazarentzos** of Hagerstown, Md., was second in 2:52:18. She missed the US Olympic Trials by 2 minutes 18 seconds. Kay Panfile of Sparta, NJ, was third in 2:53:06.

Maria (Pazarentzos) Spinnler went out with the goal of making the Olympic qualifying time of 2:50. Her first marathon was in 1993 where she placed fourth (2:58:43) in the Charlotte Observer. Her goal was to gain experience and break three hours. In 1994, she attempted to break 2:50 but dropped out in Atlantic City. At the US Women's Marathon Championships in February 1995 in South Carolina she placed 11th in 2:53:19. In June that year she ran the Grandma Marathon in 2:54:36. The Marine Corps Marathon was going to be the last stand.

Photo: George Banker

Bill Mayhugh –
The Voice of the Marathon
Hall of Fame Inductee 2003

It is easy to give up, but it takes determination to keep going. She recounts, "I went out very smart and never did anything stupid. I remember halfway through the race feeling so easy and thinking to myself I can do this."

"At around mile 22, from my waist up, I was always so positive but my legs would just turn to cement, but it was frustrating for me since I didn't go out hard and die. I was always in control from the beginning and I never did anything stupid. I went from 6:09 on mile 21 to 7:04 at mile 22. It was a gradual death for me. I would always run out of glycogen and there was never anything I could do about it. After a disappointing 2:52:18, I said that's it for me, I'm going to start my family," she added and so ended her marathon career, though she continues with the middle distances.

The female master winner was **Loraine Provost** of Springfield, IL, with 3:00:26 (13th place). In second was **Joy Hampton** of Clarksboro, NJ with 3:17:39 (48th place).

Rolling for a fourth victory was **Ken Carnes** of Snellville, GA with 1:48:41. The second finisher was **Cisco Jeter** of Woodbridge, Va., in 1:48:53.

The female chair winner was **Susan Katz**, age 16, from North Potomac, Md., with 2:45:35. The second place finisher was **Darla Alinovi** of Flushing, NY with 2:48:08. She was making her wheelchair marathon debut and was accompanied by 10-time winner **Ken Archer**. She is a six-year breast cancer survivor and has been paralyzed from the waist down since 1989 as a result of a tumor on the spine.

The Heart of the MCM is in the Runners 1996-2006

The 21st Marine Corps Marathon was held **October 27, 1996**. The race continued a modest growth to 19,234 registrants with 15,219 finishers (10,950 males and 4,269 females). The entry fee was $30. The Marine Corps Marathon was ranked fourth in the nation behind New York, Los Angeles, and Honolulu.

The leader emerged from the sea of runners, **Isaac Garcia**, age 28, a Navy Petty Officer in the Mexican Navy. Garcia had a best time of 2:10:54. At the halfway point, the elapsed time was 1:05:35. Garcia was going for the record and had been training up to 150 miles per week. At the start of the race, the weather was deceiving as the winds were keeping the temperature around 60 degrees before the start. However, the warmer weather was going to ruin many dreams of the day. The winds diminished over the course of the morning and set the stage for another warm race.

Garcia was allowed to go unchecked the entire race and won with the second fastest time of 2:15:08. **Samuel Lopez**, the training partner of Garcia and member of the Mexican Navy, placed second in 2:23:01. **Mark Croasdale** of the Royal Navy/Royal Marines team was third in 2:25:24. The fourth place went to **Mark Cucuzzella**, with the U.S. Air Force stationed in Portugal; he finished in 2:27:20.

Since 1991, the Mexicans had made their mark at the Marine Corps Marathon by taking first place in 1991 (2:17:54), 1992 (2:24:09), and 1994 (2:22:51).

The women's event had an early making of a win by the leader for the first 14 miles, **Kelly McDonnell** of Arlington, Va. The lead was taken over by Sharon Servidio of Arlington making her debut. She was in a nursing program at Georgetown University. The other part of the Mexican Navy was about to land. The eventual winner, **Emma Cabrera**, a Navy Petty Officer pulled ahead of Servidio at mile 22 after leaving Hains Point. Cabrera had run 29 marathons with 12 wins. Cabrera sailed in for the win in 2:48:34, the 13th slowest winning time in the history of the race.

Servidio managed to retain second in 2:53:04 and **Jennifer McNerney-Schretzmayer** of Bellport, NY with 2:55:00. McDonnell faded to sixth place in 3:01:34. There was a price from the blisters and the heat but the determination remained.

"It was my first marathon post collegiate. I was giving it a shot with very little knowledge on how to run a marathon. I went out slow, feeling good, and just kept running a little faster along the way. I remember hooking onto a guy for most of the race; he took me through the halfway point when I was like the fifth woman. I just kept passing people left and right," stated **Sharon Servidio**.

The marathon can lure you into friendship and slowly it can changes. Servidio continues, "The day was getting nicer and nicer but warmer and warmer as the race went on. I remember feeling really good around mile 16 and started to get excited. Then at one point I made it to first place and got really excited. I started to pick up the pace and then hit Hains Point where the heat and anticipation got to me."

1995

8th Mark Plaatjes, 35
Boulder, CO (2:31:24)

"I ended up walking a bit around mile 22-23 and that is where Emma passed me and kept on going. I was trying to finish the race at that point in disbelief that I was in second place – unbelievable. I started running shortly thereafter and finished the race in awe of Emma, – having heard that she had qualified for the Olympics but was unable to run because of an injury. At the finish, the temperature was in the 70s and I was thrilled to have finished my first marathon," adds Servidio.

Pete Kaplan of Charlotte, NC was the top master in 2:33:35 (13th place). **Ginge Gough** of the Royal Navy/Royal Marines was second in 2:35:46 (17th place). In third was **Victor Cuevas** of Las Marias, PR in 2:37:07 (23rd place). The master's record was sent in 1981 by **Bill Hall** of Durham, NC at 2:24:36.

The lead female master was **Barbara Bellows** of Ithaca, NY in 3:04:44 (8th place). The record was set in 1983 by **Diana Palmason** of Ottawa, Canada in 2:50:51. In second was **Trish Steelman** of Bowling

Green, KY in 3:07:27 (15th place). In third was **Helen Visgauss** of Port Jefferson, NY in 3:14:28 (26th place).

Rolling in another class was **Carlos Moleda** of Falls Church, Va., in 1:55:32 to win the wheelchair division. The leading female was **Julia Wallace** of Rumson, NJ in 2:21:09.

No win is easy, Moleda explains. "The '96 MCM was great race and a memorable one. Yes, it was hot but I usually do better in the heat than the cold. Overall, the race was uneventful until the finish line. I was climbing the last hill at the memorial with the crowd going crazy and screaming. At the end of the climb there was a right turn towards the finish line on the grass. When I turned and went over the transition from the pavement to the grass, my tire peeled off the rim and my chair literally locked in place.

The crowd fell into a silence. I was within sight of the finish line and stuck. No one could touch me to help with the fear I could be disqualified. I frantically ripped the entangled tire of the rim and once I succeeded the crowd started to cheer again and with the crowd screaming I proceeded to cross the finish line. It was awesome. I went on to do many races but every time the subject of 'race moments' comes along that race is always my number one."

Moleda was born in Sao Paulo, Brazil and came to the U.S. at the age of 18 and subsequently became a U.S. citizen and joined the U.S. Navy where he qualified to become an elite Navy Sea, Air and Land (SEAL). He was one of the 11 of the 130 trainees who started the class. On December 20, 1989, his unit was assigned a mission (Operation Just Cause, President George Bush) to disable a private jet at Patilla in the Republic of Panama that was used by its President General Manuel Noriega.

The 10-man squad lost the element of surprise and was met with heavy resistance and, during the fire fight, one bullet hit the pack he was wearing that had explosives. Another bullet hit him in the left leg and others hit his equipment. Four in his unit was killed in action. Petty Officer Moleda was in rehabilitation and recieved treatment for a leg infection for nine months and in 1990 he was medically discharged from SEAL Team FOUR.

In subsequent years, he became a four-time Hawaii Ironman Triathlon and World Record Holder (1998, 1990 – 10:55:22). He won again in 2004 (11:18:07) and in 2005 (10:30:54).

The Marines saw the Challenge Cup slip away at the feet of the British. The duel was close with the average time of the 2:33:40 to 2:36:10 in favor of the British. The score stands at 12 to 7 and the Cup was on display at the British Embassy in Washington, DC.

The 22nd Marine Corps Marathon was held **October 26, 1997**. The temperature was in the high 40s and a light rainfall. Miss District of Columbia, Sonya Gavankar, an American University student, sang the National Anthem. Last year she sang as Miss Federal City and she would compete in the Miss America Pageant. The official starter for the race was Secretary of State **Madeleine Albright**.

This year, the race introduced the ChampionChip for race scoring, which was provided by Burns Computer Services. The core of the system is Texas Instrument Registration and Identification System (TIRISTM) technology. A transponder about the size of a quarter is attached to the shoe lace. The information contained includes the runner's name, age, gender and other vital information. When the runners reach the start, an antenna embedded in a mat captures each transponder's unique code and sends it to a central computer.

When the runner crosses the finish line, another antenna captures the ID code and the computer instantly calculates the runner's time to within one-tenth of a second. The runners are provided with a "Chip Time," the time from when the runner crosses the mat at the start line until reaching the mat at the finish. The "Gun Time" is the time from when the starter's gun is fired. This system allowed the directors to know exactly how many people started the race. Also, mats were placed along to course as "checkpoints" to ensure that all runners run the entire distance. Race results could be posted to the Internet within seconds of verification.

The race was dedicated to the memory of triathlete **Judith Marie Flannery**, 57, of Chevy Chase, Md., a mother of five. On April 2, 1997, she and two other bikers were preparing for a 3,000-mile Race Across America. The training was not completed. About 11 a.m., a car driven by an unlicensed 16-year-old crossed the center line and struck Flannery head-on and dragged her 100 feet. The other two cyclists were able to avoid the car. The father was in the car and there were allegations that he had been drinking.

Flannery was the oldest female to be awarded the Master Female Triathlete of the Year (1996). There were six U.S. and four world championships awarded. She ran the Marine Corps seven times with the first in 1984 (3:33:51) and the last in 1993 (3:52:48). Her best marathon time was 3:32:51 at the 12th Marine Corps Marathon (1987).

The race favorite was the 1995 winner (2:16:34), **Darrell General** of Mitchelleville, Md. He went through the first mile 5:11 and by the fifth mile his split time was 5:07 (30:49). The goal was to set a new record but the changing weather conditions were going to be a factor. At mile seven he was 36:04 (split of 5:15). The halfway time was 1:08:29.

General had led wire-to-wire to win with 2:18:21 (the eighth fastest winning time). He commented, "I was prepared to run alone. I was ready to go. I was strong and fit and went out fast by myself. I got cold and my hip was hurting a

Courtesy Marine Corps Marathon

Courtesy Marine Corps Marathon

Darrell General (2:18:21)

Secretary of State Madeleine Albright

little but I had to stay focused. After mile 17 I was trying to pick up to make sure no one was on me. I had to refocus on winning. I was feeling good at mile 20. I was in a rhythm on the HOV lanes and the crowds got me pumped up."

Donna (Elliot) Moore from Kensington, Md., led wire to wire. At the halfway, she was 1:23:25 and the time at mile 20 was 2:08:20. Moore won with 2:53:42 and her personal best is 2:49:30. The second place went to **Selena Smart** of Washington, DC, 2:55:34. **Claire Norsworthy**, a member of the Royal Navy/ Royal Marine female team was third in 2:55:45.

"At miles five to seven, I felt like I am up here and if anyone was back there they would be up with me. I was running to pace and not to win. If I had picked it up, I may not have finished. The last three miles I was getting tired and I was beginning to slow down a lot," said Moore. This was her fourth time running the Marine Corps, 1980, 1984 (3:17:42), 1987 (3:07:16). She added, "I led the race the entire time. However, the last 5 miles were difficult because I went out too fast (imagine that). I was fortunate to win in spite of the drastic time loss in the last few miles."

The master's battle was between **Steven Ward** of Reston, Va., and **Ginge Gough** of the Royal Navy/Royal Marines. Ward had closed in at mile 23 along the HOV lanes and assumed the lead from Gough to take the win in 2:34:32. Gough was second master in 2:35:07. Ward had a halfway split of 1:14:13.

Ward stated, "I wasn't going to concede anything in the race. At mile 15 my body started to shut down. I had stuff on my body cramping that I didn't know could cramp. I was on the 5:40 express. I got on the bridge and chased one guy down. I dialed in on him and at mile 23 one guy came by me on the British team. I passed him back around mile 24."

A month prior, at the MS Challenge Half-Marathon, the winners were General (1:05:46) and Moore (1:19:39), with Ward the master's winner (1:12:29).

The top wheelchair winners were **Mike Postell** of Dunwoody, Ga., in 1:58:49 and **Julia Wallace** of Rumson, N.J. in 2:21:00. Wallace was defending champion; her 1996 time was 2:21:09.

There were problems with results days after the race. The ChampionChip is only as useful as the data entered into the system and runners wear the correct chip. There were three rounds before the correct female master was located. The announced winner, **Bridget Dunn** of Denver, Colo., ran an impressive 3:08:17 at age 60. It was discovered later she was 30 years old. The next in line was **Sara Dawyer** of Alexandria, VA., who ran 3:14:35. Dawyer had been notified by a friend that her name was in a local newspaper that she was the declared master's winner. Dawyer stated that her husband was trying to qualify for the Boston Marathon and he was listed as running 5:11:25 and she was listed with 3:14:35. The times were correct but the two had their chips mixed and she ran with his chip. The next in line was **Linda Russo** of Flushing, NY, in 3:20:15. This was not finalized until a couple of weeks after the race.

In 1988, **Alejandro Cruz Maya** of Mexico, at the age of 20, won the Chicago Marathon in 2:08:56 was caught up in an embarrassing moment for the Marine Corps. He was the runner up in 2:23:25 and reportedly identified as being disqualified for being seen cutting the course in two places. This proved to be false and he was reinstated.

Courtesy Marine Corps Marathon

1997
Vice-President Al Gore, Kristin Gore (4:54:25)

1997
Karenna Gore-Schiff 4:54:26

Maya was given the credit as being the first military finisher as a member of the Mexican Navy and edged out Marine **Steve Schmid** of Chester, Va., ninth overall (2:32:39). Maya was not in the Navy but a student and Schmid received the award.

Two other Mexicans were disqualified for failing to cross a check point, 17th place **Samuel Juan Lopez** who was runner up in 1996 (2:23:01) and 18th place **Carlos Espinoza**. At the halfway point, Lopez's time was 1:14:17 and Espinoza had 1:16:36. The two finished in 2:35:15.

Vice President **Al Gore**, age 49, wearing race number 17, completed the race in 4:54:25 along with his daughters, **Karenna Gore Schigg**, 24 and **Kristin Gore**, 20. Their halfway time was 2:19:06 and the 20-mile time was 3:37:18

The start of the race was delayed until 8:47 a.m., because an elderly spectator went into cardiac arrest and was taken to Arlington Hospital were he later died.

On race day before adjustments, 14,389 started the race, 14,341 were recorded at the halfway point, and 13,965 finished.

Courtesy Marine Corps Marathon

Miss District of Columbia, Sonya Gavankar

The 23rd Marine Corps Marathon was held **October 25, 1998**. The race had closed out June 17, which was two months earlier than in 1997. Applications were being processed at 1,600 per week. The weather was sunny and a warm 68 degrees. Secretary of Defense William S. Cohen was the official starter. There were 13,700 starters and the last runner reached the start line in 11 minutes. The lead runner **Weldon Johnson** of Washington, D.C. had passed mile two in 10 minutes 54 seconds. Johnson was going unchallenged as his twin brother accompanied him along a portion of the race before dropping out.

It was a runaway for Johnson as he passed the halfway point on Capitol Hill in 1:11:30. His time at mile 15 was 1:21:32, along the Mall towards The Lincoln Memorial. Johnson continued his pace back to the Iwo Jima Memorial where he crossed the line in 2:25:13, the slowest winning time in the history of the race.

Johnson stated, "Winning was in the back of my mind. I thought I could run 2:20. I didn't think I would win. I thought someone would be in front of me. My calves started to tighten up going into mile 18. I knew I was pretty far ahead. I was worried about my calves. After mile 18, I got scared, I felt good. To win was great; a great experience."

The next two places were taken by members of Royal Navy / Royal Marines, **Mark Croasdale** in second with 2:31:33 and third was **Gary Gerrard** with 2:32:43. Another runaway was in the making; **Kimberly Markland** of San Antonio, Texas, a 34-year-old Air Force major took the first mile in 6:04 and never looked back. At mile five her time was 31:14 and halfway she was

Courtesy Marine Corps Marathon

23rd MCM 10-25-98

Weldon Johnson, 25

1:22:19. She was a member of the Air Force World Class Athlete Program. This was the first year of the Armed Forces competition and she was representing the Air Force. The marathon distance was added by the Armed Forces Sports Council. Markland passed mile 20 in 2:06:14 and took the win 2:49:07, the 15th fastest winning time in the history of the race. She met the U.S. Olympic marathon trials standard of 2:50:00.

"I'm a great runner up to 18 to 19 miles. I started to feel a slowing in my pace. I realized that I was several minutes ahead. The 22 to 24 was tough, buddy, that was a killer. At mile 25, the motorcycle cops hit the sirens and the lights and I wanted to savor it. The crowd was so critical in keeping you going. Oh, this is great, I always wanted to break the tape," stated Markland.

Hidden in the memory banks along the course, Markland was having thoughts of a prior patient, retired Marine, Lt.Col. Patrick Shrunk who was under her care back in 1994 for leukemia. "At the time I mentioned to him that I was running the Marine marathon, he said, 'I've always wanted to run it.' Upon my return, I gave him my medal and told him to keep it until he got his own. He died in December. During the lonely tough time across the bridge I said, "This is for Patrick," she added.

In 1994 Markland was third in 2:53:22. "I was better trained than in 1994. I had a goal of trying to get a lower time. This time I knew I could do it; before it was a dream."

The second place and first master was captured by **Patti Shull** of Ashburn, Va., in 2:55:18. Shull states, "I had this image of qualifying for the Olympics Trials. At mile 20 I was in fourth place. I had passed one girl at mile 24 and another, **Kelly Keller**, at the bottom of the hill before going to mile 26. I pushed as hard as I could. I started off really good and the support was great, people were screaming."

She continued, "I'm glad I did this, this is where I live. At mile 14 I thought it was going to get bad, I just hunkered down and tried to finish. It was neat today, people knew who I was and I didn't know them. I felt proud of what I did."

Third place was captured by **Kelly Keller** of Fairfield, Ohio with 2:55:34.

Jason Fowler of Boston, Mass., was the winner of the wheelchair division in 1:58:18. The first female was **Holly Koester** of Cleveland, Ohio, in a time of 3:08:18. She is an elementary school teacher.

The Challenge Cup competition resulted with the final score of 13 wins for the British and eight for the Marines. The Victorian Cup traveled to the British Embassy.

This was the first year for the Challenge Cup for the women and the Marines took the win. The leader was fifth place **Patricia Bouvatte** in 2:59:29, Captain **Bridget Brunnick** in 3:11:44, and Captain **Rhesa Ashbacher** in 3:26:01. A separate Cup was presented to the Marines, which will be on display at Headquarters Marine Corps.

The British team was led by **Lindsay Gannon** in 3:08:42, **Aji Buchanan** in 3:18:21 and **Sally Donnelly** in 3:42:13.

The Air Force collected the Armed Forces Team Award with a total time of 10:51:29, the Marines were second in 11:18:42, the Army third in 11:22:01, and the Navy fourth in 11:22:37. The teams were composed of five men and three women. It was designed to foster competition among the U.S. military teams.

"We place 18,500 chips in envelopes with bib numbers. Once the event ends, we place 200 chips to a string and by Wednesday 10,000 will be in Japan and another 5,000 will be in the Netherlands for other races. I like the people, the staff and all of the Marines are courteous. I have not met anybody who was not willing to help to the fullest extent. The Marines get into it, the start was exhilarating," said **Mike Burns** of Burns Computer, supplier of the ChampionChip.

Thomas Bernard of New London, Conn., ran 3:13:41. He was the 1985 winner with a time of 2:19:16, the 10th fastest winning time to date.

"Listen—I know it was bad (speaking about her time 4:47:39), but it's all good to me. First of all, that was the most fun I have had ever at a marathon (although

Photo: Courtesy of George Banker

L - Col. Jim Fowler - Marathon Founder
Hall of Fame Inductee 2000
R - George Banker, Ad Hoc Publicity
Committee

Maj. Kimberly Markland, U.S. Air Force
Eventual Winner 2:49:07
Victor Cuevas 2:51:27

I've only done three). I talked the whole way, I saw all of my friends, and I ran with most of my group. I knew some of our group members were going to go down in flames, but what fun is it to run alone? So I ran easy and enjoyed it," said **Emily Reichman** of Atlanta, Ga. Her group consisted of husband, David in 4:47:39, **Michelle Fried** in 4:12:20 and **Adam Elrod** in 4:15:06.

"I had to lose 15 pounds and I think I did. At mile 23 it was rough, I think I hit the wall, others were walking and it was hard to run through that," said **Dan Morrison** of New York, with a time of 4:58:14, a speech writer for the Chairman of IBM, Lou Gerstner.

Courtesy Marine Corps Marathon

1998

Maj. Kimberly Markland,
U.S. Air Force Winner

Courtesy Marine Corps Marathon

1998

MCM 1998 HOV Lanes
Marine With Flag

The 24th Marine Corps Marathon was held **October 24, 1999**. The temperature was in the high 50s to low 60s, but the winds were gusting throughout the morning. It was another record number of registered runners, 21,899, 14,500 made it to the start line and there were 14,368 finishers (8,712 males and 5,656 females).

"How dreams come true: find your desire, know yourself and then comes success. The pursuit of excellence takes you to success. That's what took me to the Olympics. What I took away from the sport is displayed in the U.S. Marine Corps, unity through diversity," said **Billy Mills**, the race starter.

Mills, an Oglala Sioux and former Marine Lieutenant and is the only American to win an Olympic gold medal in the 10,000 meter run, Tokyo, 1964 in 28:24.4. He was a long distance runner at the University of Kansas and he joined the Marines in 1962.

The contenders were **Mark Croasdale**, a corporal in the Royal Navy; he works logistic supply for commando units. He was out to win and a member of the Royal Navy / Royal Marines competing for the Challenge Cup. He was third in 1996 (2:25:24) and runner up last year (2:31:33). **Mark Coogan**, a 1996 Olympian, was a University of Maryland graduate and professional runner.

A pack of five runners led the charge from the Iwo Jima towards Pentagon City. The group maintained pace while working off each other. They made their way back across the start line. The cheering crowds were lined along both sides of the road.

"Winning was my thought. I was willing to go 2:17 – 2:18. I wasn't going to make a move until after Hains Point. You need consistency and not have ups and downs. Then you look for the extra edge to improve," stated Croasdale.

"By mile 10 the pack was down to three including Jeb Meyers of Camden, N.J., who was up front. At mile 11, Coogan came up from behind and at mile five he was way back," stated Croasdale.

"I started to pick up the pace when we hit Hains Point. I had to go on my own because the others were closing down on me. I could look across and see others. I was surprised that Mark was able to close down on me each time. I wasn't slow, I was maintaining. I knew in order to win it I would have to put in a good stead. At mile 25, I knew he could not catch me," added Croasdale as he took first in 2:23:27.

Coogan was second in 2:24:18. The Mexicans picked up the next two places with **Maximino Ayala** in 2:24:38 and Juan Lopez in 2:26:47.

Bea Marie Altieri, of Columbia, Md., established an early lead over the 1997 winner (2:53:42). **Donna Moore** of Silver Spring, Md., was running her fifth Marine Corps.

"At the halfway point, I was 1:21:21 and I was visually seeing the finish line. I don't know what went wrong. I felt great until mile 20 (2 hours 6 minutes). I've never fallen apart like that before; my legs buckled going up the ramp after mile 22. I stopped and stretched. I almost thought about dropping out. I'm happy that I did well, but I'm frustrated. I know I can run under 2:50. There is no way that my body finished that race, it was my mind," said Altieri.

"I knew that Bea Marie was running and I was expecting her to qualify. On Capitol Hill, I felt that it was getting hard. I was wearing new racing flats and you don't do that, and I was getting a blister," said Moore.

She added, "A guy said I was 60 seconds behind. It woke me up and I was happy to be second, that changed my whole attitude. I wasn't going to drop out. It was great and I kept saying that I had to keep running."

Moore took the lead just before mile 23 on the 14th Street Bridge. She continued a steady pace and collected her second win in 2:51:53. Moore, age 39, became the oldest female to win the race. Altieri was second in 2:56:48.

"The weather was a perfectly sunny 50 degrees with slight winds. I was hoping that running an even pace would be less painful and maybe I would pass others later in the race who went out too fast. I ran a consistent 6:30 pace and ended up effortlessly passing the lead woman runner on the 14th St. Bridge. She looked how I felt back in 1997, and I felt really bad for her. Hitting the wall is a horrific experience. I finished the race strong. However, it was an Olympic qualifying year, and I missed the qualifying time by less than 2 minutes. But winning MCM

1999

Courtesy Marine Corps Marathon

C - Mark Croasdale #21
Royal Navy/Royal Marines (Challenge Cup)
Eventual Winner 2:23:27
R - Mark Coogan #102

1999

Courtesy Marine Corps Marathon

Key Bridge from Rosslyn into Georgetown, DC

for the second time nixed any disappointments and needless to say, I was a happy and again a lucky winner of the MCM," Moore said.

The third place went to **Christi (Constantini) Ireland** of Burke, Va., running in her first marathon finished in 2:57:58.

"Last year I came out to watch so I said that I would run it this year. My goal was to break three hours and to be in the top five. I tried not to get caught up in people or places. I was concentrating on my pace. The wind on Hains Point was tough, but it wasn't as bad as I expected. I think the last push uphill at the finish was worst than Hains Point," stated Ireland.

Kenneth Carnes of Snelville, Ga., collected his fifth win in 1:59:57. He set the record in 1990 (1:40:22). The female winner was **Holly Koester** of Walton Hills, Ohio, in 3:21:52. She made a defense of her 1998 win (3:08:16).

The defending master's champion (1998-2:35:33), **Francisco Lugo** of Mexico, made a defense of his title with a 2:31:10 (8th place). In second place was **Steve Payne** of the team Royal Navy/Royal Marines in 2:33:53 (9th pace), and teammate **Ginge Gough** was third in 2:34:18 (10th place).

Deborah Barnett of Columbia, Md., was the winning female in 3:11:25 (19th place). **Mary Catherine Malin** of Arlington, Va., was second in 3:15:50 (29th).

Colonel **Paul Puckett**, USMC, Director, Operations Division, Marine Corps Base, Quantico, Va., was second in charge at the marathon, and visiting from Japan. He ran his first Marine Corps Marathon in 5:06:45.

"One thing I wanted to do was ride the Metro and run the race to experience what the runners do. It worked out well today. It was motivating, and I was running with some Marine Vietnam veterans. It was a tremendous experience. The crowds were yelling and screaming," said Col. Puckett.

In 1999, **Jenny Bradshaw** and **Bryan Drummond**, who were dating at the time, ran the 24th Marine Corps Marathon. They did so at the suggestion of her father (Charles Bradshaw) who had a friend living near Washington. They decided to go for it. Their time was 5:28:12.

When you accomplish something for the first time, you either want to repeat or forget the experience. Drummond recounts, "It was incredible crossing the finish line and we knew that we had to come back. You don't know what to expect. We crossed with jubilation and the goal to train hard and to finish."

He continues, "You find out that you are a lot tougher than what you think you are and you find out that you may be weaker. You hold onto what you learn."

In the fall of 2001, a tragedy entered into their life that would alter their lives and test their faith. The newlyweds would have to delay the plans for the marathon. Jenny was diagnosed with Wilson's disease, which causes the body to retain copper. The liver does not release the copper into the bile, which helps with digestion. The intestines absorb copper from food; the copper builds up in the liver and injures liver tissue. Eventually, the damage will cause the liver to release the copper directly into the bloodstream, which ultimately can cause death.

They were informed by Dr. Robert Sawyer that the only way to save her life was through a liver transplant, which was performed in November 2001. It was a five-hour operation and within two weeks she was home. Their faith, prayer and belief in God helped to pull her through.

The marathon was not out of the picture throughout all of this as Drummond states, "Jenny still wanted to do it and it was one of the first things she wanted to do. We knew what it was going to take. She has never used the transplant as an excuse to quit anything, she's a fighter. We received a miracle from the Lord that she lived."

The road to recovery was short-lived and within two weeks of being home an infection set in that was life threatening. Once again, they called upon their faith, a test of what God can do by having faith. She never lost sight of her desire to run the Marine Corps Marathon, even her weight after the infection dropped to 80 pounds. She explains, "My dad is a runner and I was encouraged by him and I was his little girl. My friends thought I could do it. I knew that I was not a quitter. When I was in the hospital, Bryan had my running shoes hanging up in my room."

"She is no quitter and training for the marathon is incredibly demanding and few people can understand that. The first couple of long runs were the gut check. The running in the dark, rain, cold and hills near Charlottesville, those were tough runs. After the third long run, she came in to rest about an hour and then she was up moving around. This was the turning point, and I wanted to see her through the training," he said.

Jenny Drummond has faith but it is stronger and the race in 2003 was a test and part of her healing process. She comments: "The last race was very tough. Going into Hains Point was the hardest part and I did think about getting on the bus a few times. The marathon has changed my life and taking on that feat I know that I can do anything I set my mind to."

Bryan recounts 2003 coming around the Iwo Jima Memorial. "Up the last hill, I was in awe and running beside Jenny and I could not help but think back to when she was lying in the hospital bed with the doctor telling me that she was not going to live without the transplant. All of those images flashed through my mind. All of the emotions came to the forefront, it hit home. I broke down a little. It represents so much of our lives; it is very personal for us." Their finish time was 7:41:39.

The 25th Marine Corps Marathon was held **October 22, 2000**. Registration opened February 15, 2000 and the maximum capacity of 24,588, was reached February 18, 2000 in celebration of the silver anniversary (a record for the race). The weather was ideal for the spectators but warm for the runners. At 8:00 am it was 61 degrees with 73 percent humidity and by 2:00 pm it was up to 68 degrees with 59 percent humidity. There were 17,641 starters and 17,168 finishers (10,376 males and 6,672 females), the highest in the history of the race.

In order to ease the congestion at the start, along the course and at the water points, there was the implement of a wave start. At 8:20 am the wheelchairs started, 8:30 am the top runners in the red wave, the white wave was off at 8:38 am, and the blue wave was off at 8:45 am. The timing of each wave was handled by the ChampionChip.

In a special ceremony held at the Washington Post building, the first inductees entered into the Marine Corps Marathon Hall of Fame. The first year, six were to be inducted for achievement and contributions. Colonel **Jim Fowler**, USMCR (Ret) for the vision of being the founder of the marathon. The former Secretary of Navy and Ambassador **J. William Middendorf II.**, for providing the endorsement for the first Marine Corps Reserve Marathon in 1976 and for the contribution of the top Middendorf Trophy, which is awared to the top winners. **Joanna Martin**, while on active duty as a Lieutenant was the first female Marine winner in 1979 (2:58:14). GySgt **Farley Simon**, was the only male active duty Marine to have won the race overall in 1983 (2:17:46)

Kenny Carnes, a five-time wheelchair winner and the record holder (1990- 1:40:22) was inducted. Finally, **Steve Bozeman**, a former Marine wounded twice and who runs with the American flag every year was the last inducted.

A special acknowledgement was given to five who have run each year; they are called the Ground Pounders (Will Brown, Roger Burkhart, Al Richmond, Charles Stalzer, and Mel Williams). Each was given special t-shirts to wear with the inscription, "Marine Corps Marathon Veteran, 25 years, 1976-2000."

Navy pilot, Lt. **Richard Cochrane** of Harpswell, Maine was the winner with 2:25:50, the slowest winning time in the history of the race. Cochrane had a pack of ten runners going into Crystal City after mile two. The pack included defending champion (2:23:27) **Mark Croasdale** and **Farley Simon**, the 1983 winner (2:17:46) and the only male Marine to have won the race. The pack was averaging a 5:25 pace per mile.

In the pack was Air Force Captain **Mark Cucuzzella**, a 1988 graduate of the University of Virginia (Ellicott City) now stationed in Colorado Springs. Cucuzzella was the Air Force Male Athlete of the Year in 1997 and has run in the Marine Marathon seven times with a best finish time of 2:27:20. He was the winner of the first Air Force Marathon in 1997 in 2:33:05.

Cochrane was out of range, and second place was at stake. Croasdale held a slight lead that had dissipated at the hill going up to the Iwo Jima Memorial where he was passed by **Juan Lopez** of Mexico, second place in 2:28:33, and Cucuzzella, third in 2:28:55. Croasdale was fourth with 2:29:38. Lopez was fourth last year in 2:26:47.

"It's difficult to get a marathon right every time. I had a groin muscle injury which did not affect me but you lose your edge without speed work. I wanted to stay with the group and I found out that if you don't do the work, you don't get the win. The crowd was big going back to mile six, it was deafening," said Croasdale.

"I did walk at mile 23 and 24 and up the last hill were I was passed. I just wanted to finish the race. If it were not for the Challenge Cup competition against the Marines, I would have dropped out," added Croasdale.

Elizabeth Ruel of Laval, Quebec led the race wire to wire without any competition and took first with 2:47:52, the 11th fastest winning time. The record was set in 1990 by Olga Markova of Russia in 2:37:00.

Giving chase for second place, **Liz Speegle** of Woodbridge, Va., who finished with 2:52:04. Last month, Speegle was first in the Quantico Half-Marathon in 1:19:13, in 1999 she was third with 1:25:19. **Connie Davis** of Cronton, NY, was third with 2:58:05.

The wheelchair competition was won by **Kamel Ayari** of Huntington, NY in 1:46:48 and second was five-time winner and record holder (1:40:22- 1990) **Kenny Carnes** of Fayetteville, NC, in 2:13:29.

"The start was good, Kamel made two good attacks at me, one before mile two and the other at the hill going into Crystal City. It was disappointing, being inducted into the Hall of Fame and not winning. My mind and head wanted to win but not my body and I can't take anything away from Kamel," said Carnes.

The female winner was **Holly Koester** of Cleveland, Ohio, in 3:40:04. This was Koester's third consecutive win ('98-3:08:16, '99-3:21:52).

Lt. Richard Cochrane (US Navy) (2:25:50)

The British took the first two master places: **Steve Payne** in 2:31:53 (8th place) and **Ginge Gough** in 2:38:28 (19th place). The two-time defending champion ('98- 2:35:33, '99-2:31;10), **Francisco Lugo** of Los Cipreses, Mexico was third with 2:40:47. **Chuck Moeser** of Sterling was fifth with 2:44:36.

Leslie Rideout of Malden Mass., was first with 3:10:04 (17th) and **Leah Whipple** of Kimberton, Penna., was second with 3:11:15 (18th).

"I served six and half years in the Marine Corps. I felt a little chill when they played the Marine hymn. I always race my events and I keep moving and think about what I am doing. I do about 40 races a year. It was my first time here and I had a chance to see the sights. And I like the course," said **Bob Dolphin** of Renton, Wash., first in the 70-74 age group with 4:05:28.

On a somber note, two miles into the race, 54-year-old **William Edler** of Delmar, Md., collapsed from a heart attack and was pronounced dead upon arrival at Arlington Hospital.

The U.S. Surgeon General, **David Stacher** finished his first marathon in 4:56.

"We have time to be physically active, we have time to eat and sleep. It was not part of my plan to run a marathon. In the last two months, I've traveled 100,000 miles and I've managed to train. I ran along the Great Wall in China and I got lost," said Stacher.

Photo: George Banker

Surgeon General, David Stacher
Marathon Time 4:56:00

"I lost contact with my pace group when I had to stop for a portolet. I started talking with a young woman from Boston who had similar issues…so we talked. She wanted to quit on the bridge, I talked her over it. I wanted to stop behind the Pentagon, she talked me past it. We made it to that turn up the hill – only the Marines would think of a hill like that to finish a marathon. When I finished and one of those Marines put the medal around my neck, shook my hand and said, 'Congratulation, Ma'am, on a job well done,' it was one of the highlights of my life…and I tell everyone that asks that the MCM is one of the best first marathons for that reason," said **Rita Trimarchi** of Sterling, Va. She finished her first MCM in 4:49:43.

Chris Fillio, age 38, of Alexandria, Va., was considered to be an avid runner. He had never raced longer than a 10K. In February 2000, he registered for the Marine Corps Marathon. He realized the challenge and the significant difference between a 10K and a marathon. In May, he started his formal six-month training program.

He recounts an incident. "On June 25th, a day I can't forget – I fractured a bone in my left leg during a men's soccer game. It occurred in a non-contact situation in which I attempted to stop and change direction. The result was a hypertension in which the femur compressed backwards and downwards, crushing the top of the tibia known as the tibial plateau, just behind the knee. My immediate thought as I crumpled to the turf in pain was that my hopes of running in the marathon were over."

The next four weeks were spent on crutches and in late July he was given his "walking orders," and thus began six weeks of physical therapy. "The doctors were doubtful that I would be ready to run the marathon," he said. For the exercises specified by the therapist, he doubled the number of repetitions. He did not drive to work but biked and would walk nine flights of stairs to his office instead of taking the elevator. He focused on a full and expeditious recovery.

His physical therapy session ended in August and the orthopedist cleared him to resume exercising. The primary advice he was given was to use "pain" as his barometer- if the leg started to hurt, don't push it. There were eight weeks before the marathon, but he was still unsure if he could accomplish his goal of completing the race. He gave himself two weeks to train and then make his final "go-or-no-go" decision.

On Sunday, September 10, he gave himself the green light. "I had some major concerns about possible additional injury, fear of embarrassment with my performance and personal questions about whether this whole thing was just a bad idea in general."

The decision was in place. "I had to establish this effort in my own mind as a personal challenge. It was not simply overcoming an injury or running a race. It was something that I decided meant more than that to me; something whose whole was greater than the sum of its parts. It became a challenge about which I was deeply passionate and committed to meeting head on 150%. In short, it became a statement to me about who I am and what I was made of."

Race morning started early for Chris Fillio. "It came extremely early, 4:03 a.m., to be more specific. As one other running colleague predicted, I didn't get much sleep the night before due to the anticipation and excitement. In spite of little sleep and my compressed training schedule, I knew I was ready. Whatever nervousness or trepidation I had that morning disappeared as soon as I took my first step. The race went slowly at first, more difficult at some points, but overall quite well. I finished in a time of 3 hours 38 minutes. Contrary to my public statement that 'breaking 4-hour barrier' was no longer my goal, and rather that my goal was to finish, I blatantly lied. Secretly I'd hoped to finish with a sub-four hour time. In short, I was pleased with the results."

The stress of running a marathon affects each person differently. He met his girlfriend, Val, near the finish where they exchanged a few pleasantries. The exact words escape him as he confesses to perhaps having been somewhat delirious. He recalls, "We were standing in the shadow of the Iwo Jima monument, a testament itself to one of the greatest challenges in modern U.S. history. During the course of the conversation, I casually dropped down on one knee and presented Val with the diamond engagement ring I'd been carrying with me for twenty-six point-two miles, and asked her to spend the rest of her life with me. She said, 'Yes,' and my challenge was complete."

"I ran the 2000 MCM (5:33:55) in memory of my mom's distant cousin, Sergeant Michael Strank, who was one of the six who raised the American flag atop Mount Suribachi. My maternal great grandmother and his paternal grandfather were sister and brother. That side of the family came from what would now be Slovakia and ended up settling around Franklin Township and Connemaugh, Pennsylvania. My own grandmother ("baba") was named Tesse Deitz (nee Kovalcik). Eventually, my grandparents and their children moved from PA to New York City where my mom was born and where my grandfather (who had contracted miner's asthma) died," said **Anne Pastorkovich**, team coordinator for the Washington RunHers Club.

Pastorkovich ran again in 2002 (5:37:17) with her brother and in 2004 (5:32:54) in memory of her cousin on her father's side, Sergeant Michael J. Esposito, Jr., U.S. Army, 2nd Battalion, 22nd Infantry Regiment of the 10th Mountain (Fort Drum, NY), "Climb To Glory," who was killed while clearing a village in Dehrawood, Afghanistan. She ran with the Running in Honor of Fallen Heroes program. The Fallen Heroes Memorial is an on-line memorial for all of the fallen service members of Operation Iraqi and Operation Enduring Freedom. The runners donate their finisher's medal to the serviceman's family. The medal was presented to his parents, Michael Sr. and Dawn.

The 26th Marine Corps Marathon was held **October 28, 2001**. The race was, "Dedicated to the memory of our fellow citizens who lost their lives, the survivors of these tragic events, and the selfless heroes who worked tirelessly to save lives on September 11, 2001," stated Race Director, Rick Nealis.

The race was started by the Mayor of Washington D.C., Anthony Williams. Sunday morning, the temperature was ideal, mid 40s with a high in the low 50s with the winds gusting 10-15 miles per hour. Due to construction, Hains Point was not in the course but instead included a long section of Rock Creek Parkway, up and back. Over a period of miles, the twists and turns along the course were felt in the ankles. The HOV lanes along the 14th Street Bridge had more concrete than asphalt than in previous years; this was a little harder on the legs. There were 20,739 registered runners; 15,011 started and 14,606 finished.

There were hundreds of flags being carried by runners – some had tattoos of the flag on their faces, others had shirts and running shorts. It had to be a record crowd for the flag-waving spectators as they were scattered along the 26.2 mile course cheering for friends and family.

"I'm 46 now. I don't think any of the guys will pay me any mind. I'll not try to go out and hammer those guys. You have new tires and you have retreads and you can't go but so fast on retreads. I'm here to have fun and intermingle with old friends," said retired Gunnery Sergeant **Farley Simon**, U.S. Marine Corps.

Simon returned to run and won in 2:28:28, and was the first master. Simon has been the only active duty Marine to have won the marathon overall (1983-

Photo: Courtesy of George Banker

Start Line

Courtesy Marine Corps Marathon

GySgt Farley Simon, USMC (Ret)
Winner (2:28:28)
Only USMC Male Winner 1983 (2:17:46)
Hall of Fame Inductee 2000

2:17:46, age 28) and now he adds being the first retired Marine. In 1989, Simon was second in 2:22:37. In 1995, Simon was the first master (2:25:250).

"When I run, I don't look at the master's division, I run towards the front. Master running is competitive. Any master who has a chance to steal the show will and they will take a shot. People don't look at master runners as second fiddle," added Simon.

There were about fifteen runners in the lead pack. **Paul Zimmerman** of Cedar Creek, TX was pressing to the front and passed the first mile in 5:26 and mile two in 11:02. Simon was in contact along with two-time runner up (1995-2:23:01, 2000 2:28:33), **Juan Samuel Lopez** of Mexico. The runners raced along Route 110 towards Crystal City and then over to the Pentagon parking lot. A hush came over the runners as all eyes turned to look at the devastation from September 11, 2001; no one was speaking.

It was not until mile five that Simon realized that a lone runner was in control of the race, **Paul Zimmerman**, age 40, of Cedar Creek, Texas. At the Boston Marathon this year, Zimmerman ran 2:23:25. The first mile for Zimmerman was 5:26 and at mile five the elapsed time was 27:10.

"When he went out I felt that he had to settle down. I was counting on him slowing. I didn't think he could hold that tempo by himself," said Simon.

Lori Stitch-Zimmerman was following the example of her husband, Paul. The competition was not closing in as Zimmerman enjoyed a solo lead.

"On the bridge, near mile 23, I could see a lot of flashing lights and then I saw Zimmerman. It was a new ball game. I started to push more and I could see him weaving on the road. My focus turned to the guy behind me (Lopez), I didn't know how strong he was. I wanted to do a mental test to see how strong he was. I pushed by Zimmerman, I had nothing to lose. I take a shot and loose, no big deal," said Simon.

"When I came through the finish lines, the Marines were grabbing me. Coming up the hill was unbelievable, the energy from the crowd," added Simon.

Simon has run the fastest time in the history of the race for the age group 45-49. The old time was 2:31:51 set in 1985 by **Bill Fuller**. Lopez was second for a third time in 2:29:31 followed by **Steve Payne** in 2:31:27 and the second master. Last year, Payne was eighth in 2:31:53. In fourth was **Felipe Cabello** of Chile in 2:32:57, the third master. **David Howe** of Silver Spring was fifth in 2:33:14. Zimmerman had faded to 15th in 2:38:24.

For the women, Zimmerman led wire-to-wire in a time of 2:48:13, the 14th fastest winning time. **Tara Pointin** of Raleigh was second in 2:53:57. **Lindsay Gannon**, a member of Royal Navy/Marine team finish in third in 2:54:46. Last year, Gannon was 10th in 3:05:27.

The first master was **Sherry Thompson** of Harrisburg, NC, in 3:05:57 (9th place), the 16th fastest winning time, and **Kimberley Layman** of Nantucket, Mass., was second in 3:08:00 (10th place). **Beth McCann** of Falls Church was third in 3:10:46 (12th place).

Kamel Ayari of New Rochelle made a successful defense of the wheelchair title in 1:58:17. Last year, his time was 1:46:48. In second was **Patrick Doak** of Alpharetta, Georgia in 2:04:00. Last year, Doak was 2:19:29.

"I was happy to be here and to be an American; it made me feel proud because the flag was flying high as I ran by the Pentagon. It's an honor to run this race and to have the Marines around. There is a saying which anyone in the military understands, 'the pride is inside,' said **Jennifer Whitlow**, finishing in 5:40:35, the winner of the Boot Camp series as seen on Fox television. Whitlow ran the race in utilities.

"I knew that I wasn't going to have a good time but I wanted to feel it. It's important to let yourself feel those feelings. There are times to dig deep and other times you need to step back and reflect," said Whitlow.

Whitlow ran the race with the Texas Stars (Marilyn Bullard, Anne Steinbach, Elena Fress and Ellen Vitro) who were dressed up as Uncle Sam in red, white and blue.

Photo: George Banker

Lft-Rht - Elena Fress (A98),
Ellen Vitro (A97),
Jen Whitlow (B1423)
Winner 2001 Fox Boot Camp show,
Marilyn Bullard (A99),
Anne Steinbach (A96), 5:40:35

Photo: George Banker

2001

Jennifer Whitlow (5:40:35)
2001 Fox TV show Winner Boot Camp

"The biggest thing was crossing the finish line. What one person can do is a lot and what a lot of people can do will be off the chart. Running with the Texas Stars was symbolic. The moment we crossed the line, it was worth it," added Whitlow.

Keeping his streak going, Ground Pounder, and marathon hall of fame inductee, **Mel Williams** of Norfolk, finished in 3:11:18 and first in the age group 60-64. Williams has taken first place in age groups a total of 14 times and included every year in the 1988-1992. Williams finished the Ironman World Championship on October 9th in 14:44:07.

"I was impressed with all of the patriotism shown during the race, not only among the Americans, but the foreign runners as well. My thighs were still fatigued from the bike portion of the race from mile one, but having gone over most of this course 25 times previously they just had a mind of their own and got me through it. Only 24 more to the golden anniversary," stated Williams.

Linda Kennedy of Metro Run & Walk of Falls Church, Va., finished in 4:10:21, "going by the Pentagon was very emotional, I said a prayer to all of the people who were lost. The entire group around me was quiet. This was my 17th marathon and the only race that I didn't lose my focus. I was fired up the whole race."

"You see the pictures on TV and it looks like a movie, but when you see it, it brings it all home and you realize that it really happened. Your mind is the picture of what you see. It was shock and awe at how big the whole was. The feeling was indescribable said **Jason Koczur** of Oakton, Va., finishing his first marathon in 5:04:00.

"I still try different things. I have a PhD in Child Psychology. I was trying to play with things in my mind; it didn't work. I'm still thinking about the entire event of 9/11. I stayed for an hour after I had finished the race. I was happy," said **Sil Tomlin** of Reston, Va., finishing his 18th Marine Marathon in 4:45.

Victoria Vasenden of Annapolis, Md., wanted to make some changes. "October 2001 I ran my very first marathon, the Marine Corps Marathon. I am a mother of three beautiful girls, and at the age of 37 I decided it was time to quit smoking. So I started running. I remember the first outing around the block. I was dying! But I kept on, and before I knew it I was up to 2 miles. I decided to join the local running club just to meet people and get a better edge on this whole new challenge. Well, before I knew it I signed up for my first marathon not remotely knowing what I was in for. It was a lot more than I anticipated, although I didn't know for sure what to anticipate; the challenge far exceeded my expectations."

The weeks began to pass as the conditioning improved and the smoking was a thing of the pass. She recounts, "September 11th came. That morning I was in

2001

Jennifer Whitlow (5:40:35)
Winner Fox TV Boot Camp show 2001
George Banker

Photo: George Banker

2001

Robert Hoey (5:19:34),
Kimberly Austin (5:19:32)

Photo: George Banker

New York City. You see, I'm a flight attendant with a major U.S. airline and we were sitting on the runway at LGA on that fateful morning waiting for our departure clearance. We finally taxied into our spot on the runway and took off at approximately 8:15 a.m. that morning. I was sitting on the back jump seat and right after take-off, I got up and went to the last row of seats, aircraft left, to look out the window at the Manhattan skyline. I remember how magnificent that day was. It was a perfect fall day, sunny, cool, clear and beautiful. As the aircraft banked to the left, I remember the Manhattan skyline coming into view and looked right at the World Trade Towers. All I could think of was wow! How many times had I looked at those Towers and on that particular day, they seemed even more beautiful."

She continues, "By 9:50 we knew that something was horribly wrong and then of course everything that subsequently followed. It was hard on the world, hard on the families, but it seemed especially hard for the 'Airline Families.' The days followed and we didn't know whether they were going to cancel the Marathon. Of course everyone would have understood, so I was elated when I heard the race was on. What I didn't realize was that the course would take us right in front of the Pentagon, right where the airplane had flown in.

I don't think there was a dry eye on anyone of the thousands of runners that day. Seeing so many folks carry the American flag, and hearing the chants 'U.S.A' under every overpass. The helicopters were flying and the servicemen and women standing guard to protect us. I never felt more proud to be an American. It just was so monumental, all of it, and if it was the only marathon I ever ran in my lifetime I am honored that my 1st one was the Marine Corps, 2001." Her finish time was 4:15:16.

The 27th Marine Corps Marathon was held **October 27, 2002**. It was another record year with 20,900 registered runners and 14,621 starters. Last year, the race was ranked as the sixth largest with 14,341 finishers. Over the history of the race, there have been 360,133 registered runners. The morning air was cool and it was promised to be almost ideal but the temperature and the wind was like a yo-yo. There were periods of a cooler wind followed by warmth. It was difficult to gauge the fluid intake. It was a difficult day to know what to wear.

"Well, I was on target for a 3:05 at mile 19.5 when I had a horrible cramp in my left calf... I was running with a limp when I passed one of the aid stations and they pulled me off the course, much to my dismay. They (the Marines) insisted that I go to the tent and get the cramp rubbed out. I was so upset as I counted the minutes this was taking! The Marine told me that he thought I would not be able to finish the race (I was frustrated and upset at this point, although, I know they were doing what they were instructed to do). I told him I would finish even if I had to crawl across the line. I hobbled the next mile but soon after got right back into my groove, trying to make up for lost time. End result ... 3:33:53, not bad but not great," stated **Lisa Rhodes** of Fairfax, Va., the 94th female finisher. There was one prior year winner (1999 – 2:23:27), **Mark Croasdale** of the Royal Navy/Royal Marines team. Croasdale had an impressive list of previous times, 2:29:38 (2000, 4th), 2:31:33 (1998 - 2nd) and 2:25:24 (1996 – 3rd). In each year he was first in his age group.

The other top male contenders were **Retta Feyissa** of Ethiopia, now living in Washington. Feyissa placed second in November 2001 at The Marathons In The Parks (Rockville, Md.) with a 2:29:56 and a second place at the D.C. Marathon

2002

Rick Nealis – Race Director

Photo: George Banker

2002

Farley Simon – Team Manager USMC
Two-time winner 1983, 2001
Hall of Fame Inductee 2000
Only active duty male Marine to win

this year in 2:24:58. **John Sence** of Cincinnati, Ohio was returning after a few years of not-so-good performances. At the California International Marathon, he ran a 2:17:11 (December 1996).

There were no returning female winners. A top contender was **Alisa Harvey** of Manassas, Va. Harvey was a bronze medalist in the 1500 meters at the 1991 Pan American Games. In her debut marathon, in 2000 in Richmond, Va., Harvey was second in 2:49:26. Also, a two-time winner of the Army 10 Miler, Washington, DC (1998-58:56, 1999-57:47). Making a third debut was U.S. Air Force officer, **Christopher Juarez** of Nellis AFB, Nevada. Juarez was 14th in 1999 (2:35:58, 4th 25-29) and 22nd in 1998 (2:42:23, 6th 25-29).

The Howitzer bellowed out smoke, and the front ranks broke free. Immediately a pack of four took control. The first mile was passed in 5:11. The leaders included Juarez, **Mike Farrell** and **John Sence**. The pack moved down Route 110 towards the Crystal City area where they would loop and then circle around the Pentagon. At mile five, the elapsed time was 26:40 a split time of 5:18. The 10K time was 33:15. At mile eight the elapsed time was 42:50 a few meters from the starting line. The crowds lined the roadway as the procession of runners made their way towards the Key Bridge to go into Georgetown. Going into the ninth mile it was Sence and Juarez. The 10th mile elapsed time was 53:38 at the end of M Street before the runners turned to head up along the winding Rock Creek Parkway.

The women's race was under the leadership of **Alisa Harvey** of Manassas, Va., who had given birth to her second child, Kyah, on February 22 of this year. The first mile split was 6:12. At the halfway point, the elapsed time was 1:09:34 on the return along Rock Creek Parkway. Going into mile 14, the leaders were **Terrence Mahon** and Feyissa with the others within striking distance.

Harvey had a halfway split of 1:25 and two minutes back was **Elizabeth Scanlon** of Alexandria, Va. Scanlon was the winner of the Army 10 Miler in 1:00:19, held a week earlier. Scanlon was making her fourth appearance, 1998 (11th-3:05:56), 1999 (13th-3:08:11) and 2000 (7th-3:03:30). At mile 17 near Union Station by the U.S. Capitol, the time was 1:31:07 with Feyissa, Sence and Juarez sharing the lead. At mile 20, near the Tidal Basin, crossing the Kutz Bridge the time was 1:47:34. The pace was being held. Before heading towards the HOV lanes, near mile 22, Feyissa dropped out of the race. The time at mile 22 was 1:58:38 (5:31 split). It was a solo race as Juarez was where he wanted to be, in the lead. The remaining miles began to pass quickly. It was down the home stretch and around the Marine Corps War Memorial to the finish with a time of 2:25:01.

John Sence came in second with 2:26:31 followed by **Benjamin Sandy** of the U.S. Army from Fort Riley, Kansas in 2:29:20. **Mark Coasdale** was fourth in 2:30:46. **Steve Payne** of the Royal Navy/Royal Marines was the first master in 2:33:35, the 19th fastest master's winning time. **Bryan Smith** of New Orleans, La., was second in 2:35:54 (14th place).

The women's race took a turn near mile 18 where Harvey began to have muscle cramps and eventually dropped out. The reins were picked up by Scanlon; at mile 18 her time was 1:59:51. Scanlon went on to win with a 2:57:27, the 25th fastest winning time.

"I was impressed at how I was able to stay where I wanted. The first mile was 6:20 and the second mile was 6:35. At mile 15 something didn't feel right. At mile 18, I stopped and I cramped up," said Alisa Harvey.

"I was averaging 6:30. I was not pushed and I felt smooth. At the half I was 1:25. Hydration may have been the problem. At mile four I missed the water and did not get any more until mile seven. It was a major disappointment, the weather didn't cooperate. The times showed it was a tough run," Harvey said.

"My main goal was to break three hours. I didn't think I was going to finish. I was third for the first 10 miles. I was second until mile 18 when I saw Alisa walking. I got my second wind for a couple of miles," said Scanlon.

"Up to mile 18 I was going back and forth. At mile 15 I thought I wasn't going to make it. The temperature seemed okay, it was windy. The Army 10 Miler gave me confidence going into the marathon, and I felt comfortable the whole way," added Scanlon.

Second place was taken by **Jacquline Chen** of the U.S. Army in 3:00:53. In addition, Chen was the first master with the ninth fastest winning time in the history of the race. The week prior, Chen placed sixth at the Army 10 Miler in 1:01:55. Third place was taken by Marine **Mary Kate Sullivan-Bailey** of Stafford, Va., in 3:02:24. Sullivan-Bailey was 20th in 2000 (3:11:21) and 8th in 2001 (3:04:34). Chen was 8th in 2000 (3:04:30) and 7th in 2001 (3:04:09).

Holly Koester of Cleveland, Ohio, captured her fourth win in the wheelchair division with a 3:06:32, her best finish time. **Vincent Orlando** of Debary, Fla., was the first male in 3:17:10.

"I think it's rewarding that we were able to move forward especially since two years in a row we have been involved with terrorists and a sniper and dealing with runner safety and risk management. We get complacement and we never know what is going to come next. You have to think it through and you need volunteers who can think on their feet. When you want the best, you get the Marines," said Race Director Rick Nealis.

"I think my confidence level for all the organizations was lifted after the news on Thursday, the capture of the sniper. The plans started to come together. The group of runners who were crossing after 5 hours showed no signs of tiring with the smiles on their faces and hands in the air," added Nealis.

The 28th Marine Corps Marathon was held **October 26, 2003**. This year, 16,456 started the race and 15,965 finished (9,754 males, 6,211 females). The weather was ideal for the speculators. Each year, hundreds of well-wishers line up along the course.

In the 28-year history of the race, seven local men and three women have won this event. This year, the tide turned. Two Olympic trial qualifiers were leading the pack, **Aaron Church** of South Riding, Va. (qualified time 2:21:47), and **Peter Sherry** of Great Falls, Va. (qualified time 2:20:38). Sherry is a 1991 graduate of Georgetown University, former member of the Reebok Enclave and co-owner of the Gotta Run Shop in Pentagon City, which is located along the marathon course.

Church was enjoying an early lead for 14 miles until blisters forced him off course to an aid station. An opportunity was presented to **Eric Post** of Fairfax, Va., and he took the lead. Sherry was holding back in the wings. Into the 24th mile, Sherry began to reel Post in and took the lead. Sherry made his way around the Marine War Memorial to capture the 28th crown in a time of 2:25:07 (ranked 25th). Post came in second 2:27:49 followed by Church in 2:28:24. **Benjamin Lopez** of Mexico was fourth in 2:29:58 and **Mark Croasdale** was fifth in 2:30:20.

"A pack of females went out from the start and I took the lead at half a mile. Once I had the lead that was all I had to focus on. If I had run a 2:50 I would have been upset. Hitting the time was more important than winning," said **Heather Hanscom** of Team Pacers/New Balance, making her debut marathon. Hanscom does bio-medical research (working with cells) for the American Red Cross in Rockville, Md. When Hanscom takes to the races she has that mental concentration needed to reach her goal. The competition served as a catalyst and once the females were passed she started to work on passing the males.

The female record was set in 1990 (2:37:00) by Russian Sergeant Olga Markova. The temperature on race day was 75 degrees. Markova had a PR going into race of 2:38 (Hamburg International Marathon). Hanscom was on a record setting pace with a first mile in 5:54 and by mile five her time was 29:11. Going into mile 10 the time was 59:15 and 1:17:17 by mile 13.

"I just wanted to run relaxed and hammer the last few miles. I was focused every step of the way and I have never been that focused. I didn't want the wheels to fall off," said Hanscom.

Hanscom is a 2001 graduate of James Madison University where she majored in health sciences with majors in pre-medicine and health communications. In high school, she was All-Cardinal District and All-Northeast Region for three years. During her senior season at James Madison she was All-East (ECAC), indoor 5000m, a NCAA provisional qualifier, outdoors 10000m (34:48.64). The move up to the marathon was well thought out. At the Philadelphia Distance Run Half Marathon, she was the second American and seventh place in 1:14:11.

"My heart is competitive and I'll race anything. I do have some unfinished business with 10,000 meters. I want to be as competitive as possible. I've never really run a good 10K. I want to see what I can do this spring," added Hanscom.

Going into mile 20 (1:59:19) there were 10 splits under six minutes per mile. The last 10K was covered in 38:40. Hanscom won in 2:37:59 and missed the record by one minute. The winning margin over second place, **Lindsey Gannon** of the United Kingdom, was 20 minutes 47 seconds; her time was 2:58:46. This was the largest winning margin in the history of the race among the men and the women.

"Going into and coming out of the race, I was just me. I was able to run my race and my sister, Marie, also ran her first marathon that day (5:37:37). It meant so much to me to be able to run hard and then to watch her finish. She has always supported my crazy love for running and competing," she said.

"It does not matter to me that people know who I am, but maybe that they remember my story (recovered from a brain tumor). That someone struggling with cancer, a cancer survivor or some young girl who's maybe not so fast yet will think 'if she can do it so can I!' That maybe I can inspire someone else to follow their dreams also," she closes.

Kristin Van Eron of Timonium, Md., was third in 3:00:14. The fourth place went to **Victoria McFarland** of Washington in 3:02:26 and **Sage Stefiuk** of Highlands, NJ was fifth in 3:03:34. The Royal Navy landed the first two master places, **Dai Roberts** in 2:34:21 (12th place) and **Steve Payne** in 2:35:39 (14th place). **Francisco Medrano** of Mexico was third in 2:45:19 (27th place).

Joseph Wilbert (2396),
Jeffrey Wilbert (2395) (5:25:52)

Photo: George Banker

Michael Benbow (#10407) (5:16:20),
Thomas Simonetti (#1198) (5:16:19),
Matthew Ruane (#13893) (5:16:34)

In the sea of runners were 24 runners clad in bright orange shirts, "Team Connal," along with countless cheerleaders spread along the course. In every race you always find numerous touching stories, which can cause you to pause. The nucleus of Team Connal **Jon Andrew Connal**, was carried in the hearts of his supporters. Jon loved the sport and completed four marathons; Marine Corps Marathon 1999 (4:35:16) and 2000 (4:54:13), Vancouver Marathon 2002 (4:15:13) and the New York City Marathon 2002 (4:47:35). On February 18, 2003, Jon crossed his final finish line.

The day was about friends and family gathering for a journey for Jon and each person knew why he was running. Heidi, Jon's wife, was not enthusiastic about running at first and would just watch Jon. "He loved to run, and I didn't. Now I get it," said Heidi.

"We wanted to run for him. It started to feel good. We had 24 signed up and for 13 was their first time. We had a good success rate, 23 finished. It was a way to pay tribute to Jon. I didn't expect to get that much enthusiasm. All had a part in it. It was such a touching experience. When I ran with Jon, I didn't feel good and Jon said it was 10% physical and 90% mental," said Heidi (finished in 5:16).

Mentally, Jon crossed the line 23 times and his memory lives. The thoughts from his friends can be viewed at http://www.connal.com. "Running the Marine Corps Marathon was my worst marathon time wise, but my best experience! For some reason I hit a wall in Georgetown, only mile ten. Going up a hill before the turn into Rock Creek Parkway Jon's spirit kept me moving ... throughout the race I felt like giving up repeatedly, but the amount of support from all those that

Robert Rosenthal (#3064) (5:26:14),
Dylan Sharrock (#16117),
Angela Clarke (#1261),
Paul Woods (#24161)

Rupert Finke (#11783) (5:23:57),
Landon Leming (#7981) (5:23:55)

Photo: George Banker

Photo: George Banker

came to support Team Connal, in our orange shirts, and all those that learned of Team Connal, kept me moving through pain that would have knocked me out of another marathon. Every time I would feel defeated, there would be more triangular orange 'Go Team Connal' signs bouncing over the crowd," said **Gabe Crerie** an alumni of James Madison University (1994), and Assistant Principal at Union Grove High School, in McDonough, Ga.

"Heidi and a friend caught up to me walking at mile 24, and seeing Heidi running through a loss I could never dream of experiencing got me through that 14 mile wall ... there was still pain, but I feel like I coasted through the cheers for the last two miles ... even up that cruel hill that precedes the Iwo Jima Memorial. I don't even remember what my time was (5:13:32), but I finished feeling more of a thrill of accomplishment as part of a group than if I had finished in under 4 hours without the team," he added.

"In 2002 I ended up with the pregnancy from hell with my second child. Basically I ended up enduring many long hospital stays and was put on complete bed rest for months. For a high-energy person, this experience was somewhat akin to being in prison. Fortunately my daughter is now doing well. I made a decision during one of my hospital stays that once I could run again I was going to run my first marathon)," said **Andrea Keane-Myers** of Bethesda, Md.

In the summer of 2003 she joined the first-time marathon training program with the Montgomery County Road Runners Club (Maryland). It is a strong and supportive club. She learned the proper way to train and made a number of long-lasting friendships. She wanted not only to finish but to qualify for Boston.

She looks at MCM, "When I started the Marine Corps Marathon, I felt great and did the first half in 1:48 and was on my Boston target pace. Unfortunately, I tore my hip flexor during mile 15 and could no longer lift my leg without excruciating pain. My husband Trevor (who was also running his first marathon) came back to get me and walked me in the last 11 miles as I was determined to finish the marathon. He gave up his chance to run a great marathon in order to hold my hand and encourage me to the finish line. I finished in 4:42 and didn't qualify for Boston, but did earn my medal. I couldn't have done it without the support of my husband and the fantastic volunteers and spectators."

She closes, "While I hope that I never have to reenact the last 11 miles of the first MCM, I now know that I can accomplish my dreams."

The 29th Marine Corps Marathon was held **October 31, 2004**. A major change was made to the marathon course, as the runners did not go towards Crystal City as in the past 28 years. The direction was towards Rosslyn with a couple of slight rolling hills where the course merged back to the Key Bridge at the four-mile mark instead of the seven-mile mark. The other change was the return of Hains Point and the addition of running along Crystal Drive.

According to a study completed by the George Washington University International Institute of Tourism Studies, the Washington, D.C. metro area received $19.6 million in spending over the race weekend. There were more than 76,000 people who came into the area as part of the MCM.

"I knew I was going to win after I passed the two women at mile 14. I felt strong and knew that I could keep on pace. It started to feel hot around mile 23 but it wasn't bad. I felt the course was more challenging this year and Hains Point was pretty windy. I think being a Marine has made me mentally tough and I did not doubt myself. I was really proud to be able to run for the USMC," said winner Captain **Mary Kate Bailey**.

Captain Bailey became the second active duty Marine to win the prestigious Marine Corps Marathon in its 29-year history with a 2:48:31 (16th fastest winning time). She is a 1998 graduate of the U.S. Naval Academy where she played soccer and started racing six years ago. The conditions were ideal for the spectators with the temperature reaching towards 70 degrees under a sunny sky. There were 16,987 starters and 16,400 finishers.

At the 29th Annapolis 10 Mile Run last August, she was awarded the Commander Willie McCool Award for being the first Naval Academy Alumni finisher. Commander McCool was the pilot of the space shuttle Columbia. Capt. Bailey was the first female finisher in 1:00:42. Her previous performances include a 20th place finish in 2000 (3:11:21), 8th place in 2001 (3:04:34), 3rd in 2002 (3:02:24) and last year 3:26:17, six weeks after giving birth to her daughter.

The military presence was among the top leading women going through the 10K mark, with 1stLt. **Jennifer Ledford** (US Marine Corps) passing in 39:35. Lt. Ledford is a student aviator in Pensacola, Fla., and making her marathon debut. At Oklahoma State University, she ran cross-country and track with a best at 1,500 meters in 4:58.

Navy Lt. Cmdr. **Kimberly Fagan**, a Navy flight surgeon in San Diego, passed the 10K mark in 39:38. She was the winner at the Big Sur Trail Half-Marathon (October 2nd, 1:37:21) in California.

Army 1st Lt **Sage Stefiuk**, stationed at Fort Bragg, NC, was fourth through the 10K mark in 41:50. The week prior, she led the Fort Bragg women's team to capture the Commander's Cup at the 20th Army 10-Miler at the Pentagon with a time of 1:04:52. She was the first servicewoman at the Marine Corps Marathon last year in a time of 3:03:34 (PR) and was in fifth place. Stefiuk is from Westfield, NJ and graduated from Dickinson College (2002), Lady Red Devil, where she ran cross-country and track.

At the halfway mark on Capitol Hill, Fagan moved up into the lead and crossed with 1:22:39 followed by Ledford in 1:22:48. Bailey was holding in third with 1:23:33. A gap separated the trailing runners with **Suzanne Clemmer** crossing at 1:26:42 followed by Stefiuk in 1:27:52 and **Eleanor Stewart-Garbrecht** at 1:27:57. Coming off Hains Point at mile 20, Bailey finished in 2:07:25 with Fagan trailing in second with 2:08:08. Ledford who once had the lead had drifted back to a 2:12:47 with Clemmer at 2:13:37. Garbrecht was in sixth place but moved up to fifth and finished in 2:14:57. Stefiuk dropped from fifth to sixth and finished in 2:17:07.

The closing miles for the ladies brought the experience to the surface. Bailey held fast to the conservative game plan to be the victor in the showdown by capturing first place in 2:48:31. Fagan for the most part stayed in second place except for a brief moment when she had the lead between the 10K and the half. Fagan finished with 2:51:17. Clemmer had moved from an earlier fifth place start to finish in third with 2:59:11. The first master and in fourth was Garbrecht in 3:05:47. **Laurie Hanscom** of Eden Prairie, Minn., was the second master in 3:11:24 followed by **Leisa Ensle** of Virginia Beach, Va., in 3:11:35.

There were three returning champions seeking top honors, including British **Mark Croasdale**, 1999 winner (2:23:27). He commented in 1999, "Winning was my thought. I was willing to go 2:17-2:18 pace. I wasn't going to make a move until after Hains Point. You need consistency and not have ups and downs. Then you look for the extra edge to improve."

Major **Christopher Juarez** was the winner in 2002 (2:25:01) after making two prior attempts, 1998 (22nd place 2:42:23) and 1999 (14th 2:35:58).

Peter Sherry, co-owner of Gotta Run Shop at Pentagon row in Crystal City, was the 2003 winner (2:25:07). Sherry was seeking an opportunity to join the select club of consecutive-year winners.

Making a second appearance was Ethiopian **Retta Feyissa**, now living in Bronx, NY. In 2002, he was on contention but did not finish due to an injury. At mile 20 (1:47:34) near the Tidal Basin crossing the Kutz Bridge, it was Feyissa, **John Sence** and Christopher Juarez.

They were two members of the Hanson-Brooks Project, **Carl Rundell**, a graduate from Vanderbuilt University with a personal best of 2:19:58 (February 2003), and **Terrance Shea**, a graduate from Bucknell University, a 1995 Patriot League Scholar Athlete, with a personal best of 2:21:51 at the 2003 LaSalle Bank Chicago Marathon.

Chase Baker (#6995) *Carlos Coffman (6:06:55)* *Kermit the Frog (5:06:23)*
(6:35:37) *Jumps Rope Entire Marathon*

At the halfway point on Capitol Hill, Rundell remained in control with 1:10:01 followed by Miranda in 1:11:26. Shea moved into third place up from sixth in 1:11:39. Rounding out the top seven, Feyissa (1:11:46), Sherry (1:11:52), Juarez (1:11:58), and Croasdale (1:11:59).

Rundell was keeping a hard and fast pace as the temperature began to rise. Going through mile 20 after Hains Point, Rundell had 1:48:31 and Miranda was 1:48:37. Juarez had closed the gap and moved up into third place (1:49:58), and Shea and Feyissa were in fourth (1:49:59). Rounding the top was Croasdale (1:51:42), sixth, and Sherry (1:53:19).

The race took a different shape after the 20th mile. The pace Rundell started out with was beginning to fade as the others began to reel him in. Feyissa staged the significant move from fifth to take the lead along with Shea who moved from fourth to second place. Feyissa had more at stake. Miranda faded from second to fourth. Rundell started to fade back to fifth place and Croasdale and Sherry both had dropped back out of contention.

Feyssia became the 29th winner in 2:25:35 with Shea taking second in 2:25:57. Juarez was holding in third from mile 20 and finished in 2:26:03 and Miranda was fourth in 2:26:26. Rundell was fifth in 2:26:48. Croasdale finished in eighth (2:32:54) and Sherry was 15th (2:36:23).

The leading master through 10K was **James Bresette** of Clinton, Arkansas in 37:26. **Steve Payne** of the Royal Navy / Royal Marines was in second in 37:29 and two-time master winner (1998-2:35:33, 1999-2:31:10) **Francisco Lugo** of Mexico was in third with 37:30.

At the halfway point, Bresette had dropped to third (1:17:22) and Payne moved into the lead (1:17:02) followed closely by Lugo (37:03). The gap started to close by mile 20 with Payne still leading (1:57:34), Lugo in second (1:58:00) and Bresette in third (2:01:43).

Lugo was the fourth master in 2001 (2:37:42) and third master in 2002 (2:41:58). In the closing miles, Lugo started to make a move to take the lead and was successful in collecting his third title in 2:38:56. Payne was second in 2:39:31.

Paul Okerberg of Leesburg, Va., was 38:32 through the 10K mark, remained in fourth through mile 20 and closed the gap to take third in 2:48:27.

"I chose the MCM to be my first marathon partly because I am a retired Marine. I plan to run the MCM every year as long as I'm able to do so. I treated myself to a personalized license plate to shamelessly plug the race. My motivation was two-fold to run a marathon late in life. I retired at 38 after 20 years. I had always entertained the idea of running the MCM. I was diagnosed with high blood pressure at age 40. That made up my mind to run it for myself and to prove to others that my diagnosis was not a death sentence," said **David Strong** of Woodstock, Va., who finished the race in 3:43:59.

"I chose the MCM to honor my father's service in the Corps when he enlisted from 1966 to 1968 and was stationed at Camp Pendleton, Calif. I read a story about the active duty service personnel from Quantico putting the medals around the necks of the finishers. That conjured up the image of having my Dad to be that 'Marine,'" said **Jon Walk** of Spring, Texas.

Walk had brought his father and daughter, Waverly, to the MCM. His father was in his element as he was taking pictures. Once he passed mile 20, his quads started to lock up. He adds, "I had to walk the next three miles 70% of the time and almost 100% the rest of the way there because I went there to 'finish' – and not upset the plan – and not end up in the medical tent or with a DNF.

"I was able to gut it up the hill, make a right turn and run it on in, in front of my daughter and Dad who were waiting in the stands. Then he surprised me by giving me his dog tags that he wore everyday while in the Corps. This was a moment in my life that still brings tears to my eyes every time I think about it." Walk finished the race in 5:39:06.

The 30th Marine Corps Marathon was held **October 30, 2005**. The race accepted a record number of entries, 30,000. On-line registration filled up in a record time, 25,200 entries in 62 hours, 19 minutes on April 8, 2005. During the first hour, 3,220 runners registered. The weather for race day was sunny and the temperature was in the mid 50s with a light wind. There were 20,072 starters with 19,211 finishers. A two-wave start was utilized with the wheelchairs going out after the first wave. This was the second year for the modified course where the runners went through Rosslyn and not Crystal City in the opening miles of the race.

On the start line, **Carl Rundell** from Birmingham, Mich., led for 23 miles last year but he started to fade and finished in fifth place in 2:26:48. **Eric Post** of Centreville, Va., was the runner up in 2003 with 2:27:49.

Going into the 10K mark (along the Rock Creek and Potomac Parkway towards Connecticut Avenue) a pack of three clocked 34:34 (5:33 pace) – Rundell, **Ruben Garcia** a corporal in the Mexican Navy, **Sergio Perez** of Mexico. A couple of seconds back were **Andreas Carlborg** (34:35) and **Benjamin Palafox** of Mexico (34:36). The women's race started off with a dominant runner, **Susannah Kvasnicka** and she passed the 10K mark in 38:26 (6:11 pace) and the closest runner was **Kaitlin Nelson** of Ithaca, NY in 39:11 followed by **Marlene Farrell** of Leavenworth, Washington in 39:41. Rounding the top five were **Tara Smith** in 39:52 and Amanda Tate in 40:40.

Kvasnicka is a 1994 graduate of George Mason University and a mother of two. "Each season I find out something new about myself that I didn't know before and each season I see a new potential. I am not sure at this point what I am capable of. I ultimately see myself as a marathoner and I hope that will eventually hit the Olympic qualifying standard. But, as I try new things I make new goals." At the 2005 Twin Cities Marathon, she ran 2:47:57 (17th place).

Trailing in the top, **Liz Wilson**, was born in Taiwan and a graduate from University of Oregon, a two-time Pac-10 cross country champion, and a seven-time NCAA All-American. She was a member of four U.S. World Cross County teams. She placed in the top 15 in both 2000 (5th-2:37:27) and 2004 (14th-2:38:18) U.S. Olympic Marathon Trials. At the 2004 Twin Cities Marathon, she placed 5th in 2:38:15

Kvasnicka was not slowing and had steady pacing going through the halfway point with a time of 1:21:20 (6:12 pace). Nelson was holding in second place with 1:24:00 and Farrell in third with 1:24:34.

Going into mile 23 (Along Crystal Drive and 18th Street, South), the front runner was Garcia (2:04:25, pace 5:24) followed closely by Rundell in 2:04:34. Eric Post of Centreville, Va., had been steadily moving up in the ranks and was in third position (2:05:36). **John Mentzer** of Monterey, Calif., was in fourth place (2:06:16), and Palafox was holding his fifth place (2:07:19).

Kvasnicka maintained the hold on the lead going through mile 23 in 2:24:37 (6:17 pace). With three miles to go, she was in an excellent position. Nelson was not closing down the gap and finished in 2:31:25, followed by Farrell in 2:31:55.

Garcia was trying hard to drop Rundell as hard as he was trying to close down the gap. It was two-man race to the finish along Route 110 from the Pentagon to the Iwo Jima Memorial and screaming crowds. Garcia proved to be the stronger runner and Rundell was denied twice. Garcia finished in 2:22:18 to Rundell's 2:22:26. Eric Post captured third in 2:23:54 followed by Mentzer in 2:24:26. Kvasnicka's heart led her to a victory and a personal record in 2:47:10 with the 13th fastest winning time. Liz Wilson held in for second place in 2:50:03 followed by **Emily Brozozowski** with 2:54:58.

"I knew early on that I had a substantial lead. I knew if I could hold on that I would win, I was pretty sure of it at 15 miles. Because I hadn't put a lot of thought into a particular marathon, I really didn't have a game plan. I really just went out and ran how I was feeling," said Kvasnicka.

"Looking back, I am pleased with my decision to run. One of the only people who encouraged me to run was Jim Hage. He told me that I could probably win and that people would remember it forever. So far, I have been amazed at the response that I have gotten to winning the MCM. People have been so excited and interested in the story," she added.

The top two male masters were dominated by members of the Royal Navy/Royal Marine Challenge Cup team, **Dai Roberts** in first with 2:30:39 followed by Steve Payne in 2:35:55. **Jon Schoenberg** of Harvard, Mass., was third in 2:40:59

Winner Ruben Garcia (2:22:18)

Winner Susannah Kvasnicka (2:47:10)

Alisa Harvey of Manassas, Va., was the first female master in 3:10:11 followed by **Brenda Wilson** of Stuart, Fla., in 3:10:49. **Nancy Hendrickson** of Park City, Utah was third in 3:15:48. The record was set in 1983 by Diane Palmason of Ottawa, Ontario in 2:50:51.

"The most challenging thing on the course was the frequent turns. My splits varied from 6:34 (too fast!) to 8:36. I was challenged by the first couple of miles of hills. I ran as well as could be expected for my conditioning. My only mistake was not to fuel myself soon enough. The temps were cool enough, but the radiant factor was tough," stated Harvey.

Harvey ran her first marathon in 1999, the Crestar Richmond Marathon (2:49:26) and is a three-time winner of the Army Ten-Miler (1998, 1999, and 2000). She is also a gold medallist at the 1991 Pan American Games in the 1500 meters.

The top wheelchair winner was **David Swope** of New Windsor, Md., in 2:22:53. **Adrian Miller** of Bogotá was second in 2:36:31. **Holly Koester** of Cleveland, Ohio, was first in 4:06:12. This was her 6th win with a best time of 3:06:32 in 2002.

The 28th Challenge Cup competition was a match up of the Royal Navy / Royal Marines against the U.S. Marine Corps. The scoring was different this year; the teams were composed of five males and three females. The scoring was based upon the chip time of the top three males and first female. The score stands at 20 for the British and 8 for the Marines. The last win for the Marines was in 1997. The score this year was 10:48:37 to 10:59:01. The British team members were **Dia Roberts** (2:30:39), **Steve Payne** (2:35:55), **Peter Belcher** (2:42:53), and **Wendy Scott** (2:59:09).

2nd 2005 Carl Rundell 2:22:26

Top 3 2005 MCM
2nd Liz Wilson (2:50:03)
1st Susannah Kvasnicka (2:47:10)
3rd Emily Brozozowski (2:54:58)

The Team Marine members were **Alexander Hetherington** (2:35:23), **William Edwards** (2:35:33), **Andrew Bartle** (2:36:05), and **Tara Smith** (3:12:00).

"I thought the start was well organized and all the points along the Mall. I liked the friendliness and Marines like I have never seen around the world. I am always amazed at how much motivation you can have in a marathon, the people can motivate you. I did this race to prove to myself that I could do it and to take responsibility for my health," said **Wim Elfrink**, Vice President for Customer Advocacy, Cisco Systems, Inc. He finished in 5:44:18. Last year he ran 5:53:39.

"I have done 42 marathons around the world. I will always try to improve and make friends and social contacts because everyone has a story. I travel 80 percent of the time and the Galloway method works best for me because I can't train the way I want to and I am big supporter. I do 15-20 miles a week and every other week I try to do some long run of about 15 miles," he adds.

"A little piece of advice: Don't drink and sign up for marathons. I was out with two of my girlfriends, Stephanie and Lisa, in April of 2005 who'd run the MCM in previous years and they were preparing to run in the 30th anniversary this past October. They were diligently trying to convince me to do it with them ... well my really good friend, Cabernet, made it a reality. I signed up online that night through a charity partner. The minute I hit the 'submit' button, I sobered up pretty quick," said **Elizabeth Bailey** of Braintree, MA (6:23:09).

Once you take on a challenge larger than life, your focus changes. "No one could believe I was doing this ... my grandmother wisely pointed out that I'm the girl who doesn't like to sweat and used to take 2 showers a day in my younger years. I'm no elite athlete. I have a love/hate relationship with the gym, I love to eat, I love my wine, I really love my wines," she adds.

The morning of the race was an inspiring experience looking around and seeing the crowds of runners and spectators. Elizabeth and Stephanie were running along with Scott, Matt and Sean, who were in the Marines with the girls' husbands, and Scott's sister Denise. Lisa had unfortunately broken her foot and couldn't run but was there on the support team, which consisted of the runners' spouses, girlfriends and Elizabeth's father and in-laws.

"Team Turtle" (Stephanie and Beth) had a good pace going, but near mile seven Beth started to feel light headed, dizzy and sick to her stomach. She hates sports drink and had taken a few sips of the Powerade, which may have caused the problem. Steph continued on at her pace. Mile ten was the first contact with the support crew and later she was told that she looked like death warmed over.

She explains the next miles. "By mile 14, I had rebounded nicely, had a good clip going and thought that this was my push to catch Steph. A quarter mile later, I put my left foot down and the pain from my left foot was excruciating, it felt like muscle tearing off my ankle bone. I had to slow to a walk, which then made everything else tighten up."

The reality of the race was taking hold as she adds, "At this point EVERYTHING hurts...my feet feel like they're in vice grips that keep tightening, my legs are like lead and I'm certain that I'm going to need both hips replaced at the end of this. The bridge is the longest, lonliest stretch of road in the entire world. I stopped to stretch my back a couple of times because it was so tight you could bounce quarters off it. Every step I took, my feet were screaming at me with sharp tingly pain to stop."

She was on the other side of the "The Wall." "At the bottom of the bridge, I rounded the corner to start mile 21. What I saw was like an oasis in the desert. Hunky Marine men were handing out the most decadent ham & cheese sandwich squares I'd ever had ... Of course, I could've eaten tar at this point and thought it was gourmet dining."

She met up with a fellow St. Jude runner, Laurel, from Plattsburgh, NY. They ran together and talked until she began to drop back at mile 25 and she was going to run the last of it.

Realizing the end is near, the adrenalin starts to work. "As I'm running along, I'm passing people who are in obvious better shape than I am; Two men on either side of this, one woman who looked like if they let her go, she'd crumble. Another two women arm in arm, both limping; The folks pushing along, alone in their reserve to finish no matter how they get there. The last 1/2 mile the band at the end was playing 'Eye of the Tiger', which put at least a half spring in my step and I soldiered on."

"The end of the marathon is up this sadistically steep hill. It's probably not that bad, but after 26.1 miles, it became my enemy. I was passing folks walking up it who were probably thinking, what does this chick have to prove so many hours into it. But I knew that Matt, Sean, Stephanie and Denise ('the runners') along with the 'support team' would be there and I was not going to walk by them. I also wasn't going to allow myself to walk across the finish line," Bailey stated.

"As I crested the hill and came around the corner, there they were yelling my name and cheering, which was a better high than the actual crossing of the finish line. I hobbled over to the Marine handing out the medals and humbly said, 'Thank You, Lieutenant.' I could've kissed the Marine who took the chip off my sneaker. I don't think I could've bent down and my fingers were swollen like sausages, I wouldn't have had the dexterity to do it myself." She made it in 6 hours 23 minutes and the goal was not a time but to finish. She had not run more than a six mile months prior. "The loops my body threw at me that day, I'm pretty damn proud of myself when far better athletes than I were being taken off the course or couldn't finish," she said.

The 31st Marine Corps Marathon (MCM), Sunday, **October 29, 2006**, had three capable winners but the day would end with only one victorious. Each would claim a piece of Marine Corps history. The record of 2:14:01 set by Jeff Scuffins in 1987 was a goal of **Jared Nyamboki** of Kisii, Kenya. Nyamboki made his mark by winning the 22nd Army Ten-Miler (October 8, 2006) in a time of 48:24. **Carl Rundell** of Birmingham, Ala., was making his third attempt at the elusive title. In 2004, he was fifth in 2:26:48 and 2006 he was denied by **Ruben Garcia** and placed second in 2:22:26. Garcia, a corporal in the Mexican Navy, was first last year in 2:22:18. In January 2006, he won his first marathon (ING Miami) in a time of 2:18:15.

The Marine Corps Marathon is the fifth largest U.S. marathon. This year there were 30,074 registered runners (18,328 males, 11,746 females) the largest in the history of the race so far. There were 20,925 finishers (11,791 males, 9,134 females).

The start of the race was delayed for a second time (the first was in 1997) in the history of the race because a spectator suffered a cardiac arrest.

Nyamboki wasted no time getting out to a fast start along with Foot Solutions teammates, **Belay Kassa** and **Tamrat Ayalew**. Into the fifth mile (along 30th Street, after turning right off M Street in Georgetown), Nyamboki clocked 25:37 (5:07 pace).

At the half-marathon mark (along the Mall on Jefferson Drive before 15th Street), Nyamboki enjoyed the lead with a time of 1:07:38 (5:09 average split). Garcia and Rundell were both holding at 1:10:13.

At mile 20 (off Ohio Drive prior to Maine Avenue before reaching the HOV ramp), Nyamboki was averaging a 5:16 pace (1:45:30). Garcia had moved up into second place (1:46:51) with Kassa in third (1:47:00). Ayalew was fourth in (1:47:19) followed closely by Rundell in fifth (1:47:59).

The turning point was along the HOV Lanes as Nymaboki began to slow and was overtaken by Garcia as the lead was assumed. Rundell was giving chase to Garcia. Nyamboki was out of the race.

Along Crystal Drive after the turn before 18th Street at mile 23, Garcia enjoyed the lead with a time of 2:03:20 followed closely by Rundell in 2:05:11. The stretch along Route 110 and up the hill saw Garcia clock 2:21:20 (the 16th fastest winning time) for his second win. He is the second two-time consecutive year winner and joins Jim Hage (1988-2:21:59 19th fastest winning time, 1989-2:2:20:23 14th fastest winning time) in that honor. Rundell settled for runner up for a second year in 2:24:22. **Jose Miranda** of Mexico was third in 2:26:24.

The women's race unfolded in a similar fashion as the men's. **Kirsten Ward** of Arlington, Va., set the pace early and went through five miles in 32:32 (average pace 6:28). In 2004, Ward placed seventh in 3:07:25. Trailing in 33:18 (average pace 6:39) was U.S. Navy Commander **Suzanne Himes** of the Navy-Marine Corps Intel Training Center at Virginia Beach, Va. She had placed eighth in the 2003 MCM with a 3:07:37, and she ran 3:07:37 at Boston in 2003.

Going into the 10th mile, the average pace of Ward slowed to 6:32 (split time of 1:05:24). **Laura Thompson** of Boise, Idaho had moved up into second place with a split time of 1:06:37 (6:39 pace). She was making her MCM debut. In 2004, she ran the Chicago Marathon in 2:58:24 (placed 36th). Himes was holding in third place with 1:06:47 (6:40 pace).

Into the 15th mile along the East Basin Drive, Ward clocked 1:38:58 (6:35) with Thompson still in pursuit with 1:40:30 (6:42). Himes had a firm grip on third place with 1:40:38 (6:42) followed by Viger with 1:41:48 (6:47). Cairns had pulled back up into fifth place with 1:41:49 (6:47).

By the 23 mile along Crystal Drive, Ward was no longer a factor in the race as it was under the control of Thompson. She went through mile 23 in 2:36:52 (6:49). Air Force Major **Brenda Schrank** of Winchester, Va., had moved up into second place. Her prior MCM times included: 2000 – 3:13:10 25th place, 2001 – 3:02:58 6th place, 2002 – 3:04:39 4th place, and 2005 – 3:06:33 11th place. Himes held third place in 2:38:23 (6:53) as Cairns trailed in 2:40:00 (6:57).

The final push out of Crystal City and then by the Pentagon onto Route 110 toward the finish had Thompson on her way to victory – the race was hers. Thompson crossed the line in 3:00:22, the next-to-the slowest winning time since 1978 (3:01:34), which was run by Jane Killion of New York.

Second place went to Schrank in 3:02:34, followed by Himes in 3:02:56.

The two-time master's champion (2003-2:34:21, and 2005 – 2:30:39) **Dai Roberts** of Marlow, England was on hand to defend his 2005 title. The top challenger was Air Force LtCol. **Mark Cucuzzella** of Shepherdstown, WV. His performances date back to 1988 at age 22 with 2:34:02, 1989-2:32:41, 1990-2:31:52, 1994-2:31:01, 1997-2:35:21, 2000-2:28:55 (3rd place), 2002-2:34:36, 2004-2:33:28, and 2005-2:34:46.

Mark Sullivan of Freeburg, Pa., another competitor has run the following times: 2000-2:49:49, 2001-2:50:35, 2002-2:49:12, 2003-2:53:28, 2004-2:53:23, and 2005-2:48:24.

Roberts was a member of the British team competing for the Challenge Cup against Team Marines and Cucuzzella was in competition for the Armed Forces top team.

The three were within minutes going through five miles with Cucuzzella at 29:22, Roberts 28:08, and Sullivan with 31:37. Going into the half, the gap began to widen as the advantage remained with Cucuzzella at 1:13:59, Roberts with 1:16:31 and Sullivan with 1:22:29. At mile 20, off Ohio Drive, there had not been any change as each runner was holding fast to his pace with Cucuzzella at 1:54:53 followed by Roberts in 2:13:59 and Sullivan in 2:03:19.

Going into the closing miles with the stamina remaining to capture first place, Cucuzzella crossed in 2:32:46, the 18th fastest master's winning time in the history of the race. Roberts was second place with 2:34:57 and Sullivan was third in 2:46:54.

The race for the females started off with less than a minute between the top three finishers. **Becky Backstrom** of Sammamish, Wash., and **Jeannie Ballentine** of Darien, CT passed the five mile mark in 36:10. **Barbara Holcomb** of Cullman, Ala., was seconds off in 36:22. Going into 10 miles Backstrom clocked 1:11:10 followed by Ballentine in 1:11:50 and Holcomb was 1:11:44. It was still too close to call early in the race. By the halfway mark, the gap widened slightly as Backstrom enjoyed the lead with 1:32:53 followed by Holcomb in 1:33:38 and Ballentine in third with 1:34:31. Going into mile 20, the final stage was set with the lead enjoyed by Backstrom with a 2:21:04, Holcomb with 2:22:57 and in third was Ballentine with 2:25:59.

Backstrom was able to sustain her pace to capture first place in 3:06:34, the 20th fastest winning time in the history of the race. Holcomb captured second in 3:11:27 followed by Ballentine in 3:15:29.

The top wheelchair finisher was **Grant Berthiaume** of Tucson, Arizona with a time of 2:11:59. **David Swope** of New Windsor, Md., was second in 2:14:33. He was denied a repeat win from last year where he rolled to a 2:22:53 finish for first. In third place was **David Swaim** of Wake Forest, NC in a time of 2:16:04. He was the 2004 winner in 2:33:58. The record was set by Hall of Fame athlete Ken Carnes in 1990 with a 1:40:22.

The top female was **Leah Mullen** of Timonium, Md., in 4:11:32 and in second was **Mary Thompson** of Delmar, CA, in 4:27:08. The record was set in 1994 by Rose Winand of Boston, MA, with 2:16:25.

On a sad note, **Earl Seyford**, age 56, of Olney Md., died near the 17 mile mark, about halfway down Ohio Drive going to Hains Point in East Potomac Park along the river side. Seyford completed the following MCMs : 2000 – 6:14:51, 2001 – 5:58:22, 2002 – 5:42:26, 2003 – 6:19:12, and 2004 – 5:57:25. Sympathies are extended to his family.

Dean Karnazes was taking on the North Face Endurance 50 (50 marathons in 50 states in 50 days), which started with the Lewis and Clark Marathon in St. Louis, MO on September 17, 2006 (3:51:10) and the New York City Marathon was the final marathon. Eight of the 50 would be official marathons and the others he ran the same course. The MCM was number 43 on his list as he wore bib number 43. He finished the race in 3:37:307. The elapsed times were 5-Miles 41:07, 10-miles 1:22:44, Half-marathon 1:49:08, 15-miles 2:05:11, and 20-miles 2:48:09. (Note the finish time at New York was 3:00:30).

The 2006 MCM Running Store Team Competition was won by Pacers of Virginia with a combined time of 9 hours 25 minutes 40 seconds. The team members were **Robert Wolfe** 2:28:33, **Matt Sciandra** 2:44:42, and **Stephanie Burns** 3:52:25. The Gotta Run store placed second with a time of 10:34:00.

The charity partners of the Marine Corps Marathon continue to serve a vital role within the community. The Tragedy Assistance Program for Survivors (TAPS) is the only organization set up to heal the hearts of those left behind and it closes its arms to no one who has been affected by the loss of a loved one in the military. TAPS is not a one-time organization; they help the survivors however long, no matter how many times they need TAPS.

TAPS had 85 runners in the Marine Corps Marathon. **Aymber McElroy** of Washington was running in the memory of her husband, Staff Sgt. **Brian McElroy** who was stationed with the 3rd Security Forces Squadron at Elmendorf AFB, Alaska. On January 22, 2006, SSgt McElroy and his friend TSgt. Jason Norton were killed when their humvee was destroyed by an IED while escorting a convoy near Taji, Iraq.

"In the aftermath of Brian's death, my daughter and I found TAPS. The Good Grief Camp for Young Survivors allowed Kaley to express her loss through age-appropriate activities in a safe environment, while the Survivor's Seminar allowed me to find other military widows who simply understood," said Aymber McElroy. Her chip time at the MCM was 5:53:53.

For full details of TAPS, call 1-800-959-8277 or visit http://www.taps.org. TAPS was created in 1994 by a military widow named Bonnie Carroll and it is a registered not-for-profit corporation.

Appendices

1st PLACE FINISHERS OPEN DIVISION

YEAR		NAME	AGE	TIME	HOMETOWN
1	11/07/76	Kenneth Moore	32	2:21:14	Eugene, OR
2	11/06/77	Kevin McDonald	27	2:19:36	Greenville, SC
3	11/05/78	Robert S. Eden	25	2:18:07	Richmond, VA
4	11/04/79	Phil Camp	31	2:19:35	Pensacola, FL
5	11/02/80	Michael Hurd	34	2:18:38	Great Britain
6	11/01/81	Dean Matthews	26	2:16:31	Atlanta,GA
7	11/07/82	Jeff Smith	27	2:21:29	Cumberland, MD
8	11/06/83	Farley Simon (USMC)	28	2:17:46	Aiea, HI
9	11/09/84	Brad T. Ingram	29	2:19:40	Mansfield, OH
10	11/03/85	Thomas E. Bernard	37	2:19:16	Hayes, VA
11	11/02/86	Brad T. Ingram	31	2:23:13	Mansfield, OH
12	11/08/87	Jeff Scuffins	25	**2:14:01** *	Hagerstown, MD
13	11/06/88	Jim Hage	30	2:21:59	Lanham, MD
14	11/05/89	Jim Hage	31	2:20:23	Lanham, MD
15	11/04/90	Matthew Waight	27	2:21:32	New Britain, PA
16	11/03/91	Carlos Rivas	28	2:17:54	Mexico City
17	10/25/92	Rene Guerrero	28	2:24:09	Mexico City
18	10/24/93	Dominique Bariod	29	2:23:56	Morez, France
19	10/23/94	Graciano Gonzalez	34	2:22:51	Mexico City
20	10/22/95	Darrell General	29	2:16:34	Mitchelleville, MD
21	10/27/96	Isaac Garcia	28	2:15:09	Mexico
22	10/26/97	Darrell General	31	2:18:21	Mitchelleville, MD
23	10/25/98	Weldon Johnson	25	2:25:31	Washington, DC
24	10/24/99	Mark Croasdale	21	2:23:27	Chivenor, England
25	10/22/00	Richard Cochrane	27	2:25:50	Harpswell, ME
26	10/28/01	GySgt Farley Simon	46	2:28:28	Honolulu,HI Rtd
27	10/27/02	Christopher Juarez	32	2:25:01	Las Vegas, NV
28	10/26/03	Peter Sherry	35	2:25:07	Great Falls, VA
29	10/31/04	Retta Feyissa	29	2:25:35	Ethiopia
30	10/30/05	Ruben Garcia	34	2:22:18	Mexico
31	10/29/06	Ruben Garcia	35	2:21:20	Mexico

	YEAR	NAME	AGE	TIME	HOMETOWN
1	11/07/76	Susan Mallery	22	2:56:33	Columbus, OH
2	11/06/77	Susan Mallery	23	2:54:04	Columbus, OH
3	11/05/78	Jane Killion	29	3:01:34	New York, NY
4	11/04/79	1stLt.Joanna Martin	23	2:58:14	Oceanside, CA
5	11/02/80	Jan Yerkes	23	2:41:54	Buckingham, PA
6	11/01/81	Cynthia Lorenzoni	23	2:50:33	Charlottesville
7	11/07/82	Cynthia Lorenzoni	24	2:44:51	Charlottesville
8	11/06/83	Suzanne Carden	23	2:45:55	Stroudsburg, PA
9	11/09/84	Pamela Briscoe	29	2:43:20	Chevy Chase, MD
10	11/03/85	Natalie Updegrove	24	2:44:42	Richmond, VA
11	11/02/86	Kathy Champagne	24	2:42:59	Plattsburg, NY
12	11/08/87	Mary Robertson	25	2:44:36	Richmond, VA
13	11/06/88	Lori Lawson	22	2:51:26	Philadelphia, PA
14	11/05/89	Laura DeWald	32	2:45:16	Grand Rapids, MI
15	11/04/90	Olga Markova	22	**2:37:00** *	Leningrad, USSR
16	11/03/91	Amy Kattwinkel	24	2:44:27	Charlotte, NC
17	10/25/92	Judy Mercom	33	2:47:58	Clearwater, FL
18	10/24/93	Holly Ebert	32	2:48:41	Ogden, UT
19	10/23/94	Susan Malloy	29	2:39:34	Charlottesville
20	10/22/95	Claudia Kasen	38	2:49:21	Williamsburg, VA
21	10/27/96	Emma Cabrera	32	2:48:34	Mexico
22	10/26/97	Donna Moore	37	2:53:42	Kensington, MD
23	10/25/98	Kimberly Markland	34	2:49:07	San Antonio, TX
24	10/24/99	Donna Moore	39	2:51:53	SilverSprg, MD
25	10/22/00	Elizabeth Ruel	33	2:47:52	Laval, Quebec
26	10/28/01	Lori Stich-Zimmerman	31	2:48:13	Beaverton, OR
27	10/27/02	Elizabeth Scanlon	31	2:57:27	Alexandria, VA
28	10/26/03	Heather Hanscom	25	2:37:59	Alexandria, VA
29	10/31/04	Capt Mary Kate Bailey	37	2:48:31	Arlington, VA
30	10/30/05	Susannah Kvasnicka	33	2:47:10	Great Falls, VA
31	10/29/06	Laura Thompson	31	3:00:22	Boise, ID

Joanna Martin active duty USMC
Mary Kate Bailey active duty USMC

1st PLACE FINISHERS MASTER DIVISION

	Year	Pl	Name	Age	Time	Hometown
1	1976	7	Glynn L. Wood	42	2:28:28	Washington, DC
		860	Ali Fatima	43	4:26:19	
2	1977	25	Rusty S. Lamade	40	2:32:30	Norfolk, VA (USN)
		392	Trudy J. Rapp	40	3:01:58	Alexandria, VA
3	19/78	22	Rusty S. Lamade	41	2:32:17	Norfolk, VA
		1372	Sue Medaglia	43	3:24:33	Bronx, NY
4	1979	54	Charlie Ross	41	2:33:01	Waldorf, MD
		2	Trudy J. Rapp	42	2:58:53	Alexandria, VA
5	1980	47	Richard Jamborsky	44	2:33:06	Reston, VA
		7	Trudy J. Rapp	43	2:53:17	Alexandria, VA
6	1981	9	Bill Hall	41	**2:24:36***	Durham, NC
		6	Trudy J. Rapp	44	2:58:05	Alexandria, VA
7	1982	36	Don Davis	40	2:30:22	Woodbridge, VA
		1447	Lolita Bache	40	3:07:51	Annandale, VA
8	1983	24	Bill Hall	43	2:25:49	Durham, NC
		427	Diane Palmason	45	**2:50:51***	Ottawa, Ontario
9	1984	63	Mel Williams	46	2:36:48	Virginia Beach, VA
		51	Carolyn Cappetta	48	3:16:25	Concord, MA
10	1985	29	Norm Green, Jr	53	2:31:20	Wayne, PA
		1483	Marcia Collins	40	3:18:57	Rockaway, NJ
11	1986	20	Lucius Anderson	40	2:29:14	Silver Spring, MD
		695	Georgia Gustafson	40	3:07:47	Anchorage, AK
12	1987	26	Rick Thompson	40	2:31:19	Virginia Beach, VA
		17	Charlene Groet	40	3:02:42	Demotte, IN
13	1988	54	Don Rich	43	2:39:27	Mechanicsville, MD
		566	Patricia O'Brien	40	3:02:54	Severna Park, MD
14	1989	8	Cmdr. Phil Camp	42	2:28:25	Sigonella NAS, Italy
		18	Rose Malloy	41	3:03:45	Annapolis, MD
15	1990	17	Lucius Anderson	44	2:32:28	Silver Spring, MD
		6	Rose Malloy	42	2:58:11	Annapolis, MD
16	1991	24	Alvin Rich	41	2:34:02	Dorchester, UK
		12	Rose Malloy	43	2:55:13	Annapolis, MD
17	1992	23	Alvin Rich	42	2:34:55	Dorchester, UK
		6	Rose Malloy	44	2:56:42	Annapolis, MD
18	1993	28	Michael Zeigle	42	2:34:32	Sun Prairie, WI
		11	Sandra Jensen	43	3:01:45	Milwaukee, WI
19	1994	7	Huitzil Austin	40	2:30:28	Mexico
		35	Eileen Telford	42	3:13:56	Aiken, SC
20	1995	4	GySgt Farley Simon	40	2:25:25	San Diego, CA
		13	Lorraine Provost	44	3:00:26	Springfield, IL
21	1996	13	Pete Kaplan	40	2:33:35	Charlotte, NC
		8	Barbara Bellows	42	3:04:44	Ithaca, NY
22	1997	14	Steven Ward	42	2:34:32	Reston, VA
		63	Linda Russo	40	3:20:15	Flushing, NY
23	1998	11	Francisco Lugo	40	2:35:33	Los Cipreses, Mexico
		2	Patti Shull	40	2:55:18	Ashburn, VA
24	1999	8	Francisco Lugo	41	2:31:10	Los Cipreses, Mexico
		19	Deborah Barnett	40	3:11:25	Columbia, MD
25	2000	8	Steve Payne	44	2:31:53	Plymouth, England
		18	Leslie Rideout	40	3:09:46	Malden, MA
26	2001	1	GySgt Farley Simon	46	2:28:28	Honolulu, HI
		9	Sherry Thompson	41	3:05:58	Harrisburg, NC
27	2002	8	Steve Payne	46	2:33:35	Stubbington, UK
		2	Jacquline Chen	40	3:00:53	APO, Europe
28	2003	12	Dai Roberts	42	2:34:21	United Kingdom
		6	Janiced Flynn	44	3:04:17	Redding, CT
29	2004	19	Francisco Lugo	46	2:38:56	Mexico
		4	Eleanor Stewart-Garbrech	42	3:05:47	Jacksonville, FL
30	2005	8	Dauvio Roberts (Dai)	43	2:30:39	Plymouth, UK
		14	Alisa Harvey	40	3:10:11	Manassas, VA
31	2006	11	Mark Cucuzzella	40	2:32:46	Shepherdstown, WV
		5	Beck Backstrom	49	3:06:34	Sammamish, WA

1st PLACE FINISHERS WHEELCHAIR

YEAR		NAME	AGE	TIME	HOMETOWN
1	11/07/76				
2	11/06/77				
3	11/05/78				
4	11/04/79	Bob Hall		2:26:00	Belmont, MA
5	11/02/80	Ken Archer			Bowie,MD
6	11/01/81	Ken Archer	32	2:44:16	Bowie, MD
7	11/07/82	Ken Archer	33	2:21:11	Bowie, MD
8	11/06/83	Ken Archer	34	2:20:36	Bowie, MD
9	11/09/84	Wannie Cook	37	2:23:04	Richmond, VA
10	11/03/85	Ken Archer	36	2:15:30	Bowie, MD
11	11/02/86	Ken Archer	37	2:10:01	Bowie, MD
12	11/08/87	Ken Archer	38	2:04:02	Bowie, MD
13	11/06/88	Ken Archer	39	2:13:48	Bowie, MD
14	11/05/89	Ken Carnes	33	1:54:23	Morningside, MD
15	11/04/90	Ken Carnes	34	**1:40:22***	Morningside, MD
16	11/03/91	Steve Lietz	39	2:02:58	Salisbury, MD
17	10/25/92	Ken Carnes	36	1:48:56	Morningside, MD
18	10/24/93	Ken Archer	44	1:49:12	Bowie, MD
19	10/23/94	Ken Archer	45	1:53:31	Bowie, MD
20	10/22/95	Ken Carnes	39	1:48:41	Snellville, GA
21	10/27/96	Carlos Moleda	34	1:55:32	Falls Church, VA
22	10/26/97	Michael Postell	29	1:58:49	Dunwoody, GA
23	10/25/98	Jason Fowler	24	1:58:18	Boston, MA
24	10/24/99	Kenneth Carnes	43	1:59:57	Snellville, GA
25	10/22/00	Kamel Ayari	32	1:46:48	Huntington, NY
26	10/28/01	Kamel Ayari	33	1:58:17	New Rochelle, NY
27	10/27/02	Vincent Orlando	44	3:17:10	Debarby, FL
28	10/26/03	David Lowe	53	2:19:53	Somerville, NJ
29	10/31/04	David Swaim	58	2:33:58	Wake Forest, NC
30	10/30/05	David Swope	39	2:22:53	New Windsor, MD
31	10/29/06	Grant Berthiamume	44	2:11:59	Tucson, AZ

	YEAR	NAME	AGE	TIME	HOMETOWN
2	11/06/77	Cindy Patton	21	4:44:48	Boston, MA
9	11/09/84	Charla Ramsey			
13	11/06/88	Rose Winand	28	3:12:08	_____,PA
14	11/05/89	Leah Hann		3:24:59	Edinboro, PA
15	11/04/90	Diana McClure		2:33:57	_____, WV
16	11/03/91	Brenda Smith		2:41:33	Rockville
19	10/23/94	Rose Winand	31	**2:16:25***	Boston, MA
20	10/22/95	Susan Katz	16	2:45:35	N. Potomac, MD
21	10/27/96	Julia Wallace	34	2:21:09	Rumson, NJ
22	10/26/97	Julia Wallace	35	2:21:00	Rumson, NJ
23	10/25/98	Holly Koester	38	3:08:16	Cleveland, OH
24	10/24/99	Holly Koester	39	3:21:52	Walton Hills, OH
25	10/22/00	Holly Koester	40	3:40:04	Cleveland, OH
26	10/28/01	None			
27	10/27/02	Holly Koester	42	3:06:32	Cleveland, OH
28	10/26/03	Holly Koester	43	3:11:16	Cleveland, OH
29	10/31/04	None			
30	10/30/05	Holly Koester	45	4:06:12	Cleveland, OH
31	10/29/06	Leah Mullen	17	4:11:32	Timonium, MD

TOP THREE PERFORMANCE BY YEAR – OPEN DIVISION

1 November 7, 1976

1 Kenny Moore	2:21:14
2 Samuel Maizel	2:25:02
3 F. P. Builtron	2:26:10

Female

1 Susan Mallery	2:56:33
2 Jennifer White	2:58:03
3 Bobbie Moore	3:16:32

2 November 6, 1977

1 Kevin McDonald	2:19:36
2 Phil Camp	2:20:09
3 Max White	2:21:32

Female

1 Susan Mallery	2:54:04
2 Gail Jones	2:59:09
3 Trudy Rapp	3:01:58

3 November 5, 1978

1 Robert (Scott) Eden	2:18:07
2 Kevin McCarey	2:21:54
3 Charlie Maguire	2:23:21

Female

1 Jane Killion	3:01:34
2 Kitty Consolo	3:05:33
3 Peggy Kokernot	3:05:35

4 November 4, 1979

1 Phil Camp	2:19:35
2 William Albers	2:20:14
3 David McDonald	2:20:45

Female

1 1stLt Joanna Martin	2:58:08	USMC
2 Trudy Rapp	2:58:53	
3 Laura DeWald	2:59:25	

5 November 2, 1980

1 Michael Hurd	2:18:38	(Adjusted Time)
2 Mike Geehan	2:17:46*	
3 Phil Camp	2:18:02*	

Female

1 Jan Yerks	2:41:54	(Adjusted Time)
2 Laura DeWald	2:42:55*	
3 Majorie Tennyson	2:46:28	

6 November 2, 1981

1 Dean Matthews	2:16:31
2 Hank Pfrifle	2:17:52
3 Craig Holm	2:22:22

Female

1 Cynthia Lorenzoni	2:50:33
2 Beth Dillinger	2:53:48
3 Norma Franco	2:54:36

7 November 7, 1982

1 Jeff Smith	2:21:29
2 Bill Stewart	2:21:54
3 Terry Sullivan	2:21:56

Female

1 Cynthia Lorenzoni	2:45:51
2 Vicki Randall	2:45:07
3 Patricia Sher	2:51:07

8 November 6, 1983

1 Sgt. Farley Simon	2:17:46	USMC
2 Bill Stewart	2:19:40	
3 James Knight	2:19:47	

Female

1 Suzanne Carden	2:45:55
2 Julie Burke	2:47:19
3 Juleann Quigley	2:50:25

9 November 4, 1984

1 Brad Ingram	2:19:40
2 Thomas Bernard	2:20:45
3 Jim Hage	2:22:40

Female

1 Pamela Briscoe	2:43:20
2 Susan Stone	2:45:47
3 Charlene O'Brien	2:46:31

10 November 3, 1985

1 Thomas Bernard	2:19:16
2 Brad Ingram	2:19:47
3 Jim Hage	2:23:30

Female

1 Natalie Updegrove	2:44:42
2 Susie Patterson	2:47:47
3 Deborah Dye Favor	2:54:54

* Course was short

11 November 2, 1986

1 Brad Ingram	2:23:13	
2 John Stevens	2:24:05	
3 Rudy Robinson	2:24:32	

Female

1 Kathy Champagne	2:42:59	
2 Lucia Geraci	2:48:58	
3 Sally Strauss	2:52:08	

12 November 8, 1987

1 Jeff Scuffins	2:14:01	Event Record
2 Darrell General	2:19:08	
3 Thomas Fries	2:21:44	

Female

1 Mary Robertson	2:44:34	
2 Mary Salamone	2:26:18	
3 Elizabeth Andrews	2:47:46	

13 November 6, 1988

1 Jim Hage	2:21:59	
2 Brad Ingram	2:22:18	
3 John Stephens	2:22:27	

Female

1 Lori Lawson	2:51:26	
2 Ann Wehner	2:51:44	
3 Mary-Lynn Patizzo	2:55:24	

14 November 5, 1989

1 Jim Hage	2:20:23	
2 Sgt. Farley Simon	2:22:37	USMC
3 Paul Okerberg	2:25:16	

Female

1 Laura DeWald	2:45:16	
2 Lori Lawson	2:48:26	
3 Christine Snow-Reaser	2:50:16	

15 November 4, 1990

1 Matthew Waight	2:21:32	
2 Robert Rollins	2:26:41	
3 Barry Holder	2:26:45	

Female

1 Olga Markova	2:37:00	Event Record
2 Suzanne Ray	2:44:48	
3 Lynn Patterson	2:51:03	

16 November 3, 1991

1 Carol Rivas	2:17:54	
2 Rene Guerrero	2:21:12	
3 Craig Fram	2:23:33	

Female

1 Amy Kattwinkel	2:44:27	
2 Julie Foster	2:46:12	
3 Christine Snow-Reaser	2:47:50	

17 October 25, 1992

1 Rene Guerrero	2:24:09	
2 Michael Whittlesey	2:25:26	
3 Ricardo Galicia	2:26:23	

Female

1 Judy Mercon	2:47:58	
2 Kelly Flanagan	2:50:25	
3 Denise Metzgar	2:53:33	

18 October 24, 1993

1 Dominique Bariod	2:23:56	
2 Esteban Vanegas	2:24:20	
3 Chuck Lotz	2:24:50	

Female

1 Holly Ebert	2:48:41	
2 Mary Gaylord	2:53:33	
3 Patricia Ford	2:56:16	

19 October 23, 1994

1 Graciano Gonzales	2:22:51	
2 Gordon Sanders	2:55:06	
3 Bob Schwelm	2:25:37	

Female

1 Susan Molloy	2:39:34	
2 Callie Malloy	2:49:46	
3 Kimberly Markland	2:53:22	

20 October 22, 1995

1 Darrell General	2:16:34	
2 Hernandez Francisco	2:20:19	
3 Nelson Shertzer	2:24:11	

Female

1 Claudia Kasen	2:49:21	
2 Maria Pazarentos	2:52:18	
3 Kay Panfile	2:53:06	

21 October 27, 1996

1	Issac Garcia	2:15:09
2	Samuel Lopez	2:23:01
3	Mark Croasdale	2:25:24

Female

1	Emma Cabrera	2:48:34
2	Sharon Servidio	2:53:04
3	Jennifer Schretzmayer	2:55:00

22 October 27, 1997

1	Darrell General	2:18:21
2	Alejandro Crus Maya	2:23:25
3	Patrick Phillips	2:29:55

Female

1	Donna Moore	2:53:42
2	Selena Smart	2:55:34
3	Claire Norsworthy	2:55:45

23 October 25, 1998

1	Weldon Johnson	2:25:31
2	Mark Croasdale	2:31:33
3	Gary Gerrard	2:32:43

Female

1	Maj. Kimberly Markland	2:49:07 USAF
2	Patti Shull	2:55:18
3	Kelly Keller	2:55:34

24 October 24, 1999

1	Mark Croasdale	2:23:27
2	Mark Coogan	2:24:18
3	Maximino Ayala	2:24:38

Female

1	Donna Moore	2:51:53
2	Bea Marie Altieri	2:56:48
3	Christi Ireland	2:57:58

25 October 22, 2000

1	Lt. Richard Cochran	2:25:50 USN
2	Juan Lopez	2:28:33
3	Capt. Mark Cucuzzella	2:28:55 USAF

Female

1	Elizabeth Ruel	2:47:52
2	Liz Speegle	2:52:04
3	Connie Davis	2:58:05

26 October 28, 2001

1	GySgt Farley Simon	2:28:28 USMC(Ret)
2	Lopez Escorcia Juan Samu	2:29:31
3	Steve Payne	2:31:27

Female

1	Lori Stich Zimmerman	2:48:13
2	Tara Pointin	2:54:01
3	Lindsay Gannon	2:54:48

27 October 27, 2002

1	Capt. Christopher Juarez	2:25:01 USAF
2	John Sence	2:26:31
3	Benjamin Sandy	2:29:20

Female

1	Elizabeth Scanlon	2:57:27
2	Jacaquline Chen	3:00:53
3	Mary Kate Sullivan-Bailey	3:02:24

28 October 26, 2003

1	Peter Sherry	2:25:07
2	Eric Post	2:27:49
3	Aaron Church	2:28:24

Female

1	Heather Hanscom	2:37:59
2	Lindsay Gannon	2:58:46
3	Kristin Van Eron	3:00:14

29 October 31, 2004

1	Retta Feyissa	2:25:35
2	Terrance Shea	2:25:57
3	Maj. Christopher Juarez	2:26:03

Female

1	Capt. Mary Kate Sullivan-Bailey	2:48:31 USMC
2	LCMDR Kimberly Fagen	2:51:17 USN
3	Sizanne Clemmer	2:59:11

30 October 30, 2005

1	Ruben Garcia	2:22:18
2	Carl Rundell	2:22:26
3	Eric Post	2:23:54

Female

1	Susannah Kvasnicka	2:47:10
2	Liz Wilson	2:50:03
3	Emily Brozozowski	2:54:58

1	Ruben Garcia	2:21:20
2	Carl Rundell	2:24:22
3	Jose Miranda	2:26:24

Female

1	Laura Thompson	3:00:22
2	Brenda Schrank	3:02:34
3	Suzanne Himes	3:02:56

TOP THREE PERFORMANCE BY YEAR – MASTER DIVISION

1 November 7, 1976

1	Glynn Wood	2:28:28
2	Richard Jamborsky	2:39:50
3	David Seiler	2:43:51

Female

1	All Fatima	4:26:19
2	Gloria Krug	5:21:42

2 November 6, 1977

1	Rusty Lamade	2:32:30
2	David Bloor	2:37:10
3	P. Monahan	2:38:58

Female

1	Trudy Rapp	3:01:58
2	Sue Medaglia	3:20:30
3	Hannah Miller	4:08:24

3 November 5, 1978

1	Rusty Lamade	2:32:17
2	Richard Jamborsky	2:38:25
3	Fay Bradley	2:39:07

Female

1	Sue Medaglia	3:24:33
2	Annette Johnson	3:25:02
3	Joy Hubbard	3:32:59

4 November 4, 1979

1	Charlie Ross	2:33:01
2	Jeremy Clark	2:33:46
3	Charles Bolton	2:34:49

Female

1	Trudy Rapp	2:58:53
2	Natalie Buzzell	3:11:40
3	Sue Medaglia	3:19:11

5 November 2, 1980

1	Richard Jamborsky	2:33:06*
2		
3		

Female

1	Trudy Rapp	2:53:17*
2		
3		

6 November 2, 1981

1	Bill Hall	2:24:36 Event Record
2	Alton Migues	2:32:47
3	Dick Hipp	2:34:57

Female

1	Trudy Rapp	2:57:57
2	Janice Stoodley	3:09:55
3	Lynne Lauck	3:14:04

7 November 7, 1982

1	Don Davis	2:30:22
2	Roger Pflugelder	2:30:36
3	Melvin Williams	2:34:49

Female

1	Lolitta Bache	3:07:51
2	Gloria Jenkins	3:09:05
3	Joan Szarfinski	3:15:05

8 November 6, 1983

1	Bill Hall	2:25:49
2	Don Davis	2:29:39
3	Richard Harris	2:35:25

Female

1	Diane Palmason	2:50:51 Event Record
2	Joan Ullyot	2:58:41
3	Erlene Michener	3:05:24

* Unadjusted times course short

9 November 4, 1984

1	Mel Williams	2:36:48
2	Paul Sullivan	2:36:55
3	Edward Doheny	2:38:46

Female

1	Carolyn Cappetta	3:16:25
2	Jean Belton	3:18:31
3	Marcia Napoliello	3:19:53

10 November 3, 1985

1	Norm Green, Jr.	2:31:20
2	Bill Fuller	2:31:51
3	Marlin Thomas	2:37:17

Female

1	Marcia Collins	3:18:57
2	Beverly Shooshan	3:19:16
3	Wen-Shi Yu	3:25:35

11 November 2, 1986

1	Lucious Anderson	2:29:14
2	Keith Cawley	2:31:22
3	Edward Doheny	2:36:12

Female

1	Georgia Gustafson	3:07:47
2	Shirley Schmitt	3:15:40
3	Joy Hampton	3:22:57

12 November 8, 1987

1	Rick Thompson	2:31:19
2	Jack Miller	2:35:56
3	William Tobin	2:36:38

Female

1	Charlene Groet	3:02:42
2	Carol Jean Clark	3:05:32
3	Beverly Shooshan	3:07:55

13 November 6, 1988

1	Don Rich	2:39:27
2	Ed Brinkley	2:39:36
3	Mel Williams	2:40:38

Female

1	Patricia O'Brien	3:02:54
2	Patricia Dulin	3:07:36
3	Catherine Baldwin	3:11:02

14 November 5, 1989

1	Phillip Camp	2:28:25
2	Eric Bateman	2:29:51
3	Don Rowland	2:35:01

Female

1	Rose Malloy	3:03:45
2	Judith Bugyi	3:07:30
3	Judy Huber-Cogswell	3:12:01

15 November 4, 1990

1	Lucious Anderson	2:32:28
2	Bill Hart	2:32:46
3	Alvin Rich	2:34:36

Female

1	Rose Malloy	2:58:11
2	Ann Davies	3:03:53
3	Sandra Jensen	3:04:16

16 November 3, 1991

1	Alvin Rich	2:34:02
2	Mike Zeigle	2:37:33
3	Larry White	2:38:50

Female

1	Rose Malloy	2:55:13
2	Joyce Ploeger	3:06:06
3	Linda Mills	3:09:29

17 October 25, 1992

1	Alvin Rich	2:34:55
2	Bennett Beach	2:35:05
3	William Rogers	2:37:44

Female

1	Rose Malloy	2:56:42
2	Maddy Harmeling	3:01:54
3	Linda Mills	3:04:27

18 October 24, 1993

1	Michael Zeigle	2:34:32
2	David Dunne	2:38:42
3	Chuck Moeser	2:40:34

Female

1	Sandra Jensen	3:01:45
2	Eunice Phillips	3:04:09
3	Ann Davies	3:09:19

19 October 23, 1994

1 Huitzil Augustin	2:30:28	
2 Ray Workman	2:35:01	
3 Randy Winn	2:36:58	

Female

1 Eileen Telford	3:13:56	
2 Lorraine Provost	3:14:00	
3 Ann McKeckley	3:17:42	

20 October 22, 1995

1 GySgt Farley Simon	2:25:25	USMC
2 Alvin Rich	2:34:44	
3 James Pryde, Jr.	2:37:49	

Female

1 Lorraine Provost	3:00:26	
2 Joy Hampton	3:17:39	
3 Georgeanne Welde	3:18:42	

21 October 27, 1996

1 Pete Kaplan	2:33:35	
2 Ginge Gough	2:35:46	
3 Victor Cuevas	2:37:07	

Female

1 Barbara Bellows	3:04:44	
2 Trish Steelman	3:07:27	
3 Helen Visgauss	3:14:28	

22 October 27, 1997

1 Steve Ward	2:34:32	
2 Ginge Gough	2:35:07	
3 Al Rich	2:42:07	

Female

1 Linda Russo	3:20:15	
2 Betty Hoshoian	3:21:53	
3 Ann Meckley	3:22:00	

23 October 25, 1998

1 Francisco Lugo	2:35:33	
2 Steve Bremner	2:40:04	
3 James Christopher	2:40:20	

Female

1 Patti Shull	2:55:18	
2 Carol Virga	3:13:27	
3 Sharon Gosha	3:17:33	

24 October 24, 1999

1 Francisco Lugo	2:31:10	
2 Steve Payne	2:33:53	
3 Ginge Gough	2:34:18	

Female

1 Deborah Barnett	3:11:25	
2 Mary Catherine Malin	3:15:50	
3 Ginger Spencer	3:19:01	

25 October 22, 2000

1 Steve Payne	2:31:53	
2 Ginge Gough	2:38:27	
3 Francisco Lugo	2:40:46	

Female

1 Leslie Rideout	3:09:46	
2 Leah Whipple	3:10:35	
3 Brenda Mitchell	3:11:47	

26 October 28, 2001

1 GySgt. Farley Simon	2:28:28	USMC (Ret)*
2 Steve Payne	2:31:27	
3 Paul Okerberg	2:36:22	

Female

1 Sherry Thompson	3:05:58	
2 Kimberly Layman	3:08:04	
3 June Ciuba	3:12:10	

27 October 27, 2002

1 Steve Payne	2:33:35	
2 Bryan Smith	2:35:54	
3 Francisco Lugo	2:41:58	

Female

1 Maj. Jacquline Chen	3:00:53	USA
2 Sherry Thompson	3:06:39	
3 Cheryl Buhre	3:09:54	

28 October 26, 2003

1 Dai Roberts	2:34:21	
2 Steve Payne	2:35:39	
3 Francisco Medrano	2:45:19	

Female

1 Janiced Flynn	3:04:17	
2 Jacqueline Chen	3:07:36	
3 Beth Moras	3:08:37	

* O'All Winner

29 October 31, 2004

1 Francisco Lugo	2:38:56
2 Steve Payne	2:39:31
3 Paul Okerberg	2:43:39

Female

1 Eleanor Stewart-Garbrech	3:05:45
2 Laurie Hanscom	3:11:24
3 Leisa Ensle	3:11:35

30 October 30, 2005

1 Dauvio Roberts	2:30:39
2 Steve Payne	2:35:55
3 Jon Schoenberg	2:40:59

Female

1 Alisa Harvey	3:10:11
2 Brenda Wilson	3:10:49
2 Nancy Hendrickson	3:15:48

31 October 29, 2006

1 Mark Cucuzzella	2:32:46
2 Dai Roberts	2:34:57
3 Mark Sullivan	2:46:54

Female

1 Becky Backstrom	3:06:34
2 Barbara Holcomb	3:11:27
3 Jeannie Ballentine	3:15:29

Best Performance By Five-Year Age Groups

Age Group <19

Males

Pl	Year	Name	Age	Time	City/State
1	1977	Marshall Fortenberry	19	2:25:55	Celburne, TX
2	1982	James Davis III	19	2:38:26	Restburg, VA
3	1983	Chris Chattin	19	2:28:35	College Park, MD
4	1979	Edward Hume	18	2:34:02	Monroe, VA
5	1981	Michael Gagne	19	2:34:10	Nashua, NH

Females

1	1984	Janine Franko	19	3:06:08	Bloomburg, PA
2	1978	Donna Anderson	19	3:10:38	Pittsburgh, PA
3	1979	Tina Valverde	18	3:13:47	Washington, DC
4	1982	Karen Wiggins	19	3:15:53	West Point, NY
5	2005	Shannon Doran	19	3:18:41	North Attleboro, MA

Age Group 20-24

Males

1	1987	Darrell General	21	2:19:08	Temple Hill, MD
2	1979	William Albers	23	2:20:14	Fairfax, VA
3	1978	Kevin McCarey	24	2:21:54	Villanova, PA
4	1983	Derick Hulme	22	2:23:47	Henrietta, NY
5	1982	Jeryl Turner	23	2:24:24	Front Royal, VA

Females

1	1990	Olga Markova	22	2:37:00* +	Lennigrad, Russia
2	1980	Jan Yerkes	23	2:41:54 +	Buckingham, PA
3	1991	Amy Kattwinkel	24	2:44:27 +	Charlotte, NC
4	1986	Kathy Champagne	24	2:42:59	Plattsburgh, NY
5	1985	Natalie Updegrove	24	2:44:42 +	Richmond, VA

* Open Event Record / + Winner

Age Group 25-29

Males

Pl	Year	Name	Age	Time	City/State
1	1987	Jeff Scuffins	25	2:14:01* +	Hagerstown, MD
2	1996	Issac Garcia	28	2:15:09	Mexico
3	1981	Dean Matthews	26	2:16:31 +	Mansfield, OH
4	1995	Darrell General	29	2:16:34 +	Mitchellville, MD
5	1983	Farley Simon USMC	28	2:17:46	Alea, HI

* Open Event Record

Females

1	2003	Heather Hanscom	25	2:37:59	Alexandria, VA
2	1994	Susan Molloy	29	2:39:34 +	Charlottesville, VA
3	1984	Pamela Briscoe	29	2:43:20 +	Chevy Chase, MD
4	1987	Mary Robertson	25	2:44:34 +	Richmond, VA
5	1982	Vicki Randall	25	2:45:07	Doss, CA

Age Group 30-34

Males

1	1981	Hank Pfeifle	30	2:17:52	Kennebunkport, ME
2	1980	Michael Hurd	34	2:18:38 +	Suffolk, England
3	1997	Darrell General	31	2:18:21 +	Mitchelleville, MD
4	1979	Phillip Camp	31	2:19:25	Milton, FL
5	1985	Brad Ingram	30	2:19:47 +	Mansfield, OH

Females

1	1989	Laura DeWald	32	2:45:16 +	Grand Rapids, MI
2	2005	Susannah Kvasnicka	33	2:47:10	Great Falls, VA
3	2000	Elizabeth Ruel	33	2:47:52 +	Laval, Quebec
4	1992	Judy Mercon	33	2:47:58 +	Clearwater, FL
5	2001	Lori Stich-Zimmerman	31	2:48:13 +	Beaverton, OR

Age Group 35-39

Males

1	1985	Thomas Bernard	37	2:19:16	Hayes, VA
2	1984	Thomas Bernard	36	2:20:45	Hayes, VA
3	1983	Barry Heath	36	2:20:46	Marshall Dorset, GB
4	1979	Bill Hall	39	2:21:01	Durham, NC
5	2005	Carl Rundell	37	2:22:26	Birmingham, MI

Females

1	1990	Suzanne Ray	38	2:44:48	Anchorage, AK
2	1984	Sandra Mewett	35	2:49:11	Tuckerstown, Bermuda
3	1995	Claudia Kasen	38	2:49:21 +	Williamsburg, VA
4	2005	Liz Wilson	37	2:50:03	Eugene, OR
5	1983	Patricia Sher	36	2:51:06	Jacksonville, FL

Age Group 40-44

Males

Pl	Year	Name	Age	Time	City/State
1	1981	Bill Hall	41	2:24:36*	Durham, NC
2	1995	Farley Simon USMC	40	2:25:25	San Diego, CA
3	1983	Bill Hall	43	2:25:49	Durham, NC
4	1989	Phillip Camp	42	2:28:25	FPO, NY
5	1976	Glynn Wood	42	2:28:28	Washington, DC

* Master Event Record

Females

1	1991	Rose Malloy	43	2:55:13	Annapolis, MD
2	1998	Patti Shull	40	2:55:18	Ashburn, VA
3	1992	Rose Malloy	44	2:56:42	Annapolis, MD
4	1981	Trudy Rapp	44	2:57:57	Alexandria, VA
5	1990	Rose Malloy	42	2:58:11	Annapolis, MD

Age Group 45-49

Males

1	2001	GySgt Farley Simon USMC	46	2:28:28	Honolulu, HI USMC
2	1985	Bill Fuller	46	2:31:51	Livonia, NY
3	2002	Steve Payne	46	2:33:35	Stunnington, England
4	1983	Mel Williams	45	2:35:30	Virginia Beach, VA
5	2003	Steve Payne	48	2:35:39	Stunnington, England

Females

1	1983	Diane Palmason	45	2:50:51*	Ottawa, Ontario
2	1992	Maddy Harmeling	47	3:01:54	Merrick, NY
3	1991	Joyce Ploeger	48	3:06:06	Norfolk, VA
4	1982	Gloria Jenkins	45	3:09:05	Mount Holly, NJ
5	1993	Ann Davies	47	3:09:19	New York, NY

* Master Event Record

Age Group 50-54

Males

1	1985	Norm Green Jr.	53	2:31:20	Wayne, PA
2	1984	John Dugdale	50	2:38:21	Ridgefield, CT
3	2004	Al Rich	54	2:38:56	Dorchester, England
4	1979	Herbert Chisholm	53	2:40:32	Alexandria, VA
5	1988	Mel Williams	50	2:40:38	Virginia Beach, VA

Females

1	2001	Annette Hallett	50	3:12:44	Bermuda
2	1987	Joan Reis	50	3:16:30	Scramento, CA
3	1989	Marion Stanjones	51	3:16:35	Northport, NY
4	1998	Paula Martin	52	3:22:22	Clinton, MD
5	2000	Sandra Adams	51	3:22:27	Winchester, VA

Age Group 55-59

Males

Pl	Year	Name	Age	Time	City/State
1	1983	Phillip Gross	56	2:42:31	Birmingham, AL
2	1984	Phillip Gross	57	2:45:05	Birmingham, AL
3	1993	Oleg Morozov	59	2:48:11	Gladstone, MO
4	1982	Herbert Chisholm	56	2:48:52	Alexandria, VA
5	1992	Bernard Goldstein	56	2:51:34	Atlanta, GA

Females

Pl	Year	Name	Age	Time	City/State
1	1993	Wen-Shi Yu	59	3:24:14	Kew Gardens, NY
2	1995	Joan Ullyot	55	3:25:41	Snowmass Village, CO
3	1985	Ruth Anderson	56	3:27:05	Oakland, CA
4	1986	Whayong Semer	58	3:29:04	Fremont, OH
5	1994	Carrie Parsi	55	3:31:43	Lexington, MA

Age Group 60-64

Males

Pl	Year	Name	Age	Time	City/State
1	1984	Francis Demarco	62	2:51:17	South Windsor, CT
2	1991	Philip Watson	60	2:53:26	Simsburg, CT
3	1995	Ruben Cordon	62	2:53:42	New York, NY
4	1987	Edward Roginski	61	2:57:45	Wheaton, MD
5	1983	Francis Demarco	61	2:58:47	South Windsor, CT

Females

Pl	Year	Name	Age	Time	City/State
1	1993	Mary Wilson	63	3:18:20	St. Charles, MO
2	1994	Doris Dean	64	3:22:59	St. Charles, MO
3	1992	Doris Dean	61	3:25:19	Shrewsbury, NJ
4	1998	R. Wuthrich	62	3:25:54	Minto-Ku, Tokyo
5	1995	Wen-Shi Yu	60	3:33:55	Kew Gardens, NY

Age Group 65-69

Males

Pl	Year	Name	Age	Time	City/State
1	1979	Tom Newman	67	2:53:07	Raleigh, NC
2	1986	Anthony Napoli	66	3:05:55	Buffalo, NY
3	2000	Ben Webster	67	3:07:59	Washington, DC
4	1998	Malcolm Gillis	65	3:10:30	Toney, AL
5	1997	Robert Johnson	67	3:11:39	McLean, VA

Females

Pl	Year	Name	Age	Time	City/State
1	1993	Patti Hecht	66	3:46:15	Columbia, MD
2	1992	Shelia Barnett	66	4:00:38	Willowdale, Ontario
3	1991	Shelia Barnett	65	4:06:35	Willowdale, Ontario
4	1995	Shelia Barnett	69	4:15:06	Willowdale, Ontario
5	1985	Althea Wetherbee	66	4:18:05	Huntington Stat., NY

Age Group 70-74

Males

Pl	Year	Name	Age	Time	City/State
1	1993	Anthony Napoli	73	3:30:56	Buffalo, NY
2	1981	Ed Benham	74	3:37:07	Ocean City, MD
3	1992	Carlton Mendell	71	3:41:17	Portland, ME
4	1994	Anthony Napoli	74	3:46:50	Buffalo, NY
5	1988	James Snitzler	70	3:51:01	Potomac, MD

Females

1	2005	Gwen McFarlan	71	4:09:09	Richmond, VA
2	1992	Monica Gardner	72	4:23:14	Herndon, VA
3	1997	Betty Walker	71	4:46:59	Hun. Beach, CA
4	1999	Mary Ehrlich	71	5:15:51	Perris, CA
5	1998	Katie Seccombe	71	5:18:59	Bedlington,

Age Group 75-79

Males

1	1983	Ed Benham	76	3:34:42	Ocean City, MD
2	1985	Ed Benham	78	3:42:57	Ocean City, MD
3	1993	Karl Hackbarth	77	3:55:23	Montclair, VA
4	2005	Robert Borglund	77	4:03:16	Fort Myers, FL
5	1996	Carlton Mendell	75	4:21:22	Portland, ME

Females

1	1998	Margaret Hagerty	75	5:44:24	Concord, NC
2	2003	Mary Ehrlich	75	5:45:07	Perris, CA
3	1993	Donietta Bickley	79	5:47:28	Washington, DC
4	2005	Mary Ehrlich	77	5:47:58	Perris, CA
5	1991	Donietta Bickley	77	5:48:11	College Park, MD

Age Group 80-84

Males

1	2001	Michael Pettes	82	4:16:43	Durham, NC
2	2002	Walt Washburn	80	4:36:14	Vienna, VA
3	1994	Clifford Riordan	80	4:59:03	Gainesville, FL
4	1992	Bennett Brookstein	83	5:26:11	Huntington Valley, PA
5	2004	John Cox	80	6:00:58	Clifton, NJ

Females

1	1995	Dionetta Bickley	81	6:30:00	College Park, MD
2	2003	Margaret Hagerty	80	7:04:28	Concord, NC
3	2005	Margaret Hagerty	82	7:17:52	Concord, NC

Age Group 85-89

Males

Pl	Year	Name	Age	Time	City/State
1	2001	David Newman	89	3:56:11	Boston, MA

Females

Pl	Year	Name	Age	Time	City/State
1	1988	Ruth Rothfarb	87	4:46:25	Cambridge, MA
2	1984	Ruth Rothfarb	86	6:50:36	Cambridge, MA

Top Performance by Year — Wheelchair Division

1   November 7, 1976

2   November 6, 1977
Female
1	Cindy Patton	4:44:48

3   November 5, 1978

4   November 4, 1979
1	Bob Hall	2:26:00

5   November 2, 1980
1	Ken Archer	

6   November 2, 1981
1	Ken Archer	2:44:16

7   November 7, 1982
1	Ken Archer	2:21:11

8   November 6, 1983
1	Ken Archer	2:20:36
2	Joseph Dowling	2:29:45

9   November 4, 1984
1	Wannie Cook	2:23:04

Female
1	Charla Ramsey	

10   November 3, 1985
1	Ken Archer	2:15:30

11   November 2, 1986
1	Ken Archer	2:10:10

12   November 8, 1987
1	Ken Archer	2:04:02

13   November 6, 1988
1	Ken Archer	2:13:48

Female
1	Rose Winand	3:12:08

14   November 5, 1989
1	Ken Carnes	1:54:23

Female
1	Leah Hann	3:24:59

15   November 4, 1990
1	Ken Carnes	1:40:22 Event Record
2	Ken Archer	1:52:39
3	Michael King	2:05:15

Female
1	Diana McClure	2:33:57
2	Laura Schwanger	2:59:13

16   November 3, 1991
1	Steve Lietz	2:02:58
2	Patrick O'Brien	2:30:48
3	Skip Sanders	2:46:32

Female
1	Brenda Smith	2:41:33
2	Shelia Luellen	3:41:04

17 October 25, 1992

1	Ken Carnes	1:48:56
2	Ken Archer	1:49:31
3	David Cruse	1:57:21

18 October 24, 1993

1	Ken Archer	1:49:12
2	James Arendt	2:10:56
3	T.J. Johnson	2:28:51

19 October 23, 1994

1	Ken Archer	1:53:31
2	Larry Binger	2:14:16
3	Cisco Jetter	2:15:21

Female

1	Rose Winand	2:16:25
	Event Record	
2	Susan Katz	3:01:10

20 October 22, 1995

1	Kenneth Carnes	1:48:41
2	Cisco Jetter	1:48:53
3	Todd Robinson	2:10:59

Female

1	Susan Katz	2:45:35
2	Darla Alinovi	2:48:08
3	Courtney Motley	4:31:22

21 October 27, 1996

1	Carlos Moleda	1:55:32
2	Thomas Gorman	2:31:40
3	Michael Atkins	2:47:51

Female

1	Julia Wallace	2:21:09

22 October 27, 1997

1	Michael Postell	1:58:48
2	Dan Andrews	2:13:19
3	Steve Pietz	2:24:32

Female

1	Julia Wallace	2:21:00
2	Jeanne Prins	4:12:44
3	Kathleen Bligh	4:20:17

23 October 25, 1998

1	Jason Fowler	1:58:18
2	Thomas Gorman	2:02:49
3	James Arendt	2:03:20

Female

1	Holly Koester	3:08:16

24 October 24, 1999

1	Ken Carnes	1:59:57
2	Scott Moore	2:19:46
3	Geoffrey Hopkins	2:29:26

Female

1	Holly Koester	3:21:52

25 October 22, 2000

1	Kamel Ayari	1:46:48
2	Kenny Carnes	2:13:29
3	C. David Swaim	2:15:35

Female

1	Holly Koester	3:40:04

26 October 28, 2001

1	Kamel Ayari	1:58:17
2	Patrick Doak	2:04:00
3	Thomas Gorman	2:10:53

27 October 27, 2002

1	Vincent Orlando	3:17:10

Female

1	Holly Koester	3:06:32

28 October 26, 2003

1	David Lowell	2:19:53
2	Brian Woodyard	3:00:23
3	David Ford	3:10:18

Female

1	Holly Koester	3:11:16
2	Barbara Bowling	4:19:31

29 October 31, 2004

1	David Swaim	2:33:58
2	Marcus Krackowizer	4:43:57

30 October 30, 2005

1	David Swope	2:22:53
2	Adrian Miller	2:36:31
3	Tony Choe	2:38:36

Female

1	Holly Koester	4:06:12

31 October 29, 2006

1	Grant Berthiaume	2:11:59
2	David Swope	2:14:33
3	C. David Swaim	2:16:04

Female

1	Leah Mullen	4:11:32
2	Mary Thompson	4:27:08

WINNERS MARGINS 1st & 2nd PLACE

1	November 7, 1976	Time	Margin	Rank
1	Kenny Moore	2:21:14	3:48	24
2	Samuel Maizel	2:25:02		

	Female			
1	Susan Mallery	2:56:33	1:30	5
2	Jennifer White	2:58:03		

2	November 6, 1977			
1	Kevin McDonald	2:19:36	0:33	7
2	Phil Camp	2:20:09		

	Female			
1	Susan Mallery	2:54:04	5:05	22
2	Gail Jones	2:59:09		

3	November 5, 1978			
1	Robert (Scott) Eden	2:18:07	3:47	23
2	Kevin McCarey	2:21:54		

	Female			
1	Jane Killion	3:01:34	4:00	17
2	Kitty Consolo	3:05:33		

4	November 4, 1979			
1	Phil Camp	2:19:35	0:39	8
2	William Albers	2:20:14		

	Female			
1	1stLt Joanna Martin USMC	2:58:08	0:39	3
2	Trudy Rapp	2:58:53		

5	November 2, 1980			
1	Michael Hurd	2:18:38(Adjusted Time)		30
2	Mike Geehan	2:17:46*		

	Female			
1	Jan Yerks	2:41:54(Adjusted Time)		30
2	Laura DeWald	2:42:55*		

6	November 2, 1981			
1	Dean Matthews	2:16:31	1:20	14
2	Hank Pfrifle	2:17:52		

	Female			
1	Cynthia Lorenzoni	2:50:33	3:15	15
2	Beth Dillinger	2:53:48		

7	November 7, 1982	Time	Margin	Rank
1	Jeff Smith	2:21:29	0:25	5
2	Bill Stewart	2:21:54		

	Female			
1	Cynthia Lorenzoni	2:45:51	0:17	1
2	Vicki Randall	2:45:07		

8	November 6, 1983			
1	Sgt. Farley Simon USMC	2:17:46	1:54	16
2	Bill Stewart	2:19:40		

	Female			
1	Suzanne Carden	2:45:55	1:23	4
2	Julie Burke	2:47:19		

9	November 4, 1984			
1	Brad Ingram	2:19:40	1:05	11
2	Thomas Bernard	2:20:45		

	Female			
1	Pamela Briscoe	2:43:20	2:27	9
2	Susan Stone	2:45:47		

10	November 3, 1985			
1	Thomas Bernard	2:19:16	0:30	6
2	Brad Ingram	2:19:47		

	Female			
1	Natalie Updegrove	2:44:42	10:12	27
2	Susie Patterson	2:47:47		

11	November 2, 1986			
1	Brad Ingram	2:23:13	0:52	9
2	John Stevens	2:24:05		

	Female			
1	Kathy Champagne	2:42:59	5:59	24
2	Lucia Geraci	2:48:58		

12	November 8, 1987			
1	Jeff Scuffins	2:14:01*	5:07	26
2	Darrell General	2:19:08		

	Female			
1	Mary Robertson	2:44:34	1:42	6
2	Mary Salamone	2:26:18		

* Course was short

* Open Event Record

13	November 6, 1988	Time	Margin	Rank
1	Jim Hage	2:21:59	0:19	2
2	Brad Ingram	2:22:18		

Female

1	Lori Lawson	2:51:26	0:18	2
2	Ann Wehner	2:51:44		

14	November 5, 1989			
1	Jim Hage	2:20:23	2:04	17
2	Sgt. Farley Simon USMC	2:22:37		

Female

1	Laura DeWald	2:45:16	3:10	14
2	Lori Lawson	2:48:26		

15	November 4, 1990			
1	Matthew Waight	2:21:32	5:09	27
2	Robert Rollins	2:26:41		

Female

1	Olga Markova	2:37:00*	7:48	36
2	Suzanne Ray	2:44:48		

16	November 3, 1991			
1	Carol Rivas	2:17:54	3:18	21
2	Rene Guerrero	2:21:12		

Female

1	Amy Kattwinkel	2:44:27	1:45	7
2	Julie Foster	2:46:12		

17	October 25, 1992			
1	Rene Guerrero	2:24:09	1:16	13
2	Michael Whittlesey	2:25:26		

Female

1	Judy Mercon	2:47:58	2:27	10
2	Kelly Flanagan	2:50:25		

18	October 24, 1993			
1	Dominique Bariod	2:23:56	0:24	4
2	Esteban Vanegas	2:24:20		

Female

1	Holly Ebert	2:48:41	4:52	20
2	Mary Gaylord	2:53:33		

19	October 23, 1994	Time	Margin	Rank
1	Graciano Gonzales	2:22:51	2:15	18
2	Gordon Sanders	2:55:06		

Female

1	Susan Molloy	2:39:34	10:12	28
2	Callie Malloy	2:49:46		

20	October 22, 1995			
1	Darrell General	2:16:34	3:45	22
2	Hernandez Francisco	2:20:19		

Female

1	Claudia Kasen	2:49:21	2:57	12
2	Maria Pazarentos	2:52:18		

21	October 27, 1996			
1	Issac Garcia	2:15:09	7:52	29
2	Samuel Lopez	2:23:01		

Female

1	Emma Cabrera	2:48:34	4:30	19
2	Sharon Servidio	2:53:04		

22	October 27, 1997			
1	Darrell General	2:18:21	4:44	25
2	Alejandro Crus Maya	2:23:25		

Female

1	Donna Moore	2:53:42	1:52	8
2	Selena Smart	2:55:34		

23	October 25, 1998			
1	Weldon Johnson	2:25:31	6:02	28
2	Mark Croasdale	2:31:33		

Female

1	Maj. Kimberly Markland	2:49:07	6:10	25
2	Patti Shull	2:55:18		

24	October 24, 1999			
1	Mark Croasdale	2:23:27	2:43	20
2	Mark Coogan	2:24:18		

Female

1	Donna Moore	2:51:53	4:55	21
2	Bea Marie Altieri	2:56:48		

25 October 22, 2000

1	Lt. Richard Cochran	2:25:50	1:13	12
2	Juan Lopez	2:28:33		

Female

1	Elizabeth Ruel	2:47:52	4:12	18
2	Liz Speegle	2:52:04		

26 October 28, 2001

1	GySgt Farley Simon	2:28:28	1:03	10
2	Lopez Escorcia Juan Samu	2:29:31		

Female

1	Lori Stich Zimmerman	2:48:13	5:44	23
2	Tara Pointin	2:54:01		

27 October 27, 2002

1	Capt. Christopher Juarez	2:25:01	1:20	15
2	John Sence	2:26:31		

Female

1	Elizabeth Scanlon	2:57:27	3:26	16
2	Jacaquline Chen	3:00:53		

28 October 26, 2003

1	Peter Sherry	2:25:07	2:42	19
2	Eric Post	2:27:49		

Female

1	Heather Hanscom	2:37:59	20:47	29
2	Lindsay Gannon	2:58:46		

29 October 31, 2004

1	Retta Feyissa	2:25:35	0:22	3
2	Terrance Shea	2:25:57		

Female

1	Mary Kate Sullivan-Bailey	2:48:31	2:46	11
2	LCMDR Kimberly Fagen	2:51:17		

30 October 30, 2005

1	Ruben Garcia	2:22:18	0:08	1
2	Carl Rundell	2:22:26		

Female

1	Susannah Kvasnicka	2:47:10	3:03	13
2	Liz Wilson	2:50:03		

31 October 29, 2006

1	Ruben Garcia	2:21:20	3:02	21
2	Carl Rundell	2:24:22		

Female

1	Laura Thompson	3:00:22	2:12	9
2	Brenda Schrank	3:02:34		

GySgt Farley Simon, USMC (Ret)

Farley Simon was born on the island of Grenada, West Indies. He came to the U.S. in 1971 (age 17) with his family. They settled in New York and he later joined the Marines. In 1983, Sgt. Simon became the first active duty male Marine to win the MCM in a time of 2:17:46 (his marathon debut and his best time to date). The Marines were denied for seven years. He was fueled by a statement a reporter made in 1981 about how it was too bad that one of the Marine's own could not win the race. He set the second fastest winning time and qualified for the U.S. Olympic Marathon Trials.

He was runner up in 1989 (2:22:37), and in 1995 he was fourth in 2:25:25 and the first master.

He retired in 2000 afer 22 years of service. In 2001, at the age of 46, he became the first retired Marine to win the race overall and became the oldest winner and first master. His time was 2:28:28. He became the second person to hold and open and master title.

His personal records are: mile 4:03.5, 3000, 8:35, 10K road 29:45, half-marathon 1:06:02, and marathon 2:17:46.

Joanna Martin

1stLt. Joanna Martin is a 1976 graduate from the University of Missouri – Columbia. In 1979 she became the first active duty Marine to win the women's division of the marathon while stationed at Quantico, Va., in a time of 2:58:14. Her father was a Marine and it was a natural for her to join the Marine Corps. She had reached her first duty station in April of 1977 and her training started from ground zero. She ran her first Marine Corps Marathon in a time of 3:10:26. It was almost six months before she had a full recovery. In 1978, she returned but dropped out.

In 1979 the mission was to win. "I was really gearing up for the race and I should have run a better race. My training was 60 to 90 miles a week. I was running 10Ks at a six minute pace. In the last six miles of the race, I knew that I was in first place. I learned after that I was several weeks pregnant."

During the time she was training, there were no digital watches and in colleges there were not many options in running shoes. She would just go out and run. There is more information available today about running.

"Winning the Marine Corps Marathon was a high point for me and even today a great memory. It's also a picture of working to achieve something and to do something well. I am glad to have that," stated Martin.

Her record stood until 2004 when Captain Mary Kate Bailey was the second female Marine to win in a time of 2:48:31.

26th MCM 2001

Colonel Herb Harmon, USMCR (Ret)

In 1978 Herb Harmon assumed the position of Chairman of the Marine Corps Marathon Ad Hoc Publicity Committee. He is an advocate of change and a protector of the marathon. He went about forming a diverse body of support for the vision of Colonel Fowler and the mission of the marathon. The primary purpose was to serve as the transitional body for the transfer of the marathon from the Marine Reserves to the active duty Marines. In the early years, the marathon leadership would rotate every one or two years and the committee remained active in recruiting celebrity participants and publicity from print media, radio, and local television stations. He was instrumental in providing the leadership for the committee, (the first committee included Michael Carberry, Jim Coates, Col. Jim Fowler, Bill Mayhugh, Buff Mundale, Michael T. Harrigan and Joe Trainor), which relayed issues to the attention of the Marine Corps, such as paving the way for the changes involving trademark and sponsorship.

Harmon was born in Columbus, Ohio and is a partner of Harmon, Wilmot and Brown, LLP and a graduate of Georgetown University Law Center. In 1968, he was a platoon commander in Vietnam and retired from the Marine Corps Marine Reserve with the rank of Colonel in 1998. He served as the Reserve Officers Association National President from 1997-1998. He is a member of the Military Order of the Purple Heart, former National Judge Advocate General of the Marine Corps Aviation Association and a life member of the Marine Corps League.

Colonel Harmon has served as a former prosecutor, past president of the Bar Association of DC and as a Mediator for the District of Columbia Superior Court. He is a member of the Civil Affairs Association and the Psychological Operations Association, a former member of the International Chair of Commission II, NATO International Reserve Officers Association, and a member and former Treasurer of the Barristers and past President of the Counsellors.

Mel Williams

Mel Williams' daily running routine was part of his training while on active duty in the U.S. Army. He served from June 1955 to June 1958 with the 11th Airborne Division as a paratrooper medic.

Williams graduated from East Stroudsburg University, East Stroudsburg, Pa., (B.S. 1962), Ohio University, Athens, Ohio (M. Ed-1963) and the University of Maryland, College Park, Md. (PhD-1968). At Old Dominion University, he taught Physiology of Exercise, Kinesiology, and Nutrition for Fitness and Sport.

The active running started in 1972 with the formation of a local running club, The Tidewater Striders out of the Norfolk/Virginia Beach, Va., area.
Williams leads the group of five who have completed all 30 MCMs. When it

comes to performance, he managed over the years to dominate each of his age groups since turning a master (age 40 and over). There have been 21 sub-3 hour marathons. A back injury affected the time in 1995, which resulted in a time of 3:10:50, and a hamstring injury in 1996 resulted in a time of 3:31:26, his slowest time ever. His best performance was in 1982 with a 2:34:49, which was good for third master.

He has run seven between 2:35 – 2:40, eight between 2:40 – 2:50, six between 2:50 – 3:00, and nine 3:00 and over.

In the 40-44 age group, Williams has collected 2 third place finishes. In the 45-49 age group, there have been 3 first place and 2 second place finishes. In the 50-54 age group, there have been 5 first place finishes. In the 55-59 age group there have been 2 first place and 1 second place finishes. In the 60-64 there have been 5 first place finishes. In the 65-69 age group there have been 3 first place finishes.

The first Marine Corps Marathon (wearing bib number 206), in 1976 (his third marathon overall) was two weeks after running the New York City Marathon (2:55). There were no expectations since he was at a party until 2 a.m., race morning. He took a four-hour nap before making the trip from Columbia, Md., to Washington. The lack of sleep did not work against the performance as Williams ran 2:51:41 (86th place overall).

"My perspective on racing is simply to finish the race, particularly marathons. If I set an objective, such as a particular time, but do not make it, normally it does not bother me unless I made some mistake that contributed to my not making the objective. My distant goal is simply to continue to run as well as I can for both competition and health," said Williams.

Williams enjoys reading historical novels and loves traveling to foreign countries, especially if there is a marathon available.

27th MCM 2002
Commander Al Rich
Commander Al Rich from Dorchester, England was one of the moving forces on the British Royal Navy/Marine team. The inaugural Challenge Cup team competition started in 1978 of which he was a member and ran a 2:37:23 at the age of 27 and placed 47th. He rose from team member to team captain. He is always soft spoken and displays wit at the Challenge Cup team dinners at the Portofino Restaurant. He made 13 appearances out of the 28 years of competition. His best time was run in 1986 at the 9th Challenge Cup competition with a time of 2:33:51 (35th overall).

In 1990, he was the third master with a time of 2:34:36 and placed 35th overall. The following year he was the first master with a time of 2:34:02 (24th overall). In 1992, he made a successful defense of his master's title with a time of 2:34:55 (23rd overall). In the 30-year history of the race, only three runners have been back-to-back winners: Rusty Lamade (1977-2:32:30, 1978-2:32:17), Al Rich, and Francisco Lugo (1998-2:35:33, 1999-2:31:10).

He continued to demonstrate his athletic performance by taking first in the age group 45-49 in 1995 (2:34:44) and 1997 (2:42:09). In 2004, he ran 2:57:55 at the age of 54 and all of his times have been under three hours.

Commander Rich was instrumental in starting the Warriors of the Sea Challenge in 1997, which is held in conjunction with the Plymouth Half-Marathon in England. Each team runs for the two-foot silver mounted cup. This event is an extension of the good-natured competition between the two teams.

1978	2:27:23
1979	2:42:22
1980	2:36:33
1985	2:36:26
1986	2:33:51
1990	2:34:36
1991	2:34:02
1992	2:34:55
1994	2:37:45
1995	2:34:44
1997	2:42:09
2001	2:51:21
2004	2:57:55

Dr. Dave Brody, M.D.

Dr. Dave Brody, M.D., started his involvement with the MCM by assisting at one of the water stops along the course in 1976. He ran the race in 1977 (4:10:31) and again in 1978 (4:13:22). The third year it was unseasonably warm and at the water stop under the Whitehurst Freeway he noticed they were sharing the ladles to serve the water. This prompted him to make a phone call to the marathon office and he was asked to serve as the Medical Director for the marathon.

Dr. Brody took the initiative to form a complete medical staff with top notch clinical personnel and supplies from George Washington University and Georgetown University. All they wanted in return were t-shirts; the response was overwhelming.

One year they had the staff in West Potomac Park (between miles 18 and 19) and they had to relocate back to the finish line. He had to walk in front of their vehicle to keep from hitting the runners. He realized some changes had to be made and the process was ever evolving. The method of medical communication was through the use of HAMM radio operators. The practice was to call back to the main medical tent and they would only say "Runner Down" for any situation and he quickly realized that more detailed information was required.

"I love the Marine Corps. I have always lectured to runners. The original idea stemmed from the danger to the runners at the aid situations. The interest was primarily for the runners. I saw and the Marines realized the race was a potential for a mass casualty situation, which required multi-special personnel," said Dr. Brody.

One year a runner suffered a heart attack along the course near the Lincoln Memorial and the person was revived. The following year, at the same location, the same doctor treated the same person who suffered another heart attack, and once again he was revived.

In the mid 1980s, the medical coverage was taken over by the U.S. Navy and according to Dr. Brody they have been doing an outstanding job. He remains the civilian medical consultant.

Dr. Brody has remained involved through the series of lecture he provides each year to runners of all abilities. He stays because of the concern for all of the runners and, secondly, the Marines are wonderful and in his heart he is a Marine. He ran again at the 25th Anniversary in 2000 (6:44:14). He has written two books on running injuries.

- *Founder of the Runner's Clinic at George Washington University in 1978*
- *Member of the American Society of Sports Physicians*
- *American College of Sports Medicine*
- *American Board of Orthopedic Surgeons*
- *VP of the International Medical Marathon Director Association.*

28th MCM 2003

Jim Hage

Jim Hage was inducted into the Hall of Fame in 2003, the only back-to-back winner, 1988 (2:21:59) and 1989 (2:20:23). He had two years of placing third (1984-2:22:40, 1985-2:23:30), which was during the Ingram dynasty.

In 1987, he was coming off a good running season with a PR at the Nike Cherry Blossom 10 Mile Run in 48:35, April, Washington, DC. At the Philadelphia Distance Run, half-marathon he ran 1:04:30. He has a marathon PR of 2:15:51, Columbus, Ohio in November 1992.

At the age of 15, he ran his first marathon, the Maryland Marathon in Baltimore (1973) where 150 quit the race because it was too challenging. The following year he attempted the JFK 50 Miler and in an icy rain he dropped out after 30 miles. At the age of 44, he won the 40th JFK 50 Miler in 6:13:10 (November 2002) becoming the oldest winner in the history of the race.

He ran 2:16:27 at the 1992 U.S. Olympic Marathon Trials. In 1988 he was 26th and in 1996 he was 37th. He was a member of the U.S. World Cup Marathon team in 1989 (Milan) and 1993 (San Sebastian, Spain).

In 1998, at the age of 40, he ran the Boston Marathon and finished in 2:22. He was inducted into the D.C. Road Runners Hall of Fame in April 2005.

Hage is a legal editor at the Bureau of National Affairs and running corres-pondent to the *Washington Post, Running Times* magazine, and the *Washington Running Report*.

Bill Mayhugh

He is known as the original "Voice of the Marathon" and one of the founding members of the Ad Hoc Publicity Committee, Inc. While a broadcaster with radio WMAL, he helped to establish and promote the marathon.

29th MCM 2004

Darrell General

In 1983, at the age of 17, he ran his first MCM and placed 9th in the age group 19 and under in 2:58:55. The following year, he placed second in his age group in a time of 2:24:36. In 1985, he placed first in his age group with 2:26:52, the second fastest time in the history of the race for his age group. In 1987, he placed second overall in the race with a 2:19:08 at the age of 21. This is the MCM record for the age group 20-24. No other runner has gone under 2:20. He won the 1995 race in 2:16:34 (the fourth fastest winning time), and again in 1997 with a 2:18:21 (the eighth fastest winning time).

He was the youngest Olympic marathon trials qualifier at age 22 for the 1988 U.S. Olympic Marathon Trials. He has 11 consecutive USA Marathon Championship appearances (1992-2002): 1988- 2:20:31, 19th, 1989 – 2:14:42 (PR), 3rd, 1990 – 2:19:25, 24th, 1992 – 2:25:02, 30th; 1993-2:16:08, 6th; 1994-2:18:47, 3rd; 1995-2:19:07, 8th; 1996-2:16:30, 12th; 1997-2:22:47, 10th; 1998-2:17:58, 4th; 1999-2:25:50, 16th; 2000-2:28:41, 35th; 2001-2:20:20, 6th, 2002- 2:29:02, 18th. General was the best American at the 1990 Boston Marathon, 14th place in 2:15:28. His personal best time for the marathon is 2:14:42.

He is one of five who have qualified for five U.S. Olympic Marathon Trials (1988, 1992, 1996, 2000, and 2004). He is the first male qualifier to complete five U.S.

Olympic Marathon Trials: 1988 – 2:20:31 (19th), 1992 – 2:25:02 (30th), 1996 – 2:16:30 (12th), 2000 – 2:28:41 (35th), and 2004 – 2:33:20 (67th).

Cynthia Lorenzoni

Cynthia Lorenzoni (formerly Wadsworth), of Charlottesville, Va., grew up in Farmington, Connecticut where the foundation of her running began. In high school, she was the open champion in 1973 – 1975 in cross country (Connecticut Interscholastic Athletic Conference Girls Cross Country). At the State Open Meet she won the two-mile race in 11:03 and set a national record. Later in the day, she won the mile in 5:09.

She was a scholarship athlete (recognized for her academic and athletic abilities) and attended Michigan State University (MSU) where she was team captain in track and field and cross country. She was the top Spartan at the Big Ten Championships in 1976 (17:21 – 2nd place) and in 1979 (18:16 – 5th place). "One thing I learned in college, the longer the race was, the better I became."

She returned to competition after training with Olympian Margaret Groos (UVA graduate) who set school records from 1500 meters to 10,000 meters. The two would do long runs every weekend of 10-15 miles. In 1981, the weekend before the Marine Corps Marathon, she ran 20 miles and then decided to enter the race to see what it was all about. She ran the distance at a 6:30 pace. She won in 2:50:33.

In 1982, she felt that she could run a sub-2:40. She was running in a pair of Converse that caused problems. "At mile 19, my feet were bleeding and I was in so much pain and I was going to drop out. I saw my husband at mile 20 and he told me the leader, Laura DeWald had dropped out and that I was in the lead and had to finish," she continued for the win in 2:45:51.

At the 1984 U.S. Women's Olympic Marathon Trials (Olympia, Wash.) she ran 2:42:42 and she placed 45th out of 196 finishers. She tells her children to never have any regrets in life and is happy that she had the opportunity to make the Trials.

At the Houston Marathon in 1983, she ran her personal record for the marathon in a time of 2:38. This was a high point in her running career and she did not want to leave the sport feeling like she should have tried harder.

She worked at the Frank Shorter Running Store in East Lansing while attending MSU. She met her husband, Mark, at MSU and in 1980 they relocated to Charlottesville, Va. In 1982, they opened the Ragged Mountain Running Shop.

In the early '80s they partnered with the Charlottesville Track Club to start the Charlottesville Women's Four Miler to support the UVa Cancer Center Breast Care Program. In 2005 the race raised $100,000.

30th MCM 2005

Mary Robertson Wittenberg

Mary Robertson Wittenberg was inducted into the Marine Corps Marathon Hall of Fame in 2005. She won the 1987 marathon with a time of 2:44:34. In 1993, she placed 21st in 3:06:15.

She was raised in Buffalo, New York, the oldest of seven children. During high school she was a cheerleader until her senior year when she joined the crew team at the West Side Rowing Club.

She majored in English at Canisius College in New York (1984). She continued crew and was the coxswain at the West Side Rowing Club. In 1983 she entered the Mayor Jimmy Griffin Four Mile Race and finished first. In her senior year she trained with the men's cross country team.

In 1984 she attended law school at Notre Dame in South Bend, Indiana. There she trained with the men's cross country team in between studies. As a result she ran the 1985 Chicago Marathon and finished 16th (2:46) and qualified for the 1988 U.S. Olympic Trials.

After law school, she joined the law offices of Hunton and Williams where she specialized in international trade deals for U.S. banks. In 1994 she relocated to firm's New York office and eventually met her husband, Derek. In 1997 she was made a partner.

In 1998, Wittenberg transitioned from the law profession to accept a position as the Executive Vice President of Administration of the New York Road Runners Club. This was the highest position held by a woman in the history of the club.

On April 1, 2005, Wittenberg became the race director of the ING New York City Marathon and the president and CEO of the New York Road Runner's Club.

Allan Steinfeld the vice chairman of the New York Road Runners and executive director of the New York Marathon provides an account of Wittenberg:

"Upon the passing of my good friend and mentor Fred Lebow, I took over the leadership of the New York Road Runners and the New York City Marathon. Prior to that I was the COO/EVP and the Technical Director of the Marathon. We were essentially Mr. Inside (Allan) and Mr. Outside (Fred). I realized after many years that I could not fulfill my duties running the NYRR on a day-to-day basis and also continue to be involved with our sponsors, city agencies, national and international running governing bodies and organizations. So, in the summer of 1998, we did an executive search for a COO/EVP and my eventual successor.

"I was looking for a bright, articulate individual who possessed the skills that were needed for the position. That fall we hired Mary Wittenberg, a lawyer, who had good managerial skills, a sharp mind and could relate well to people. First and foremost I wanted a business associate, but I got something more. Mary had been a top runner and won the Marine Corps Marathon in 1987 and was passionate about running and the sport of running. Over these many years I mentored Mary, as Fred did me, and gave her the opportunity to expand her horizons of the sport first on the national scene and then the international front, while all the while running the day-to-day operations of Road Runners. Mary was a quick learner and not afraid to get her hands 'dirty.'

At the end of 2004, I was considering stepping back from my role, and I knew that Mary was capable and ready to assume the top position at New York Road Runners. So at the end of March 2005, we announced that effective April 1, 2005 Mary Wittenberg would assume the role of Presdent/CEO of New York Road Runners and Race Director of the ING New York City Marathon, and I would become the Vice Chairman of NYRR and Executive Director of the marathon. Mary is our first woman President/CEO and Race Director. She is carrying on the legacy that Fred Lebow and I left for her. I am sure that we will see great things from her as she carries out our mandate to reach out to our community, be the best running organization and, of course, continue to be the greatest marathon in the world."

Major General Michael P. Ryan

Major General Michael P. Ryan USMC (Ret) was born in Osage City, Kansas. He attended Rockhurst College in Missouri, and later George Washington University majoring in Political Science. He died at the age of 88 on January 9, 2005 of a heart attack in Northridge, Calif.

In 1933 he entered into the Marine Corps Reserves and was called to active duty in 1940 with the 15th Reserve Battalion of Galveston, Texas, and was commissioned as a second lieutenant. As a major he was Company Commander Company L, 3rd Battalion, 2nd Marines Division. He took part in Operation Galvanic, November 20-24, 1943, the Battle for Tarawa. The mission was to seize an airfield the Japanese had constructed on Betio Island, Tarawa Atoll, in the Gilbert Islands, now a part of the Republic of Kiribati.

As the Marines landed on the beachhead, they were met with strong enemy fire. Major Ryan assembled a composite battalion and over the next two days they took over the western end of Betio. This proved to be a costly battle for the Marines with 3,000 casualties and, of the 4,700 defenders of the airfield, only 17 survived.

Major Ryan was awarded the Navy Cross for action at Tarawa. In recognition of his gallantry, he was awarded the British Distinguished Service Cross. The Navy Cross citation reads:

"For extraordinary heroism, great determination and leadership, conspicuous fighting spirit, great personal bravery, and tactical skill, When his battalion commander failed to reach shore, senior officer Ryan assumed command of the badly disorganized and isolated survivors of three battalion. He organized and directed critical operations of these elements throughout the battle until he was relieved, leading assaults on enemy positions, retaining initiative in his sector, and clearing his isolated beachhead into which reinforcements could be moved."

In January 1974, General Ryan assumed duty as Director, Marine Corps Reserve Division, Headquarters Marine Corps, until his retirement July 1, 1977 – a career of 44 years. General Ryan had approved the request of Col. James Fowler to start the first Marine Corps Reserve Marathon, which was later changed to the Marine Corps Marathon. In 1976 it was unofficially called "Ryan's Run" and it was the largest first-time marathon, which attracted 1,175 runners of which 1,018 finished (994 males and 24 females). It was started as a recuiting and publicity tool for the Marine Corps. There had been a concern if anyone would attend.

31st MCM 2006

Ken Archer

He was born in Lodi, Ohio in 1949 and served in the U.S. Army from December 1967 until February 1972. As a result of being smashed between two auto-mobiles, he lost his legs.

"In 1976, Bob Hall from Boston, MA did a marathon exhibition in a parking lot of a shopping center in Toledo, Ohio. I lived near Akron at that time. He did this during a wheelchair track meet in Toledo. At that time the longest competition they had was the mile. He said, 'It was no problem,' and everyone idolized him and thought at that time he wasn't even human! I started out playing wheelchair basketball and three of the team members also competed in wheelchair track and field. I began to correspond with Bobby and he encouraged me to compete in the Boston Marathon," said Archer.

He adds, "So, I packed my bags and competed in the first National Wheelchair Marathon in Boston in 1977 as one of seven wheelchair athletes."

In 1979 he returned to Boston and placed first in 2:38:59. A controversy arose at the Glass City Marathon in Toledo, Ohio in 1979 where he crossed first in 2:22:54 and the first able-bodied runner Bob McOmber in 2:24:44. The organizers awarded the overall win to McOmber and presented Archer with a special award.

In 1979, mentor Bobby Hall won the Marine Corps in 2:26:00 and the following year Archer won his first of 10 titles. His best time at the Marine Corps came in 1993 with a time of 1:49:12. He had a five-year winning streak 1980 – 1983 and this had not been repeated.

At the 1991 Midnight Sun Ultra Challenge, a 367 mile race from Fairbanks to Anchorage, Alaska he placed first and in 1992 he was second.

In a memorable moment, from 1994, "I escorted a wheelchair athlete, Daria Alinovi from Long Island, New York to the race. I remember spending several hours with two racing buddies the day before the race one of who was Kenny Carnes (5-time MCM winner and race record holder 1:40:22-1990) helping me put it together and getting it ready for racing. It rained the next day and I remembered being excited at how well I did using an untested new wheelchair in the rain." He won the race in a time of 1:53:31.

He has collected several titles from the NPC Wheelchair Body Building Championships, 1995 first place masters, 1997 – second place men's light heavyweight, 1998 – second place men's heavyweight.

He works at the Bureau of Labor Statistics as a Mathematical Statistician. He obtained a Masters Degree in Mathematical Statistics from Akron University (1979) and in Computer Science from Bowie University (1989).

He adds, "Currently, I'm in a serious rebuilding stage after many surgeries. It's been a real long haul rebuilding muscle as they tore a rotator cuff and damaged a C-5 nerve to my right bicep. I hope to participate in live competition again soon."

Colonel H.C. "Barney" Barnum, Jr., USMC (Ret.)

Colonel Barnum was born July 21, 1940 in Cheshire, Connecticut. While attending St. Anselm College in Manchester, New Hampshire, he joined the Platoon Leadership Class. He joined the Marine Corps in November 12, 1958, received a Bachelor of Arts in Economics and was commissioned a second lieutenant upon graduation in 1962.

He served 27 years more, and retired on August 1, 1989. He was the fourth Marine to be awarded the nation's highest honor, the Medal of Honor for valor in Vietnam where he served two tours. On December 18, 1965, during his first tour in Vietnam, he displayed leadership and courage and was wounded, which led to the award.

In 1985 he joined the Ad Hoc Publicity Committee and continued after retirement. He was instrumental in moving the MCM Expo to the Sheraton Hotel where he worked.

He has served as the Principal Director, Drug Enforcement Policy, Office of the Secretary of Defense. He is the former President of the Congressional Medal of Honor Society. On July 21, 2001 he was appointed by the President as the Deputy Assistant Secretary of the Navy for Reserve Affairs.

ARMED FORCES MARATHON CHAMPIONSHIP

Since 1998 the Armed Forces Marathon Championship has been conducted in conjunction with the Marine Corps Marathon. The Armed Forces Sports programs serve under the direction of the Armed Forces Sports Council, which is under the direction of the Department of Defense.

The objectives of the Armed Forces Sports Program are to:
- Promote goodwill among the Armed Services through sports.
- Promote the positive image of the Armed Services through sports.
- Provide an incentive and encourage physical fitness by promoting a highly competitive sports program.
- Provide an avenue for military athletes to participate in national and international competitions.

The military team standings are determined by adding the chip time of the top three male finishers and the top two female finishers from each team. The team with the lowest total time wins.

1st 23rd MCM 10-25-98

1. U.S. Air Force	10:51:29
2. U.S. Marine Corps	11:18:43
3. U.S. Army	11:22:01
4. U.S. Navy	11:22:37

2nd 24th MCM 10-24-99

1. U. S. Marine Corps	10:56:15
2. U.S. Air Force	11:06:0
3. U.S. Navy	11:29:52
4. U.S. Army	11:45:40

3rd 25th MCM 10-22-00

1. U.S. Air Force		10:18:13*
Mark Cucuzzella	2:28:55*	
Jon Schoenberg	2:35:49*	
Curt Rogers	2:35:55*	
Michael Mann	2:37:34*	
Amy Nesbit	3:02:15	
Brenda Schrank	3:13:06	
2. U.S. Navy		10:35:20
Richard Cochran	2:25:50	
Michael Ferreira	2:40:37	
Mohamed Chankhte	2:42:11	
Mark Bell	2:46:42	
3. U.S. Marine Corps		10:41:07
Rob Adams	2:33:11	
Alex Hetherington	2:36:15	
Jay Belmarez	2:39:52	
Edwin Holloway, Jr.	2:51:49	

4. U.S. Army		11:10:04
Gary Brimmer	2:38:40	
Shannon Swords	2:42:33	
John Weaver	2:53:49	
Mariano Barajas	2:55:02	
Jacqueline Chen	3:04:27	

4th 26th MCM 10-28-01

1. U.S. Army		11:10:02
Gerardo Aliva	2:28:36*	
Benjamin Sandy	2:41:36*	
Shannon Swords	2:45:35*	
Jacqueline Chen	3:04:05*	
Margaret Bozgoz	3:15:32	
2. U.S. Air Force		11:11:21
Jon Schoenberg	2:37:04	
Mike Wasson	2:43:08	
Steve Bremner	2:48:11	
John Engesser	2:49:55	
Brenda Schrank	3:02:58	
Heidi McKenna	3:11:19	
3. U.S. Marine Corps		11:16:02
Alexander Hetherington	2:38:05	
Douglas Marocco	2:41:48	
Steven Schmid	2:51:38	
Charles Blaisley	2:52:38	
MaryKare	3:04:31	
Sullivan-Bailey		
Kristin McCann	3:09:01	

4. U.S. Navy INC

William Swick	2:38:50
Mohamedi Chakhte	2:41:12
Michael Ferreira	2:53:57

1. U.S. Air Force 7:39:47

Christopher Juarez	2:25:01
Mark Cucuzzella	2:34:36
Jon Scheonberg	2:40:00
Michael Mann	2:41:34
Brenda Schrank	3:04:39
Heidi McKenna	3:07:44

2. U.S. Army 7:44:23

3. U.S. Marine Corps 7:48:09

1. U.S. Air Force 11:00:01

Mark Cucuzzella	2:28:37*
Michael Mann	2:37:31*
Bob Dickie	2:40:20*
Heidi McKenna	3:08:13*
Amy Nesbit	4:03:04

2. U.S. Army 11:14:59

Gerardo Aliva	2:32:59
Ted Leblow	2:35:54
John Weaver	2:58:30
Page Karsteter	2:58:54
Jacqueline Chen	3:07:36
Margaret Bozgoz	3:11:07

3. U.S. Marine Corps 11:31:15

Alexander Hetherington	2:37:07
Greg Mislick	2:49:15
Matthew Limbert	2:53:32
Chad Walton	2:54:26
Ginger Beals	3:11:21
Kristin McCann	3:24:21

4. U.S. Navy 11:33:54

William Swice	2:43:37
Saad Elmoutawakel	2:48:00
Geoffrey Weber	2:54:40
Michael Raney	2:58:28
Suzanne Himes	3:07:37
Lori Krayer	3:31:45

1. U.S. Marine Corps 10:38:05

William Edwards	2:35:16	
Andrew Bartle	2:36:37	
Alexander Hetherington	2:37:41	
Mary Kate Bailey	2:48:31	1st Place Winner
Nathan Flores	2:50:21	
Jennifer Ledford	3:09:01	

2. U.S. Air Force 10:52:49

Christopher Juarez	2:26:03
Mark Cucuzzella	2:39:41
Michael Mann	2:40:39
Jon Schoenberg	2:50:38
Mike Lilly	2:58:47
Jill Metzer	3:06:26
Amy Nesbitt	3:09:30

3. U.S. Navy 11:12:41

Timothy Fahey	2:43:21
Richard Hayes III	2:48:48
Loren Masouka	2:49:15
Kimberly Fagen	2:51:17
Eleanor Stewart-Garbrecht	3:05:47

4. U.S. Army 11:21:49

Liam Collins	2:38:13
Timothy Vandervlugt	2:45:17
Nathan Pennington	2:51:45
Mark Davis	2:54:36
Sage Stefiuk	3:06:36
Jacqueline Chen	3:11:43

1. U.S. Army 10:36:00

Keith Matiskella	2:30:42
Liam Collins	2:34:06
Zeke Austin	2:36:13
Wayne Blas	2:41:15
Emily Brozozowski	2:54:58
Jacqueline Chen	3:19:06

2. U.S. Navy 10:39:48

John Mentzer	2:24:26
Jon Clemens	2:30:25
William Swick	2:41:01
Richard Hayes	2:47:34
Melissa Cole	3:03:56

3. U.S. Marine Corps 10:59:01
Alexander Hetherington	2:35:23
William Edwards	2:35:33
Andrew Bartle	2:36:05
Jeffrey Klemmer	2:38:55
Tara Smith	3:12:00

4. U.S. Air Force 11:29:18
Mark Cucuzella	2:34:46
Levi Severson	2:38:41
John Worley	2:39:37
Benjamin Sandy	2:40:48
Brenda Schrank	3:06:31
Jill Metzger	3:06:39

9th   **31st MCM 10-29-06**

1. U.S. Air Force 13:42:43
Ben Payne	2:28:06
Levi Severson	2:31:26
Mark Cucuzzella	2:32:45
Jason Schlarb	2:36:42
Brenda Schrank	3:02:34
Elissa Ballas	3:07:52

2. U.S. Navy 14:19:42
Philip Reutlinger	2:33:26
Timothy Fahey	2:36:04
Wallace Miller II	2:42:22
Loren Masaoka	2:48:51
Suzanne Himes	3:02:56
Cinda Brown	3:24:54

3. U.S. Marine Corps 14:34:10
Timothy Tapply	2:34:40
Alexander Hetherington	2:38:35
Andrew Bartle	2:42:12
Thomas Blackwell	2:52:04
Kyleanne Hunter	3:19:37
Ginger Beals	3:27:55

4. U.S. Army 14:41:45
Liam Collins	2:37:54
Daniel Welsh	2:38:22
Zekiel Austin	2:39:46
Shawn Dodge	2:40:03
Mary Wollschlager	3:22:08
Jacqueline Chen	3:23:35

Finisher Numbers Male and Female 1976 – 2006

No	Date	Male	%	Female	%	Finishers	Fee
1	11-7-76	994	98	24	2	1018	$2
2	11-6-77	2279	97	87	3	2366	$5
3	11-5-78	4462	95	238	5	4700	$5
4	11-4-79	5090	93	393	7	5483	$7.50
5	11-2-80	5915	95	349	5	6264	$7.50
6	11-2-81	6312	96	244	4	6556	$7.50
7	11-7-82	7513	88	1003	12	8516	$10
8	11-6-83	7285	88	1032	12	8317	$12
9	11-9-84	7441	86	1163	14	8604	$12
10	11-3-85	6640	85	1179	15	7819	$12
11	11-2-86	6719	85	1194	15	7913	$12
12	11-8-87	7505	85	1304	15	8809	$15
13	11-6-88	7504	83	1494	17	8998	$15
14	11-5-89	8430	84	1654	16	10084	$17
15	11-4-90	8821	81	2085	19	10906	$17
16	11-3-91	9224	82	2064	18	11288	$22
17	10-25-92	9078	81	2184	19	11262	$21
18	10-24-93	9570	80	2460	20	12030	$21
19	10-23-94	9795	77	2880	23	12675	$28
20	10-22-95	10902	74	3716	26	14618	$28
21	10-27-96	10950	72	4269	28	15219	$30
22	10-26-97	9655	69	4355	31	14010	$35
23	10-25-98	8365	64	4784	36	13149	$40
24	10-24-99	8712	61	5656	39	14368	$45
25	10-22-00	10376	61	6672	39	17048	$60
26	10-28-01	8567	60	5774	40	14341	$60
27	10-27-02	8624	61	5434	39	14058	$75
28	10-26-03	9758	61	6210	39	15968	$80
29	10-24-04	9699	59	6700	41	16399	$85
30	10-30-05	11159	60	7682	40	18841	$85
31	10-29-06	11791	56	9134	44	20925	$85
	Totals	249135		93417		342552	

Marathon Leadership

NO	DATE	DIRECTOR	COORDINATOR	COMMANDANT USMC
1	11-07-76	Col. James Fowler	Capt. Dorthory L. Edwards	Gen. Louis H. Wilson, Jr. 26th
2	11-06-77	Col. James Fowler	Maj. J. Drucker	Gen. Louis H. Wilson, Jr.
3	11-05-78	Col. J.P. Monahan	Capt. Jim Burke/ Capt. Dave Young	Gen. Louis H. Wilson, Jr.
4	11-04-79	Col. J.P. Monahan	Capt. Bob Dodson	Gen. Robert H. Barrow 27th
5	11-02-80	Col. J.P. Monahan	Capt. Jay M. Paxton, Jr.	Gen. Robert H. Barrow
6	11-02-81	Col. O.K. Steele	Capt. Rick W. Goodale. Jr.	Gen. Robert H. Barrow
7	11-07-82	LtGen R.E. Cary	Maj. R.G. Napier	Gen. Robert H. Barrow
8	11-06-83	MajGen D.M. Twomey	Capt. E. Sol Griffin, Jr.	Gen. Paul X. Kelley 28th
9	11-09-84	MajGen D.M. Twomey	Capt. C.N. Moody	Gen. Paul X. Kelley
10	11-03-85	LtGen D.M. Twomey	Capt. C.N. Moody	Gen. Paul X. Kelley
11	11-02-86	LtGen D.M. Twomey	Capt. Jose D. Rovira	Gen. Paul X. Kelley
12	11-08-87	LtGen F.E. Petersen	Capt. Jose D. Rovira	Gen. Alfred M. Gray, Jr. 29th
13	11-06-88	LtGen W.R. Etnyre	Capts S.D. Olmstead/ A.C. Caldwell	Gen. Alfred M. Gray, Jr.
14	11-05-89	LtGen W.R. Etnyre	Maj. S.D. Olmstead	Gen. Alfred M. Gray, Jr.
15	11-04-90	LtGen E.T. Cook, Jr.	Capt. M.H. Fields, Jr.	Gen. Alfred M. Gray, Jr.
16	11-03-91	LtGen W.E. Boomer	Capt. J.O. Thorson, III	Gen. Carl E. Mundy, Jr. 30th
17	10-25-92	LtGen CharlesC. Krulak	Capt. Leo Salgado	Gen. Carl E. Mundy, Jr.

NO	DATE	COMMANDING GEN, MCB	RACE DIRECTOR	COMMANDANT USMC
18	10-24-93	BGen M.R. Steele	Maj. Rick G. Nealis	Gen. Carl E. Mundy, Jr.
19	10-23-94	BGen M.R. Steele	Maj. Rick G. Nealis	Gen. Carl E. Mundy, Jr.
20	10-22-95	BGen E.C. Kelley, Jr.	Rick G. Nealis, Maj. USMC (Ret)	Gen. Charles C. Krulak 31st
21	10-27-96	BGen E.C. Kelley, Jr.	Rick G. Nealis, Maj. USMC (Ret)	Gen. Charles C. Krulak
22	10-26-97	BGen Frances C. Wilson	Rick G. Nealis, Maj. USMC (Ret)	Gen. Charles C. Krulak
23	10-25-98	BGen Frances C. Wilson	Rick G. Nealis, Maj. USMC (Ret)	Gen. Charles C. Krulak
24	10-24-99	Col. Lef Hendrickson	Rick G. Nealis, Maj. USMC (Ret)	Gen. James L. Jones 32nd
25	10-22-00	MajGen John F.Cronin	Rick G. Nealis, Maj. USMC (Ret)	Gen. James L. Jones
26	10-28-01	BGen Joseph Composto	Rick G. Nealis, Maj. USMC (Ret)	Gen. James L. Jones
27	10-27-02	BGen Joseph Composto	Rick G. Nealis, Maj. USMC (Ret)	Gen. James L. Jones
28	10-26-03	Col. James M. Lowe	Rick G. Nealis, Maj. USMC (Ret)	Gen. Michael W. Hagee 33rd
29	10-26-04	Col. James M. Lowe	Rick G. Nealis, Maj. USMC (Ret)	Gen. Michael W. Hagee
30	10-30-05	Col. James M. Lowe	Rick G. Nealis, Maj. USMC (Ret)	Gen. Michael W. Hagee
31	10-29-006	Col. Charles Dallachie	Rick G. Nealis, Maj. USMC (Ret)	Gen. Michael W. Hagee

Winning Times Progression grid

YR	PLC	OPEN-M	YR	PLC	OPEN-F	YR	PLC	MAST-M	YR	PLC	MAST-F
87	1	2:14:01	90	1	2:37:00	81	1	2:24:36	83	1	2:50:51
96	2	2:15:09	03	2	2:37:59	95	2	2:25:25	80	2	2:53:17
81	3	2:16:31	94	3	2:39:34	83	3	2:25:49	91	3	2:55:13
95	4	2:16:34	80	4	2:41:54	89	4	2:28:25	98	4	2:55:18
83	5	2:17:46	86	5	2:42:59	76	5	2:28:28	92	5	2:56:42
91	6	2:17:54	84	6	2:43:20	01	6	2:28:28	81	6	2:58:05
78	7	2:18:07	91	7	2:44:27	86	7	2:29:14	90	7	2:58:11
97	8	2:18:21	87	8	2:44:36	82	8	2:30:22	79	8	2:58:53
80	9	2:18:38	85	9	2:44:42	94	9	2:30:28	02	9	3:00:53
85	10	2:19:16	82	10	2:44:51	99	10	2:31:10	97	10	3:00:26
79	11	2:19:35	89	11	2:45:16	05	11	2:30:39	93	11	3:01:45
77	12	2:19:36	83	12	2:45:55	87	12	2:31:19	77	12	3:01:58
84	13	2:19:40	05	13	2:47:10	85	13	2:31:20	87	13	3:02:42
89	14	2:20:23	00	14	2:47:52	00	14	2:31:53	88	14	3:02:54
76	15	2:21:14	92	15	2:47:58	78	15	2:32:17	89	15	3:03:45
06	16	2:21:20	01	16	2:48:13	90	16	2:32:28	03	16	3:04:17
82	17	2:21:29	04	17	2:48:31	77	17	2:32:30	96	17	3:04:44
90	18	2:21:32	96	18	2:48:34	06	18	2:32:46	04	18	3:05:47
88	19	2:21:59	93	19	2:48:41	79	19	2:33:01	01	19	3:05:58
05	20	2:22:18	98	20	2:49:07	80	20	2:33:06	06	20	3:06:34
94	21	2:22:51	95	21	2:49:21	96	21	2:33:35	86	21	3:07:47
86	22	2:23:13	81	22	2:50:33	02	22	2:33:35	82	22	3:07:51
99	23	2:23:27	88	23	2:51:26	91	23	2:34:02	00	23	3:09:46
93	24	2:23:56	99	24	2:51:53	93	24	2:34:32	05	24	3:10:11
92	25	2:24:09	97	25	2:53:42	97	25	2:34:32	99	25	3:11:25
02	26	2:25:01	77	26	2:54:04	92	26	2:34:55	94	26	3:13:56
03	27	2:25:07	76	27	2:56:33	98	27	2:35:33	95	27	3:17:39
98	28	2:25:31	02	28	2:57:27	84	28	2:36:48	85	28	3:18:57
04	29	2:25:35	79	29	2:58:14	88	29	2:39:27	84	29	3:16:25
00	30	2:25:50	06	30	3:00:22	04	30	2:38:56	78	30	3:24:33
01	31	2:28:20	78	31	3:01:34	03	31	2:34:21	76	31	4:26:19

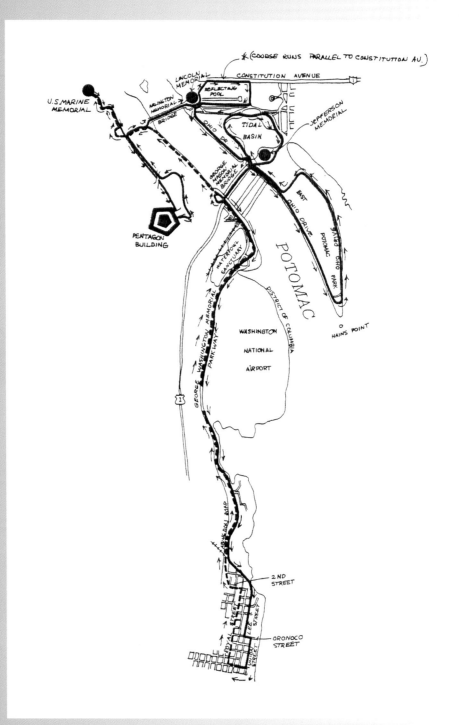

Photo & Illustrations Credits

Cover design:	Jens Vogelsang, Germany
Cover photos:	dpa Picture-Alliance, Germany
	Terry Adams, National Park Service
	Marine Corps Marathon, Chappell Studio, Inc.
Other photos:	See captions

Our Bestsellers i

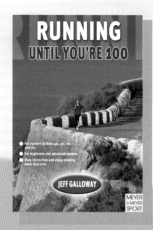

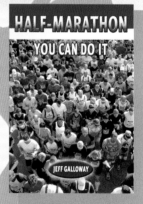